Pay Per Click Search Engine Marketing For Dummies®

The Big Three PPC Systems

The first two have been operating for years; the last is running in some countries, should be fully operational in the U.S. by the spring or summer of 2006, and will be a major player in the PPC industry once fully launched.

- ✔ **Google AdWords:** www.AdWords.com
- ✔ **Yahoo! Search Marketing:** http://Search Marketing.Yahoo.com
- ✔ **MSN Keywords:** http://adCenter. MSN.com

Content-Placement Services

Google and Yahoo!, and some of the smaller PPC systems, have *content-placement* (also known as *contextual*) ads. Here are some more services that offer content-placement ads:

- ✔ **adMarketPlace:** www.adMarketPlace.net
- ✔ **Health Central Direct** (formerly GoText): www. healthcentraldirect.com
- ✔ **IndustryBrains:** www.Industry Brains.com
- ✔ **Kontera:** www.Kontera.com
- ✔ **Quigo:** www.adsonar.com
- ✔ **TheWeddingConnection:** www.TheWedding Connection.com
- ✔ **Vibrant Media:** www.VibrantMedia.com

Plenty More PPC Systems

- ✔ **7Search.com:** www.7search.com
- ✔ **AJInteractive** (AskJeeves, iWon, Excite, and MaxOnline): www.AJInteractive.com
- ✔ **BlowSearch:** www.blowsearch.com
- ✔ **Brainfox:** www.brainfox.com
- ✔ **Business.com:** www.business.com
- ✔ **Clicksor:** www.Clicksor.com
- ✔ **Enhance Interactive** (formerly Ah-Ha.com): www.Enhance.com
- ✔ **ePilot:** www.ePilot.com
- ✔ **Findology:** www.Findology.com
- ✔ **GenieKnows.com:** www.GenieKnows.com
- ✔ **goClick.com:** www.goclick.com
- ✔ **Kanoodle:** www.Kanoodle.com

- ✔ **LookSmart:** www.LookSmart.com
- ✔ **Lycos Insite AdBuyer** (Lycos, HotBot, AngelFire, and so on): http://insite. lycos.com/adbuyer/overview.asp
- ✔ **Mamma:** www.mamma.com
- ✔ **Mirago:** www.mirago.com
- ✔ **Miva** (formerly FindWhat.com and eSpotting): www.Miva.com
- ✔ **myGeek:** www.MyGeek.com
- ✔ **PageSeeker:** www.PageSeeker.com
- ✔ **Search123:** www.Search123.com
- ✔ **S** _____chfeed.com
- ✔ **S**
- ✔

Copyright © 200___ _____ rights reserved.
Item 5494-3.
For more information about Wiley Publishing, call 1-800-762-2974.

D1361691

For Dummies: Bestselling Book Series for Beginners

Pay Per Click Search Engine Marketing For Dummies®

Glossary

Here are a few terms you should know:

- **Broad match:** A keyword matching method in which an ad is matched with searches that are similar to the specified keywords

- **Click fraud:** Clicks on your ads that were carried out for fraudulent purposes

- **Content-placement ad:** A PPC ad placed on a content page rather than on a search-results page; also called a *contextual ad*

- **Conversion rate:** The number of people at any point who carry out a particular action; in particular, who come to your site and buy from you or provide lead information; a visitor is being "converted" into a buyer

- **CPA:** Cost per Acquisition

- **CPM:** Cost per thousand ad impressions (the *M* is taken from the Roman numeral for 1,000)

- **CTR (click-through rate):** The percentage of people seeing an ad who click it

- **Exact match:** A keyword matching method in which an ad is matched with searches that include the exact keyword phrase and nothing else

- **Geo-targeting:** Targeting ads to particular geographic regions

- **Impression:** An individual placement of an ad on a Web page

- **Keyword matching:** Refers to different methods for matching keywords associated with your ads, with the search terms entered by people at the search engines; see also *Broad match, Exact match, Phrase match, and Negative match*

- **Landing page:** The page the visitor lands on after clicking an ad

- **Negative match:** A form of keyword matching in which ads are never matched with searches that include the specified negative keyword

- **Organic search results:** Nonpaid search results

- **Pay per Call:** Similar to PPC, except that the advertiser pays when the searcher calls a phone number

- **Phrase match:** A keyword matching method in which an ad is matched with searches that include the exact keyword phrase, though with other words before or after

- **PPA (Pay Per Action):** An advertising campaign in which the advertiser pays when a particular action is completed, such as a sale or a form being filled in

- **PPC (Pay Per Click):** An advertising campaign in which the advertiser must pay each time someone clicks an ad

- **ROI (return on investment):** A measure of how much profit you make for a particular advertising investment

- **SEM (search engine marketing):** Activities designed to generate business through Web search engines; some people use the term to refer specifically to PPC activities

- **SERP (search engine results page):** The page a search engine displays containing your search results

For Dummies: Bestselling Book Series for Beginners

Pay Per Click
Search Engine Marketing
FOR DUMMIES®

by Peter Kent

Author of *Search Engine Optimization For Dummies*

WILEY

Wiley Publishing, Inc.

Pay Per Click Search Engine Marketing For Dummies®

Published by
Wiley Publishing, Inc.
111 River Street
Hoboken, NJ 07030-5774

www.wiley.com

Copyright © 2006 by Wiley Publishing, Inc., Indianapolis, Indiana

Published by Wiley Publishing, Inc., Indianapolis, Indiana

Published simultaneously in Canada

For general information on our other products and services, please contact our Customer Care Department within the U.S. at 800-762-2974, outside the U.S. at 317-572-3993, or fax 317-572-4002.

For technical support, please visit www.wiley.com/techsupport.

Wiley also publishes its books in a variety of electronic formats. Some content that appears in print may not be available in electronic books.

Library of Congress Control Number: 2005935147

ISBN-13: 978-0-471-75494-7

ISBN-10: 0-471-75494-3

Manufactured in the United States of America

10 9 8 7 6 5 4 3 2 1

1B/RY/QR/QW/IN

WILEY

About the Author

Peter Kent is the author of numerous books about the Internet, including *Search Engine Optimization For Dummies,* the *Complete Idiot's Guide to the Internet,* and the widely reviewed title, *Poor Richard's Web Site: Geek-Free, Commonsense Advice On Building a Low-Cost Web Site.* His work has been praised by *USA Today, BYTE, CNN.com, Windows Magazine, The Philadelphia Inquirer,* and many others.

Peter has been online since 1984, doing business in cyberspace since 1991, and writing about the Internet since 1993. Peter's experience spans virtually all areas of doing business online, from editing and publishing an e-mail newsletter to creating e-commerce Web sites, from online marketing and PR campaigns to running a Web-design and hosting department for a large ISP.

Peter was the founder of an e-Business Service Provider funded by one of the world's largest VC firms, Softbank/Mobius. He was the VP of Web Solutions for a national ISP and VP of Marketing for a Web applications firm. He was also the founder of a computer-book publishing company launched through a concerted online marketing campaign.

Peter now consults with businesses about their Internet strategies, helping them to avoid the pitfalls and to leap the hurdles they'll encounter online. He also gives seminars and presentations on subjects related to online marketing in general and search engine marketing in particular. He can be contacted at Dummies@PeterKentConsulting.com, and more information about his background and experience is available at www.PeterKentConsulting.com.

Dedication

For Cheryl

Author's Acknowledgments

Thanks again to Wiley's staff, in particular Acquisitions Editors Terri Varveris and Tiffany Franklin and Project Editor Blair Pottenger, for putting up with my idiosyncrasies and believing that indeed they *would* finally end up with a book, more or less on time. And, of course, the many Wiley staff members editing, proofreading, and laying out the book.

Publisher's Acknowledgments

We're proud of this book; please send us your comments through our online registration form located at www.dummies.com/register/.

Some of the people who helped bring this book to market include the following:

Acquisitions, Editorial, and Media Development

Project Editor: Blair J. Pottenger

Acquisitions Editors: Terri Varveris, Tiffany Franklin

Copy Editor: Andy Hollandbeck

Technical Editor: Paul Chaney

Editorial Manager: Kevin Kirschner

Media Development Manager: Laura VanWinkle

Media Development Supervisor: Richard Graves

Editorial Assistant: Amanda Foxworth

Cartoons: Rich Tennant (www.the5thwave.com)

Composition Services

Project Coordinator: Jennifer Theriot

Layout and Graphics: Carl Byers, Andrea Dahl, Stephanie D. Jumper, Barry Offringa

Proofreaders: Leeann Harney, TECHBOOKS Production Services

Indexer: TECHBOOKS Production Services

Publishing and Editorial for Technology Dummies

Richard Swadley, Vice President and Executive Group Publisher

Andy Cummings, Vice President and Publisher

Mary Bednarek, Executive Acquisitions Director

Mary C. Corder, Editorial Director

Publishing for Consumer Dummies

Diane Graves Steele, Vice President and Publisher

Joyce Pepple, Acquisitions Director

Composition Services

Gerry Fahey, Vice President of Production Services

Debbie Stailey, Director of Composition Services

Contents at a Glance

Table of Contents

Introduction

. . . .

Welcome to *Pay Per Click Search Engine Marketing For Dummies.* If you're reading this book, you've undoubtedly heard all the talk about *Pay Per Click,* advertising for the masses. Anyone with a credit card and a Web site . . . wait, no, you don't even need a Web site anymore. . . . Anyone with *just a credit card* can place ads on major search engines and major content Web sites with just a few minutes' work.

You've probably heard how simple Pay Per Click (or *PPC,* as we insiders know it) really is. But if that's the case, how have I managed to fill an entire book on the subject?

Well, as is almost always the case, things aren't as simple as they appear. Getting started with PPC is very easy; what takes a bit more time and understanding is getting started and making it work. I know companies that are doing very well with PPC advertising — one company that even spends $2 million on PPC ads *every month.* I also know companies that are losing money with their PPC ads.

Making a PPC campaign work takes some brains, and although this is the *For Dummies* book series, the publishers of this series have always believed they were publishing for *smart people;* it's just that, at the point of picking up the book for the first time, those people don't feel so smart about the subject. In fact, they feel a little lost. They want the straight dope, and they want it fast, in an easy-to-digest format. That's just what you get with this book. By the time you finish this book, you'll be no dummy in the PPC world. You'll have a good idea of where to begin and where to go.

About This Book

This book simplifies the whole Pay Per Click advertising business for you. You find out how to make PPC ads work *for* you, not *against* you. In this book I show you how to

- ✔ Figure out where to place your PPC ads. You have *many* choices.

- ✔ Make sure that you're using the right keywords to trigger your PPC ads.

- ✔ Calculate your breakeven and gross profit numbers.

✔ Calculate your return on investment (ROI).

✔ Pick the keywords that will connect you with your customers.

✔ Write ads that encourage the right people to click your ads . . . and discourage the wrong people.

✔ Bid on your ads in a way that makes sense (and cents).

✔ Work with the major PPC systems — Yahoo!, Google, and MSN.

✔ Use geo-targeting to put your ads in front of people close to your business.

✔ Work with content-placement systems to place your ads on non-search Web sites.

✔ Track the effects of your ads, in terms of sales and other conversion types.

✔ And plenty more!

Foolish Assumptions

You and I have a lot to cover in this book, so we don't have time for the basics. So I assume that, if you're reading this book, you already know a few things about the Internet and search engines, such as

✔ You have access to a computer that has access to the Internet, and you know how to connect.

✔ You know how to use a Web browser to get around the Internet.

✔ You know how to carry out searches at the major search engines, such as Google and Yahoo!.

✔ You know how to use Web-based form systems. You'll be using a variety of online systems to create your ads.

✔ You, or someone working with or for you, know how to create Web pages. You'll probably be pointing PPC ads to those pages (although it is possible to run PPC ads, in some cases, without having a Web site).

✔ You have some basic writing skills. You'll be writing simple little text ads, so you need to be able to string a sentence or two together.

✔ You can do a little in the way of math. You'll need to carry out the simple calculations required for figuring out whether you're making or losing money on your PPC campaign.

There's actually very little in the way of nasty technical stuff in this book. I do discuss IP numbers, but don't worry; it's only in passing, and I explain what they are. Perhaps the most complicated technical stuff in the book is in the chapter on tracking conversions and sales (Chapter 15), but it's really quite straightforward. Anyone who creates Web pages should be able to understand how to enter tracking codes into those pages.

How This Book Is Organized

Like all good reference tools, this book is set up to be read "as needed." It's divided into several parts, which I discuss shortly. So if you want to jump right in and learn about working with Yahoo!'s Sponsored Search PPC system, just skip to Chapter 8. If you need to understand how to write good PPC ads that the PPC services won't reject and that will encourage the right sort of people to click through to your site, then read Chapter 6. If you need to understand the different options open to you for tracking traffic as it comes to your site and figuring out what those visitors actually do on your site, then flip to Chapter 15.

However, I really recommend that you read everything in the book because it will make a big difference to your chances of success. When I wrote the book, I put the basic foundation knowledge at the beginning, the information on how to get started in the middle, and the more-advanced details at the end. You really should understand how to write ads (Chapter 6) before you start working with the PPC systems (Chapters 8 through 14), and you need to know how different bidding strategies can hurt and hinder you (Chapter 7) before you actually invest a lot of money in your PPC campaigns.

This book contains a lot of information, and you never know what you might need. Are the clicks on the major systems too expensive? Then you might try a few lesser-known systems (see Chapter 11); have you seen a sudden surge in clicks to your site, but without an increase in sales? Maybe you should read Chapter 5. PPC can be very profitable for companies that understand how to use it, so make the most of the book you are holding in your hands.

Don't forget to visit the Web site associated with this book. At `www.dummies.com/go/payperclick`, you can find all the links in this book. And don't forget to visit my Web site at `www.PCBulletin.com`, where you can find links to special discounts on a variety of PPC services.

Part 1: Preparing for Your Campaign

I start at the beginning, getting you ready for your PPC campaign. In this part, you find out just exactly what PPC *is* and where it came from. You discover the different places you can place ads, from search engines to content sites, from the monsters of the PPC world — Yahoo!, Google, and MSN — to the second- and third-tier systems — Kanoodle, Miva, Searchfeed, myGeek, Quigo, and many more. You find out how to calculate your "return on investment," how to pick keywords for your campaign, and how to write ads that work well. You also get the lowdown about how advertisers bid for the position of their ads on the search-results page and about a number of bidding strategies. Bidding for position is not like bidding at an auction, so I show you a number of strategies that can make or save you money.

Part II: Using the PPC Systems

In this part, I explain how to work with the major PPC systems. Each one works a little differently and has its own advantages and idiosyncrasies. Yahoo!, Google, and MSN are responsible for the majority of the world's PPC ads. But what if their ads are too expensive? Or what if they work really well, but you want more clicks? I also show you other places where you can buy PPC ads — the second- and third-tier PPC systems.

But there's more! How about using the PPC systems of content-placement services such as Quigo? Or the PPC-based shopping directories, like Yahoo! Shopping, or perhaps the Yellow Pages PPC systems? You need to understand geo-targeting, too, with which you can present your ads to Internet users in particular locations, even down to circles with a half-mile radius in American cities (in theory, anyway; I explain why practice is different).

Part III: Managing Your Campaign

Your advertising campaign may be up and running, but don't think that means you can sit back and rest on your laurels as the sales pour in. There are a number of things you need to know about to make sure everything stays on track.

Running a PPC campaign without any kind of tracking is a recipe for disaster. You'll miss opportunities, as well as problems. How do you really know whether you're making money from PPC if you aren't measuring how many people come to your site and what they do when they get there? How do you know which keywords and ads work well, and which are losing you money, if you don't track? You don't. So in this part of the book, I show you how to keep track of how many visitors come to your site from the PPC services and what actions they carry out on your site.

I also point out the various bid-management tools available to you; that is, tools that are more advanced than the basic systems provided to you by the

PPC services — tools designed to make life easier for people tracking hundreds, or thousands, of keywords and thousands of PPC ad impressions every day.

Oh, and before leaving this part of the book, I examine a controversial subject: *click fraud*. Perhaps 20 percent of all clicks on PPC ads are fraudulent, according to some experts. Fraud rates have even hit as high as 80 percent for some advertising campaigns. Why would people click PPC ads *fraudulently?* For two good reasons . . . which I explain in this part.

Part IV: The Part of Tens

All *For Dummies* books have the Part of Tens. In this part, you find ten ways to make money by *selling* clicks . . . by, in effect, getting into the business of selling PPC ads. You also find out about ten useful tools for planning and managing your PPC campaigns, and ten ways to continue your PPC education and keep up with the latest information and innovations.

Icons Used in This Book

This book, like all *For Dummies* books, uses icons to highlight certain paragraphs and to alert you to particularly useful information. Here's a rundown of what those icons mean:

A Tip icon means I'm giving you a little extra, an additional snippet of information that may help you on your way or provide some extra understanding to help you really understand the concepts.

The Remember icon points out things that I may already have told you, but that bear repeating. Hey, we all forget something sometimes.

This icon indicates geeky stuff that you can skip if you really want to . . . though you may want to read it if you're the kind of person who *has* to have the background info.

The Warning icon is here to help you stay out of trouble. It's intended to grab your attention to make sure you avoid a pitfall that can harm your Web site or business in some way.

Part I
Preparing for Your Campaign

The 5th Wave
By Rich Tennant

"The top line represents our revenue, the middle line is our inventory, and the bottom line shows the rate of my hair loss over the same period."

In this part . . .

You'll hear often from the Pay Per Click (PPC) companies that you can get started with your PPC campaign in minutes, and perhaps you *can*. Whether you *should* or not is another matter. Personally, I think you'd be well-served to find out a bit before you jump in with both feet.

Perhaps you think you already know all about PPC — but do you know the difference between advertising in the search results and in "contextual" placements? How about the second- and third-tier PPC systems? How about Pay Per Call and Pay Per Action? In any case, even if you know these things, there's still work to be done before you should begin your advertising campaign.

You really do need to understand a few numbers. The PPC companies will tell you (a little) about ROI (return on investment), but they don't talk much about calculating gross profit and breakeven costs, about costs per sale and costs per action. These, and other things, are essential to any full understanding of whether a PPC campaign is working or not, and I discuss them all in this part.

You also need to understand *keywords* — and be able to pick keywords that work well for you. And there's no point beginning a PPC campaign if your Web site isn't ready, so I discuss *landing pages* and site *conversions*. Oh, and then there are your ads. Sure, you can write an ad in a couple of minutes, but you could also take your time and do it right. I give you the help you need in this part.

But no, you go ahead, skip all this "preparing for your campaign" stuff and jump right in . . . where angels fear to tread. Or, flip the page and spend a little while learning the background first.

Chapter 1

Introducing Pay Per Click Advertising

*I*f you're reading this book, you've heard the hype about *PPC*. Pay Per Click advertising is many things to many people. To some, it's a tremendously effective way to push people to a Web site and sell products to them; to others, it's a great way to lose money. To some, it's a tool into which to pour millions of dollars for *brand advertising;* to others, it's a huge disappointment.

Which side of the line you sit on — the side of success or the side of failure — and how *close* to the line you sit, depends on a number of factors. Some of those factors are under your control, and some are not, but the intention of this book is to give you a good understanding of those factors and the best chance of landing on the money-making side of the line.

Let's begin at the beginning. In this chapter, you find out what PPC is all about and why some people swear by it, while others swear at it!

The Days before PPC

Not so long ago, Internet advertising came in a couple of basic flavors. The first was very similar to print advertising. You paid someone to put some kind of advertisement on a Web site — typically what's known as a *banner ad* (you can see an example in Figure 1-1). The ad sat on the site for the specified period — a week, a month, a year — and if you were lucky, people clicked the ad and came to your Web site. You were paying for an ad *placement*.

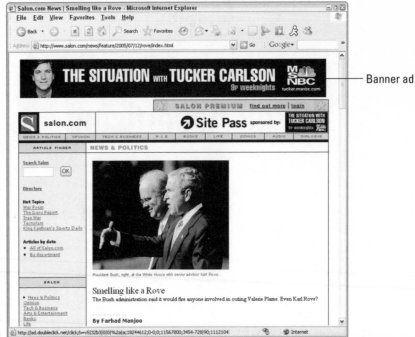

Banner ad

Figure 1-1:
Old
school . . .
the "banner
ad."

Soon, a slight refinement to this model appeared. The main problem with the ad-placement model was that you didn't really know what you were getting for your money. Sure, the ad would sit on the site for, say, a year, but what did that mean? Would a million people see it? Or a thousand? In many cases, all you had to go by was a vague promise from the site owner — "we get a million visitors a year," for instance. Does that mean the page on which the ad sat would be seen a million times? Probably not. Worse, the promise might have been something like "we get a million *hits* a year." What's a hit? Ah, you think you know, but you probably don't.

The term *hit* has come to mean just about nothing. People say *hit* when they mean *visit,* and sometimes say *hit* when they mean *hit* but hope you'll think they mean *visit.* Want to know what a hit actually is?

A hit is a Web server request. When someone clicks a link leading to a page, the browser requests the page from the Web server; that's the first hit. If the page has five images in it, those images have to be sent to the browser, too. That's five more hits. If the visitor clicks a link and requests another page, that's another hit, plus the images or other components inside the page. A hit might even be an error message, when a browser requests a page that no longer exists.

So, the next time someone tells you that his site gets, say, 100,000 hits a month, ask him what that means. Is that 100,000 visitors? Almost certainly not, unless he is misusing the term *hits* and really meant to say *visitors.* Does it mean 50,000 visitors? 10,000? Who knows?

Anyway, back to the story. If you put an ad on a site and pay for a month or year, what do you get? That's right, no one knows *what* you get. So a second mechanism was developed — ads were sold by the *ad impression.* You would pay for the ad to be displayed a particular number of times. Ads were typically sold in blocks of 1,000 impressions; they were priced by *CPM.*

CPM means *cost per thousand* (no, not per million; *M* is the Roman numeral for 1,000). If you pay, say, a CPM of $35, that means your $35 buys you 1,000 ad "impressions" — the ad will be loaded into Web pages 1,000 times. Each time an ad appears, it costs you 3.5 cents.

Hmm, still a few problems here. Just because your ad is loaded into a browser 1,000 times doesn't mean the people viewing the pages actually saw the ad. What if the ad was "below the fold," so far down the page that it wasn't visible without scrolling down? Sure, it was loaded into the page, and if the visitor scrolled down he would see it. But if he didn't scroll down, he wouldn't.

And so what if the ad *was* actually seen 1,000 times; will someone actually click it? And if people *do* click, how often will they click? In general, not very often, somewhere near 1percent of the time (and often way below that level). And that's where PPC comes in.

Understanding PPC: What It Is and Why You Should Care

With PPC, you're not paying for a promise, and you're not paying to load an ad onto a page. You're paying for an actual *result,* a *click.* With PPC, you don't pay if nobody sees your ad, and you don't even pay if someone *does* see it but doesn't click. You pay only when someone clicks your ad. In the business, people talk about *buying clicks* because that's just what they (and you) are doing. You're paying a PPC company each time someone clicks a link pointing to your Web site.

Now, I wouldn't go so far as to say you're paying for a *lead* . . . you're not. Some PPC companies have taken to referring to each click as a lead, but that's just hype. (A *lead* in sales-talk is someone who has expressed an interest in your product or service. No sales professional would regard the visitor, at this click stage, as having expressed enough interest to have risen to the level of being a sales lead.) Nonetheless, you are paying for a particular action. Someone sees your ad, clicks the ad, and (in general) views your site. Certainly, now and then, people won't arrive at your site — they may click and then cancel before your page fully loads — but generally speaking, a click is the same as a visit. It could be a very short visit, true, but it's something a bit more tangible than a *placement* or an *impression.*

Why isn't a click the same as a lead? Compare Internet advertising with direct mail. Imagine, for a moment, a direct-mail campaign that is intended to get someone to call your company. You mail a letter, someone opens the letter, reads the letter and, you hope, picks up the phone and calls you. When the person calls, the person becomes a sales lead. Most people who open the letter won't call, though. So you can't call the letter a lead, and you can't call someone opening the letter a lead. Displaying a PPC ad is the equivalent of sending the letter; and a click on the PPC ad is the equivalent of having someone open your letter. It's a step in the right direction, but it's most certainly *not* a lead.

PPC, 1-2-3

To make quite sure I'm explaining the concept of PPC adequately, let me just take you through the process of how PPC works, step by step:

1. The advertiser joins a search engine's PPC program and "loads" the account with some money — say $50 (though some companies' PPC budgets are in the hundreds of thousands, even millions, of dollars a month).

2. The advertiser creates a small text ad (in some cases, PPC *can* include images, but I describe the most common form here).

3. The advertiser specifies with which keywords the ad should be associated.

4. The advertiser specifies how much he's willing to pay each time someone clicks on the ad.

5. Later, someone arrives at the search engine, enters one of the keywords or keyword phrases specified, and clicks the Search button.

6. The search engine finds the matching ads and places them on the results page.

7. If the searcher clicks the ad, he is taken to the advertiser's Web site, and the advertiser is charged for the click.

PPC pulls the banner down

By the end of 2000, when the Internet bubble burst, banner advertising had acquired a really bad reputation. Billions of dollars had been spent on banner advertising, and most of it was wasted. Click-through rates — the proportion of ads that are clicked upon — for banner ads were very low, and many advertisers, perhaps most, spent more on the ads than they made on any sales derived from them.

Banner ads had several problems:

- ✔ **They were expensive.** Although CPMs were typically $35–$50, because only one ad impression in 200 resulted in a click, that often translated into a price of $7–$10 per click.

- ✔ **They had low click-through rates (the ratio of ad impression to actual clicks on the ad), which made them expensive.** People were sick of seeing them, so they learned to just ignore them.

- ✔ *Conversion rates* **were low.** That is, only a small percentage of the people who clicked a banner and arrived at a site actually bought anything.

- ✔ **They were in the wrong places.** Ads were often placed in front of people who simply wouldn't be interested in the offer, which meant people didn't click them much.

Which brings me to another critically important characteristic of PPC ads as opposed to the majority of banner ads — PPC ads are, often, placed in the *right* place, while most banner ads were in the wrong place. As you discover in this book, there are lots of different types of pay per click advertising, but the concept really took off when it was incorporated into search engines, and search engines' results pages are the *right* place to put your ads.

The first big move in PPC search advertising was made by GoTo.com, a company founded by Bill Gross' IdeaLab. (IdeaLab has had a huge effect on the Internet, from eToys to CitySearch, NetZero to PETsMART.) In the summer of 1998 the company began selling ad "bids" on the GoTo search engine; you'll learn more about bidding in a moment. The company changed its name to Overture, went public, began a partnership with Yahoo! and late in 2003 was purchased by Yahoo!. (Yahoo! is now in the process of re-branding Overture, calling it Yahoo! Search Marketing.) By the way, in the early days this form of advertising was often known as *CPC* — Cost Per Click (but I'll be sticking to the form that's more common these days, *PPC,* in this book).

Here's the basic concept of PPC advertising: Rather than placing banner ads on various destination and content Web sites, when you buy PPC ads, most are placed in search results. If you've searched on the major search engines — Google and Yahoo!, and MSN — and most smaller search systems, too, you've seen them: small ads that appear above and alongside the search results. In fact, the search results page contains two types of search result, as you can see in Figure 1-2.

Organic search results   PPC ads

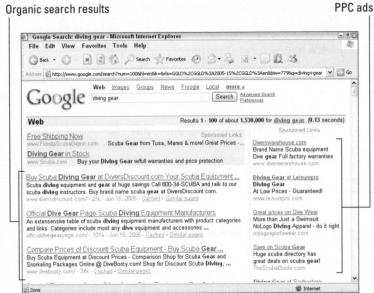

Figure 1-2: Most PPC ads are placed into search results on the major search engines.

As you can see in Figure 1-2, I searched on the term *diving gear* on Google; the words I'm searching on — *diving gear* — are known as the *search term, search query,* or *search keywords.*

Figure 1-2 shows what's known as the *search-results page;* Google takes my search term and returns information that it feels matches my search term most closely. You see two types of results in this page. The main area of the results contains *organic search results.* These are *not* ads; they are simply pages that Google found in its vast index of the Web (over 8 *billion* pages at the time of writing), pages that it thinks are the best matches for the search keywords I entered. At the top, and along the side, are *sponsored links.* These are the PPC ads.

How do you get your pages to sit at the top of the *organic* search results? This book is about PPC advertising; however you might want to read the "partner" book to this volume, *Search Engine Optimization For Dummies* for all the details on ranking well in the non-paid search results. (See `www.Get SEOBook.com`.)

One major search engine sometimes mixes organic and sponsored results — Yahoo!. At the time of writing, Yahoo! is the only major search engine that has a *trusted-feed* program, which you find out about in Chapter 14. In some cases, what appear to be organic search results are actually trusted-feed PPC ads, with no indication to the searcher that this is the case!

The power of search advertising

PPC ads on search engines are likely to be much more effective than banner ads. Why?

- ✔ **People are searching for something when they see your ad.** Banner ads are often placed onto what may be termed *content sites,* as opposed to *search sites.* On content sites, people are looking *at* information, rather than *for* information. In most cases, banner ads lead people *away* from the task at hand; PPC ads are designed to help people *with* the task at hand — looking for information.

- ✔ **Ads are delivered based on what people search for,** so there's a very good chance that if someone clicks your ad, he or she is interested in what you're selling or promoting.

- ✔ **The ads are unobtrusive and not gimmicky.** The major PPC systems have guidelines to stop the use of tricks and gimmicks. Again, if someone clicks, he or she is probably interested.

All in all, PPC ads on search sites are generally more effective than banner ads on non-search sites, in the same way that Yellow Pages ads are often more effective than newspaper ads. When people see your ad for, say, a shoe store in the Yellow Pages, chances are they're looking for a shoe store. When they see your shoe-store ad in a newspaper, they may just be reading the news.

Having said all that, it's important to understand that sometimes PPC ads are *not* placed in search results — they are sometimes placed on content sites (that's a choice made by the advertiser). You can see an example of a PPC ad on a content site in Figure 1-3. (I'm going to use the term *content match* for this type of ad, which is actually the term used by Yahoo! — other PPC systems use different terms. One common term you'll hear is *contextual advertising,* though that term is a little ambiguous in some ways.) Right now, Google is the big player in the content-match game, but other PPC systems also do it. Google's big in the content-match business because, through its AdSense program, it makes it very easy for almost any site owner to run PPC ads on his or her Web sites.

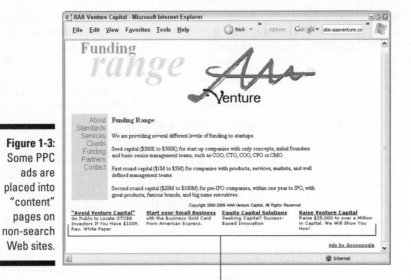

Figure 1-3:
Some PPC ads are placed into "content" pages on non-search Web sites.

Google AdSense PPC ads

It's also important to understand that these types of ads are likely to be less effective (and, therefore, more expensive from a results standpoint) than the ads in search results. I recommend that when you start your PPC advertising, you *turn off* content-match ads (you'll see how in the chapters on Google and Yahoo!) to increase your chances of success, or at the very least, track them separately so you'll know the true picture (I cover tracking in Chapter 15); if your PPC campaign is a total failure, you may find the content-match ads pulling down the average while the regular search-match ads work okay. I cover this in more detail later, in Chapter 13.

Oh, and there's another reason to avoid content-match advertising; *click fraud,* a subject you find out about in Chapter 17. Content-match ads are prime targets for fraudulent clicking, so avoiding that form of advertising may reduce your exposure.

By the way, there's no reason that a PPC ad can't be a "banner" ad. They can, and sometimes are. But at present, most PPC ads are the small text ads I've shown you here.

You pick your placement

Here's another important PPC concept — you get to pick where your ads are placed by associating your ads with various keywords.

In the past, with banner ads, you would place ads on a specific Web site or work with an ad network to place ads on a particular type of Web site. If you sold sports paraphernalia, for instance, you would place your ads on sports-related sites.

With PPC, though, you can get much more targeted than this. Rather than just placing an ad on a site related to sports, you can now display your ad to someone who has clearly stated that she has some kind of interest in . . . some keyword. When someone searches on *nfl memorabilia,* for instance, your ad may appear. You get to state, in very specific terms, when your ad appears.

More specifically, each ad you create can be combined with one or more key-word search phrases. You might have 30 different ads with 30 different groups of keywords. When a keyword in group one is typed into a search engine by a searcher, the associated ad is displayed; when a keyword phrase from group two is typed, the associated ad for that group is displayed, and so on.

Again, having said that, content-match ads are not quite as precise as regular search-result ads. Remember, with content-match ads, nobody's typing a search phrase into the page; rather, the ads are simply displayed when a page is opened in a browser. So the PPC systems try to match your chosen key-words with the text in the Web page. Sometimes they do well; sometimes they don't. In general, PPC advertisers seem to agree: The PPC traffic you get through content matches are *not* as good as the traffic from searches.

You bid for position

PPC ads vary greatly in price. On the major PPC systems, you'll pay anywhere from a minimum of 1 to 10 cents per click (Google's and Yahoo!'s minimum bids, respectively) to many dollars per click: $20, $50, $75, perhaps more. But rather than negotiating with the company selling the ads, you compete with other people who want to display ads at the same time you want to display an ad.

Here's an example: Imagine that you want to display an ad when someone searches on the term *mesothelioma* at Yahoo! (Mesothelioma is a disease caused by breathing in asbestos fibers.) You're not alone. Many other people want *their* ads to appear at the same time. Of course, everyone wants his or her ad to display at the top, so how does Yahoo! determine which goes first? By how much each advertiser bids.

You can see a list of bids in Figure 1-4; these are bids on the Yahoo! Search Marketing system for the term *mesothelioma.*

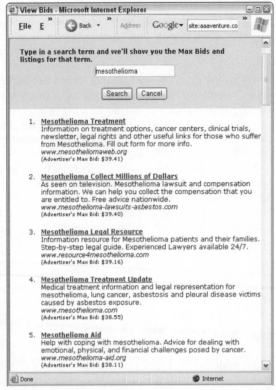

Figure 1-4:
A list of bids
on Yahoo!
Search
Marketing.
You find out
about this
bid tool in
Chapter 7.

On Yahoo!, the minimum bid is 10 cents per click, so the first advertiser to select this keyword phrase selected 10 cents. Another advertiser may have come in and tried to get a better position by placing a bid of 11 cents a click. Then another might have tried to beat that position, with a bid of 12 cents, and so on. So, with the most basic of bidding schemes, you see a bid structure like this:

Top Bidder	14 cents
#2 Bidder	13 cents
#3 Bidder	12 cents
#4 Bidder	11 cents
#5 Bidder	10 cents

Of course, bidding gets far more complicated than this. Bidders, as in any kind of auction, try to beat the competition. Bidder #5, for instance, may be determined to get the top spot, so he outbids the Top Bidder, as do #2 and #3, perhaps. Prices rise until people stop trying to keep up with the top bids.

In fact, the top bid for *mesothelioma* on Yahoo!, at the time of writing, was $39.41 (as you can see in Figure 1-4). I've seen the price well over $50, though, and I've been told it went far higher than this at one point.

When you bid on a keyword, you're saying, "This is the maximum amount I'm willing to pay when somebody clicks my ad." If you bid $12, that means if someone clicks on the ad, you may end up paying the PPC service $12. So make sure a click is really worth $12!

A PPC bid is a little different from the normal auction-type bid, however. While a bid in an auction is what you'll pay if you have the top bid, a bid in PPC advertising is what you're willing to pay, if necessary. But you generally won't pay more than one penny above the next lowest bid for the top position. For instance, look at this situation:

Top Bidder $20.00

#2 Bidder $12.00

In this case, the Top Bidder pays $12.01 per click, not $20. Bidding $20 allows the Top Bidder to hold the top position. In order for #2 to take the top position, he'll have to bid at least $20.01, but then he will have to pay $20.01 per click! But as long as Top Bidder is bidding more than anyone else, he pays only a penny more per click then the second-highest bid.

This is the case in most major PPC systems these days. It wasn't this way in the early days, when you paid what you bid, but in order to encourage more advertising and more bidding, the engines came up with this system in which you place a maximum bid but pay only a penny above the guy below you. However, some smaller PPC systems may still use the old system.

Google handles bidding a little differently. The top bidder does not necessarily get the top spot. Rather, the bid is just one criterion, and ad position is also dependent on how well the ad performs. Ads that get clicked often get a "bonus" and may actually be displayed higher than ads that are being charged more per click. (I discuss this in more detail in Chapter 9.)

You have total control

As you discover in this book, PPC systems provide a great deal of control over how and when your ad is placed. You can control characteristics, such as these:

- ✔ You can set the maximum you're willing to pay for a click.

- ✔ You can specify the maximum you're willing to spend on your ads each day, week, or month.

- ✔ You decide which keyword or keywords "trigger" the ad — from a single keyword to thousands of keywords.

✔ You control the ad wording — you can change wording from minute to minute if you really want to.

✔ You can associate different ads with different keywords or keyword groups.

✔ You can specify exactly how keywords work — if you select *shoes,* will the ad appear if someone searches on *shoe?* What about *shoes in denver?*

✔ You can specify, to some degree, *where* the ad appears — will the ad appear if the person searching is in Denver? In Chicago? In California? In Germany?

The degree of control allows you to tweak your advertising campaign. As you see in Chapter 15, you can track the effects of your ads — not only can you see how much each click costs and how many people click an ad, you can even see what people do when they come to your site. You can track how many of the people who click the ad actually buy, fill in an information-request form, or take some other kind of action. Some ad texts may work better than others. You can experiment by combining different keyword choices with different ads. This information allows you to optimize your advertising by pinpointing which keyword/ad pairs get you the best results.

Is Everyone Making Money with PPC?

No.

Why use PPC if you're losing money?

As bizarre as it may seem, many PPC advertisers are losing money on their ads. How can that be possible? The following are *real* quotes from real companies using PPC, explaining why they use PPC despite the fact that the PPC campaigns are losing money:

✔ "I know we're losing money on PPC, but I'm under pressure to provide leads."

✔ "Well, we're not really sure if we're making money on PPC or not." (They weren't.)

✔ "We experimented with PPC last Christmas . . . sure, we lost money, but we'll probably try again this Christmas, too."

✔ "It doesn't really matter if we make money directly; this is 'brand' advertising." (I talk about brand advertising in Chapter 3. Suffice it to say that brand advertising is often — perhaps usually — a good way to lose money.)

✔ "No, we're not making money right now, but we will just as soon as we improve our conversions." (The term *conversions* refers to the process of converting visitors to customers, and the last time I spoke to these guys, they were still a long way from fixing this problem.)

The fact is, despite the hype — to some degree *because* of the hype — many people working with PPC are losing money doing so. Some are in the process of finding out if PPC works for them and either will stop when the pain gets too great or will experiment and figure out a way to make it work. Others have a much higher pain threshold and are willing to lose large sums of money because they're caught up in the hype and know that PPC *must* work, if they can just figure out how! Or they really don't care much either way; PPC costs are just a small part of a large marketing budget.

Sometimes, spending money on PPC and taking a loss can make sense. PPC can be used to test your site and to test keywords very quickly. You can turn on a PPC campaign, watch for a day or two, and get a feel for how things are going — what people do on your site, how well the site converts visitors to buyers (see Chapter 5), the difference between people who had searched on keyword A and keyword B, and so on. PPC can be used as a clearly measurable system for testing and improving what happens on your site and for picking keywords (see Chapter 4).

Now, just because PPC hasn't worked for you doesn't mean you should stop and never try again. But if you do try again, there has to be a good reason. As a good friend, Joe Sabah, likes to say: "If you do what you've always done, you'll get what you've always gotten." If PPC fails, you'd better figure out why and do something to resolve the problem, rather than just banging your head against the same wall (you find out more about making your PPC campaigns more efficient throughout the book).

Reality is, PPC might work, and it might not. In Chapter 3 you'll learn whether or not it's likely to work for you. But the ultimate test is, of course, to try it. But be realistic, and test carefully.

Most advertising doesn't work

Remember also that *most* advertising doesn't make money. "I know half the money I spend on advertising is wasted," said Chicago department store owner John Wanamaker more than 100 years ago, "but I can never find out which half."

There's an adage in the advertising — wait, no, not in the advertising business, because the adage is not exactly good for the business — that goes, "most advertising doesn't work." I don't remember who said it . . . oh, wait, it was me.

Anyway, it's true, and it's worth understanding up front if you've never purchased advertising before. If you *have* purchased advertising for a large business, you may not believe this; many large business spend a fortune on advertising that doesn't work, because nobody has actually proven that it doesn't work. But having worked with small-business people over the last 15 years, I've learned that many small-biz people *do* understand this concept.

Here's how we *know* most advertising doesn't work . . . because if it did, business would be easy! Need customers? Just advertise for them! Need some more? Advertise some more. Most of the money you spend will make you money, and the longer you do it, the better you do, as you eliminate the minority of advertising that doesn't work.

Reality is very different. Most advertising doesn't work, so business is a battle, and most businesses, business experts tell us, fail in the first few years.

So can you make money with PPC?

The answer to the above question depends on what you mean. If you mean *can one make money with PPC?*, then the answer is, "Absolutely!" One can, if one happens to have the right product, the right Web site, the right ad, and the knowledge you find in this book.

If you mean *can I make money with PPC?*, the answer is a definite "Maybe!" I don't know what you're selling, what your Web site looks like, and whether you can put together the right ad, so I don't know for sure. But some people definitely are making money with PPC; perhaps you can, too.

I've worked with companies doing well with PPC, and with those doing badly. If all the planets align, if you put all your ducks in a row, and if you figure out any other folksy mottos that may apply, you can make money with PPC. But as with every New Thing, there's a lot of hype behind PPC. Just remember that the PPC companies are in the business of selling PPC ads, not of selling information about your chances of succeeding.

Why Bother Using PPC?

So why bother with PPC? There are *lots* of ways to bring people to your Web site, after all. Here are a number of reasons why PPC might be the way to go:

- ✔ **You're reaching people when they're looking for you.** The search engines are hugely popular, with more than half a billion searches *every day* (perhaps much more)! These are great prospects for your business.

- ✔ **It's fast.** While most marketing methods can take a long time to get started, you can get a PPC campaign rolling very quickly, literally within an hour or so.

- ✔ **It's a numbers game.** It's easy to measure success; count how much you spend, and how many sales you made.

- ✔ **It's a great testing tool.** As I mention earlier, even if you can't make money with PPC, it can be a useful way to test your site and test keywords.

- ✔ **It allows you to market products temporarily.** Seasonal goods, products of which you have a small supply, and so on. Want to sell or promote a product around Christmas or Easter, have decided to discontinue a product and want to get rid of it, or have a limited-time discount? PPC could help.

- ✔ **It's a good brand advertising tool . . . oh, wait a minute. No, it's not!** At least, not for most companies. Many writers and PPC pundits promote PPC as a great brand advertising tool. In Chapter 3, I explain why it generally *isn't.*

If you use *only* PPC to market your product or service, you're probably making a mistake. But PPC is often a very good first choice.

Let's compare with search-engine optimization, the practice of "optimizing" pages and links to make your Web pages rank well in the search engines. Search-engine optimization is complex — there's a *lot* to learn. The work you have to do can sometimes be quite difficult. And it can be very time consuming, both in terms of time invested and the time you'll have to wait for results. While it's sometimes possible to see results in days, more commonly it can take weeks or months. (Did I mention my other book, *Search Engine Optimization For Dummies?*)

On the other hand, PPC is quick and easy. When you know what you're doing, you can begin a PPC campaign in an hour or so.

Many people use PPC to get things rolling. While they plan to use other forms of online marketing, they can use PPC to begin bringing people to their sites within minutes of the site launch and start making sales and testing their sites right away. PPC allows you to turn on a campaign immediately, and turn it off as soon as you're finished with it.

Placing Eggs in Several Baskets

PPC is just one weapon in your marketing arsenal, just one wrench in the tool chest. You may discover that it's incredibly important, a business builder; but don't get tunnel vision and think PPC is the only way to go. You may find PPC is useful, but not enough. Or you may find that it's simply not viable for your business. Either way, don't focus on only PPC.

Even if PPC works wonderfully for you, there are two very good reasons for trying other forms of marketing, too:

✔ If there are other forms of online marketing that can make you money, why leave money on the table?

✔ Just because PPC works for you today, doesn't mean it will work tomorrow.

I think it's important to remember the second of these. There are a limited number of ads that can be placed, and two important trends at play:

1. The increase in the number of people using the Internet — and, thus, searching at the major search engines — is slowing down.

2. The increase in the number of businesses using PPC is ramping up.

Pay Per Click fees have been increasing, as PPC becomes more popular. Most businesses — the vast majority — not only haven't used PPC, they don't even know what it is. Certainly the PPC companies are constantly looking for more places to put their ads, but it seems likely to me that as more people learn about PPC, and more get online and use them, the more expensive the clicks are likely to get.

In fact even without an overall upward trend, your business could be hurt if competitors move in on your space. Here's an example (a proverbial "off the top of my head" example). Let's say you sell books about, um, rodent racing. Right now you could buy clicks *very* cheaply. It's hard to believe, but you can place an ad on Yahoo! when someone searches for rodent racing and pay only

10 cents a click! As strange as it sounds, *nobody . . . not a single company*, is currently bidding on that term.

Anyway, imagine that you are placing ads whenever someone searches on the term *rodent racing,* and making a tidy little sum. But then, a series of nasty accidents during high-profile rodent races lead to a sudden interest in insurance for racing rodents (and their jockeys). Major insurance companies realize that there are huge profits to be made . . . and start bidding on PPC ads. Rates go up, 50 cents, a dollar, five dollars. And now, you're out of business, because the click rates are so high you just can't buy them.

Many companies think that when they advertise through PPC, they are competing with, well, their competitors. But they're not, they're competing for ad space with other companies that are interested in the keywords. Look at Figure 1-5. I searched for the term *campground,* and five ads appeared.

Figure 1-5: These PPC advertisers are *not* in direct competition with each other.

The PPC ads are not directly competing with each other, as you can see below.

- ✔ Camping.com — make campground reservations and buy camping gear
- ✔ eBay.com — auctions of camping gear
- ✔ MapQuest.com — maps

- ✔ Cheap-Prices.co.uk — a British "affiliate" site with links to vacation services
- ✔ GoodSamClub.com — the world's largest RV owner's association

Not one of these sites directly competes with another. Now, the rodent-racing example earlier is rather unlikely — rodent racing is, in fact, a very safe sport — but this sort of thing *does* happen. If you're selling a $25 book, you simply can't afford to pay as much in click costs as a company selling, say, insurance policies or mortgages worth thousands of dollars over the life of the policy. Yet you may want to advertise under the same keywords.

Oh well, that's life. You have several choices:

- ✔ Find keywords that the "big boys" aren't targeting
- ✔ Find PPC systems that the big boys aren't using
- ✔ Move on! PPC won't work for you

So, let's move on. We've talked enough in generalities, let's look at the different places you can advertise using the PPC model.

Chapter 2

The Different Forms of PPC

As I mention in the previous chapter, there's more than one form of PPC ad. There are quite a few, and more types enter the market all the time. In this chapter you take a quick look at where and how you can employ PPC advertising.

The Big Two PPC Search Engines

At the time of writing, the vast majority of all PPC advertising goes through just two large, tier-1 PPC systems, owned by the two most important search companies:

> ✔ **Google AdWords:** http://AdWords.Google.com
>
> ✔ **Yahoo! Search Marketing:** http://SearchMarketing.Yahoo.com

For now, there are two big systems. By the time you read this, there may be three. Microsoft is launching its MSN AdCenter advertising system. Within that overall system, Microsoft will have its own PPC service, *MSN Keywords*.

Microsoft owns some of the world's most popular Web sites. While Yahoo! is the world's most popular site, the number 2, number 3, and number 6 most popular sites are owned by Microsoft (the ranks shown below are provided by Alexa, an Amazon-owned company — www.Alexa.com):

> ✔ Number 2: MSN.com
> ✔ Number 3: Passport.net
> ✔ Number 6: Microsoft.com

Actually, until recently, this list was larger, but Microsoft has merged various sites; the domain `Hotmail.com`, for instance, now points to Passport.net, so it isn't measured as a separate (but incredibly popular) site. In any case, my point is that Microsoft's sites get a huge amount of traffic.

Microsoft has a search engine, with its home on the MSN.com Web site, and Microsoft.com and Passport.net both use this system. This search engine has PPC ads, of course — it's big business, too big for Microsoft to ignore. But at the time of writing, the PPC ads are provided by Yahoo!'s Search Marketing PPC system.

That's all changing. Early in 2005, MSN announced that it was building its own PPC system (which was hard to hide, anyway, as people throughout the PPC business were getting calls from headhunters wanting to hire them to work for Microsoft). In the summer of 2005, MSN went live with its own PPC system — AdCenter — in France and Singapore. In the fall of 2005 it also launched an "invitation-only" service within the United States, open to large advertisers, and started mixing its own PPC ads in with the ones coming from Yahoo!. Microsoft, today, owns one of the world's three largest search systems. The change is that it will be running its own ads, not someone else's, on its search-results pages.

However, in the summer of 2005 Microsoft announced that it was *renewing* its PPC partnership with Yahoo! and signed another contract taking it through to June 2006. So it's close to 100 percent certain that by June 2006, MSN will be running its own PPC system, with full access for all advertisers.

If you want to see if MSN's system is fully open for business yet, visit this page: `http://advertising.msn.com/msnadcenter/`.

So there you go, two big PPC systems, based on the Google, Yahoo!, and a third on the way, MSN. And the vast majority of PPC ad placements and clicks go through those systems.

By the way, all PPC systems are not equal. You may find that you do very well on Google but just can't get PPC to work on Yahoo! — or vice versa. In fact, that's exactly the case for one company I recently spoke with. They've given up working with Yahoo! because, although they can buy clicks, they just don't seem to "convert" for them — that is, the visitors coming to them from Yahoo! are less likely to buy from them. This may be a function of the type of products the company sells. The company believes that its prospects (the people who could be persuaded to buy from them) are more likely to use

Google than Yahoo!, and this may well be the case (the company targets computer server administrators). So bear in mind that although the two major systems (three major systems soon) have a number of similarities, the traffic coming from the different PPC sites won't necessarily convert equally.

Who Feeds Whom?

If PPC ads placed with the major systems were placed only on the major systems' Web sites, that would result in many millions of ad impressions. But, in fact, the big systems feed *other* systems. That is, ads placed with Google and Yahoo! do not appear *only* on Google.com and Yahoo.com. (I'll ignore MSN for the moment.) Rather, the major systems sign agreements with many other sites, to feed PPC ads and share revenues from the ads.

For instance, imagine that you place ads on Google and decide to use *only* search placement (that is, you're not using content-match ads that appear on non-search sites, as I discuss a little later in this chapter). Your ads will appear on Google.com, of course. But they'll also appear on AOL.com, Earthlink.com, Netscape.com, AskJeeves.com, Amazon.com/A9.com (see Figure 2-1), Shopping.com, and many more.

These PPC ads are delivered by Google

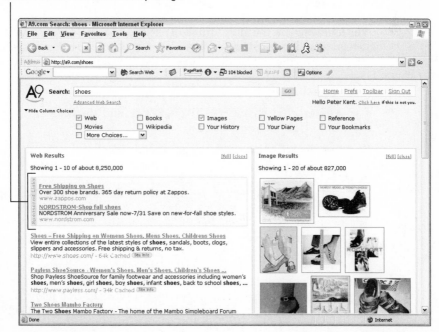

Figure 2-1:
The two ads
at the top of
A9.com's
search
results
come from
Google.

Or perhaps you use Yahoo! Search Marketing, also using only search placement. Your ads appear not only in Yahoo!'s search results, but also in MSN's (at the time of writing; as I mention before, by the time you read this, MSN might be running its own PPC system). They will also appear on Altavista.com, InfoSpace.com, CNN.com, and various other sites.

Second-Tier PPC Systems

There are, however, other PPC systems, the systems I like to think of as the "second tier." They're in no way comparable to the major three "first-tier" systems — they're far smaller and almost unheard of. Everyone's heard of Google, Yahoo!, and Microsoft, but who's heard of Kanoodle, SearchFeed, or myGeek? Regardless of their size, they are still important players in the business, and they may be important to you. Two good reasons to investigate using the smaller PPC systems are

✔ **Price:** Clicks from these second-tier systems are often much cheaper, especially if you're chasing expensive terms. A keyword that requires, say, a $10 bid for a first-place position in Overture or Google may cost only 5 or 10 *cents* on one of these smaller systems.

✔ **Volume:** Perhaps you're maxed out on the big systems; you're doing well, buying all the clicks you can, and making money. But you want more clicks! The second-tier systems may be able to provide them.

The following are the sites I think of as second-tier. This is rather a subjective category, so I'm sure that some people might pull up other systems from the *third tier* and into the second. They're listed in alphabetical order, not by size:

✔ 7Search.com (www.7search.com)

✔ AJInteractive (AskJeeves, iWon, Excite, and MaxOnline, www.AJInteractive.com)

✔ BlowSearch (http://blowsearch.com)

✔ Brainfox (http://brainfox.com)

✔ Enhance Interactive (www.enhance.com, formerly Ah-Ha.com)

✔ ePilot (http://epilot.com)

✔ goClick.com (www.goclick.com)

✔ Kanoodle (www.kanoodle.com)

✔ LookSmart (http://search.looksmart.com)

✔ Lycos InSite AdBuyer (Lycos, HotBot, AngelFire, and so on; http://insite.lycos.com/adbuyer/overview.asp)

✔ MIVA (`www.miva.com`, formerly FindWhat.com and eSpotting)

✔ Mamma (`www.mamma.com`)

✔ myGeek (`www.mygeek.com`)

✔ Search123 (`www.search123.com`)

✔ Search*feed*.com (`www.searchfeed.com`)

✔ Snap (`www.Snap.com`)

The huge advantage of the second-tier systems is that the traffic you get from them is likely to cost far less than traffic from the major systems; the clicks are very cheap, and this is definitely their main competitive advantage. In Figure 2-2, you can see an example of a table provided by Brainfox comparing clicks purchased from them with clicks purchased from a "Tier-1" system.

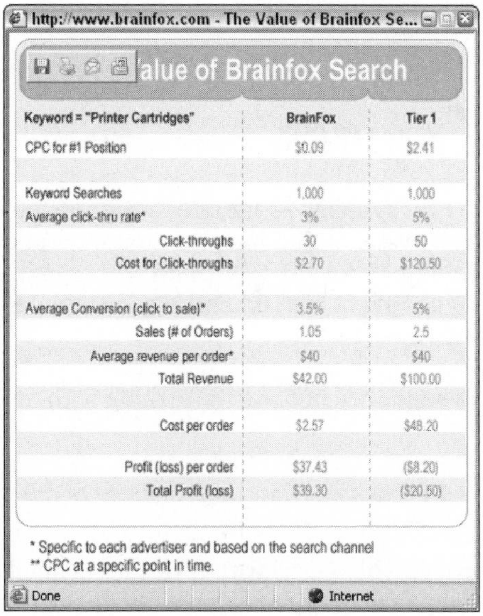

Keyword = "Printer Cartridges"	BrainFox	Tier 1
CPC for #1 Position	$0.09	$2.41
Keyword Searches	1,000	1,000
Average click-thru rate*	3%	5%
Click-throughs	30	50
Cost for Click-throughs	$2.70	$120.50
Average Conversion (click to sale)*	3.5%	5%
Sales (# of Orders)	1.05	2.5
Average revenue per order*	$40	$40
Total Revenue	$42.00	$100.00
Cost per order	$2.57	$48.20
Profit (loss) per order	$37.43	($8.20)
Total Profit (loss)	$39.30	($20.50)

* Specific to each advertiser and based on the search channel
** CPC at a specific point in time.

Figure 2-2: Brainfox compares its clicks with Google and Yahoo!.

The huge problem with such systems is that they generate far lower levels of traffic — you generally won't be able to buy as many clicks. So when you figure the cost of managing these programs into your return-on-investment (ROI) calculations, you *may* find that they are not quite so profitable. (A common complaint among companies who have tried them is "we just couldn't get any traffic out of them.")

Furthermore, the quality of traffic from the second-tier search engines is often low — it often doesn't convert as well as traffic from the first-tier systems. Despite low conversions, because the clicks are so cheap, second-tier systems can often still provide a better ROI.

If the second-tier services provide much lower click prices, shouldn't you start there? Probably not. Because volumes are so low, it's often difficult to evaluate whether a PPC campaign is going to work using the smaller systems. With the bigger ones, you can get things rolling, find out if it works, and then expand to the smaller ones. And even if it doesn't work with the bigger systems — because click prices are too high — you should have enough information to evaluate whether you could make PPC work with lower click prices, so you'll know if it's worth trying the smaller systems.

Making the second-tier systems work isn't always easy, but it's possible in some cases. I discuss, in Chapter 11, how to ensure that you have the best chance of a successful tier-two campaign.

By the way, I didn't include a number of other second-tier PPC systems because they seem to be in a category of their own: the content-match and contextual advertising systems, such as Quigo and adMarketPlace, which I look at a little later in this chapter.

Third-Tier Search Engines

There are many, many more PPC systems — literally hundreds of small PPC systems. Some are specialized systems that may be worth working with if your site matches their specialty. Unfortunately, many are scams, or nearly so, making money by getting people to sign up and pay a setup fee but never delivering much traffic, if any.

In general, these third-tier systems are not worth working with, except in a couple of circumstances:

- ✔ You can find a specialty PPC system that targets exactly the people you're after.
- ✔ You can work with a broker who works with a variety of smaller systems, "aggregating" clicks; you pay the company a set fee for each click, and that company figures out how to get them to you.

In most cases, avoid these systems. You'll quite likely spend more in terms of time — setting up and managing the programs — and setup fees than you're likely to benefit from the cheap clicks. Perhaps you can find a specialty system that targets just the people you need to reach. But most people find the third-tier systems to be more trouble than they're worth.

Want to see some of these systems? Use one of the PPC directories, such as PPC-Directory.com or PayPerClickSearchEngines.com, both of which list hundreds of systems.

Geo-targeting

Geo-targeting is an extension of regular PPC. It's simply a way to target audiences more closely, geographically. Not only do you specify which keywords you want to trigger your ads, but you also specify *where* you want the ads placed. For instance, you may want your ad to display when someone types the word *shoes* into the search engine, *if* that person is in Springfield, Illinois, but *not* if the searcher is in Springfield, Missouri.

Clearly, geo-targeting is an important development because it makes PPC advertising useful to far more people. Now, not only can people who sell shoes online buy clicks based on the keyword *shoe,* but people who sell shoes in a particular city might consider bidding on the term, too. You discover more about this in Chapter 12.

Content-Match or Contextual PPC

As I mention in Chapter 1, PPC is generally thought of as a search engine advertising tool; ads are seen by people searching for something.

Naturally, the search engine companies have only a limited "inventory" of ad space. They can't display more ads than fit on the search-results pages generated by searchers. Of course, they can try jamming more and more ads onto a page, but eventually such a tactic is self-defeating: The search engine risks losing customers, both searchers and advertisers.

If search engine companies want to grow their revenues, what can they do? They can feed ads to other search engines, of course, and the major systems do just that, as I explain earlier in this chapter. But they can also feed ads to non-search sites. The major systems do this, too. In particular, Google has managed to spread billions of PPC ads throughout the Internet through its AdSense program (which I discuss in Chapter 18). These ads are sometimes known as *contextual* or *content-match* ads, using Yahoo!'s terminology; *contextual* because they are placed according to the context of the Web page in which they are being placed, and *content-match* because they are matched up with "content" Web sites as opposed to search sites.

They work like this. A Web site signs up to join the program and puts a little bit of code on the pages in which the ads are going to be placed. This code is a "call" — it calls the PPC service asking for an ad. In other words, when you go to a Web site and open a page that contains one of these little codes, the code sends a message to the PPC service and asks for an ad, or maybe several ads, to place on the page.

The PPC service examines the page on which the ad will be placed and sends what it thinks is an appropriate ad, based on the keywords chosen by the advertiser. So if the page is related to, say, traveling to Greece, the ads are, hopefully, from companies in some way related to vacations in Greece. The trick behind these ads is figuring out what a page is all about — which the PPC service does by reading all the text on the page — and then placing ads related to that subject onto the page, so when you're reading about Greece, you see Greece-related ads. You can see an example of this in action in Figure 2-3, in which Google has placed ads from travel companies onto a page containing a forum message about vacationing in the Greek islands.

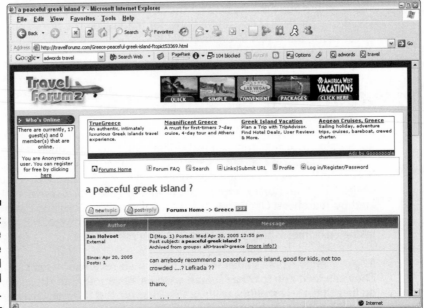

Figure 2-3:
Four Google
AdSense
ads dropped
into a travel
Web site.

First-tier content-match systems

The major PPC systems let you decide where you will run your ads: either in the search engines or in both the search engines and the content sites. I recommend that when you begin your program, you advertise only on the search engine results pages, not the content pages. Or, at least, watch both carefully. (You can see in your reports the results of both forms of placement.)

The problem is that content-match ads are likely to be less effective than search-results ads for a couple of reasons:

✔ When placing ads on search-results pages, the search engine has to match the keywords specified by an advertiser to the keywords entered by the searcher, an easy task. A search engine has a harder time looking at a page and figuring out which keywords best match it, so the ads being placed are often not very well-matched with the page content.

✔ Even if the ad is well-matched, the tendency to buy might not be as strong. When people are searching, they're looking for something — often looking for a product. When they are reading a content page, they may not be looking for anything in particular beyond information.

That doesn't necessarily mean you can't successfully use content-match ads. You might find that the numbers work well enough to allow you to use both forms, even if the ROI on the content-match ads is lower — after all, a return on your investment is still a return, even if it isn't as high as you had hoped. But it does mean that content-match should be approached with caution, particularly when starting out.

Second-tier content-mach systems

There's a new category of second-tier PPC systems: companies that focus on content-match advertising. The second-tier systems I mention earlier in this chapter grew up in the search engine phase of PPC ads, and their main focus is placing PPC ads into search results. However, a number of companies focus on placing ads into content sites rather than search sites.

For instance Quigo (`http://quigo.com/adsonarexchange.htm`) places ads on many well-known sites, such as Cars.com, USAToday.com, Discovery.com, Newsday.com, HomeStore.com, and theKnot.com (see Figure 2-4). This company is perhaps the largest well-known independent with the broadest reach in content-match, so it's one worth considering if you want to play in these waters.

Another system, adMarketPlace (`www.adMarketPlace.net`), manages eBay's keywords system, but it also has a non-eBay network of sites on which advertisers can place PPC ads. adMarketPlace's main thrust is the creation of image-based PPC ads rather than text ads. It's hard to tell right now where its ads are placed, though — adMarketPlace is definitely proud of the eBay connection but says nothing about any other sites.

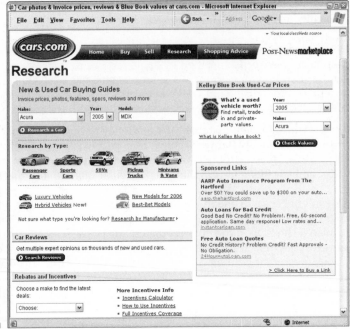

Figure 2-4:
These PPC
ads were
placed into
Cars.com by
the Quigo
content-
match PPC
system.

Underlined Words

Here's an up-and-coming system you may have seen here and there: Vibrant Media's IntelliTXT system (www.vibrantmedia.com). IntelliTXT is a form of content-match PPC — the ads are placed on content sites (currently "hundreds of sites and millions of pages"), not search sites. And the ads are pop-up ads. Here's what I mean: If you look in Figure 2-5, you'll notice a number of doubly underlined words. If you were to point at one of the words, an ad would open (see Figure 2-6). Clicking the word opens another Web browser window with the advertiser's site displayed.

These ads do get clicked; one company I know that runs these ads, along with Google AdSense ads, told me that it was actually making more money from the advertising commissions from the IntelliTXT ads than from the AdSense ads. But if you're an advertiser, that doesn't necessarily mean it's a good deal for you. Remember that these are also content-match ads, and so are likely to have a lower ROI than search-results ads. Still, many major companies have been using these, from IBM to Gateway, Sun to Microsoft. Here's how, from the advertiser's perspective, this works. You provide an Excel spreadsheet file containing the following:

✔ The keywords you want to match with your ad

✔ The text that will appear in the pop-up ad

✔ A "visible" URL, generally the domain of the site being pointed to

✔ The actual URL — the URL pointing to the page that the prospect lands on when he clicks the ad

IntelliTXT looks through the Web sites it works with, finds good matches for your keywords, and places the double-underline under words in the pages.

I recently ran across a similar system, DynamiContext, from Kontera (www.kontera.com). This company provides two types of content-match ads: text ads displayed alongside the page content *and* underlined text with pop-up ads similar to IntelliTXT. (With this system, the double-underline uses one solid line and one dotted line.)

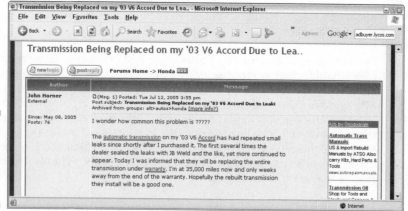

Figure 2-5: The double-underlined words are ads.

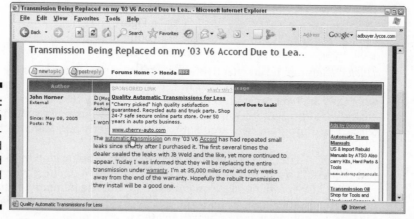

Figure 2-6: Point at a double-underlined word, and the ad pops up.

Paid Inclusion

I definitely recommend against paid inclusion for the vast majority of cases. It's a very expensive way to get pages into a search engine, but with no guarantees. Still, here's how it works:

You provide a search engine with a list of URLs pointing to pages on your site and pay an annual fee, per page, to have the search engine index your site's pages. The search engine will also come back frequently, every day or so, and reindex the pages.

Paid-inclusion services are expensive. Yahoo! charges $49 for the first URL, $29 for URLs 2 through 10, and $10 for each subsequent page. This can be extremely expensive . . . you do the math! And in most cases, it's simply not necessary because you can get the search engines to index your pages automatically for free.

I've included paid inclusion in a discussion of PPC because, although in most cases, paid inclusion is not actually a PPC system — there's a submission charge, but no click charge — the most important paid-inclusion system *is* a PPC system. Yahoo!'s Search Submit Express (formerly Site Match Self Serve) program charges you to place your pages into the index and charges each time someone clicks a link to your site. In effect, paid inclusion — and trusted feeds, which we'll look at next — are methods by which you pay for clicks coming from a search engine's *natural* search results. (That is, the search results that are not paid ads.)

I have some real problems with paid inclusion; I'll discuss this in more detail in Chapter 14.

Trusted Feeds

Trusted feeds can be an effective way to get cheap traffic to your Web site . . . but will they still be around after the Federal Trade Commission understands what they are? In a trusted feed program, a company "feeds" data to a search engine . . . at present, to Yahoo!, the only company currently running a trusted-feed program — Search Submit Pro (formerly Site Match Xchange).

Essentially, trusted feeds work like this: You create some kind of "datafeed" text that contains information about pages on your Web site. If you have, for example, 1,000 product pages on your site (about the minimum required for the program), the datafeed text contains information about 1,000 pages — the URL of each page and keywords related to each page.

This information is then searched when Yahoo! searches its organic search results; a link to your page may appear mixed in with the *organic* — that is, non-paid — search results on the Yahoo! site, with no indication to the searcher that the entry is "sponsored." You pay if someone clicks the link, though.

I explain this system in more detail in Chapter 14. For now, let me just say that trusted feeds can definitely be an effective advertising tool, but that there are some questions as to its legitimacy (is it right to mix paid ads with what appear to be non-paid search results) . . . though I guess that's Yahoo!'s problem, not yours.

Shopping Directories

Another way to buy clicks is through the shopping directories and price-comparison services. Some of these are actually free — most notably Google's service, Froogle (www.froogle.com). But most charge by the click, and some have a bidding system very similar to the normal search-engine PPC model.

Yahoo! Shopping (Figure 2-7) is one of the best-known of these services. In order to enter information about your Web site into the Yahoo! Shopping directory, you join Yahoo!'s Shopping Submit program. Various other directories channel traffic to your site in exchange for a click fee, too. PriceGrabber, PriceWatch, NexTag, and PriceSCAN charge a flat click fee, while BizRate and Shopping.com charge a click fee that depends on bidding for position. I get into the shopping directories in Chapter 14.

Figure 2-7:
When you click a link at Yahoo! Shopping, the merchant is charged a click fee.

eBay Keywords

Everyone's getting into the PPC game, including eBay. If you sell on eBay (and millions of people do), you can place PPC ads throughout the site (see www.ebaykeywords.com). As you can see in Figure 2-8, eBay has both image and text PPC ads.

All three ads here are PPC ads

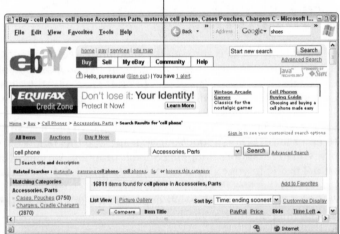

Figure 2-8: eBay's PPC service allows its merchants to place both text and image ads onto search-results pages.

eBay has three types of ads:

✔ A 120-x-60-pixel text box, shown to the right of the large banner in Figure 2-8

✔ A 468-x-60-pixel image banner at the top left of the search results

✔ A larger text box that is sometimes placed to the left of search results

Note, by the way, that eBay's keywords are mainly intended to generate traffic for eBay stores and listings, not for independent Web sites. However, at present, most of the large banners are placed by eBay itself, promoting the eBay credit card for instance, which suggests that they're not selling all their ad inventory. When you *do* find a non-eBay banner, it may point out of the eBay system, so evidently, now and then, eBay is willing to point out of the system.

Pay Per Call

Here's another great way for the PPC companies to expand the PPC market: Find a way to sell "actions" to people who don't even have a Web site or who are not trying to drive traffic to a Web site. The latest and greatest move in PPC is, um, PPC: *Pay Per Call.*

With Pay Per Call, Internet advertising meets low-cost telecommunications. The basic principle is that instead of getting people to click a link that takes them to your Web site, your ad encourages people to call you. In order to measure calls, of course, you need a dedicated phone line; all calls arriving on that line are assumed to be derived from the advertising campaign. Thanks to the drop in phone-service charges over the last few years (does anyone remember how expensive long-distance was in 1991?!), you can play games like this fairly cheaply — setting up a phone number for a particular ad is not an expensive proposition anymore.

Actually, this service has been around for a few years in the paper world; various Yellow Pages companies have sold ads linked to a particular phone number for some time. But it's just taking off in the online world, which, of course, will help to boost click prices some more. Now, not only are you competing against every other Web site that likes your keywords, you're also competing against brick-and-mortar businesses that just want their phone numbers advertised on the Internet. Several companies have Pay Per Call services, including Miva, Ingenio, and Free411.com (see Figure 2-9).

Figure 2-9:
Not only are these PPC ads, but Free411 also provides a way for people to place free calls to the business.

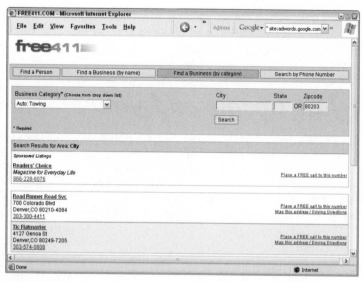

PPA — The Next Wave?

In Chapter 1, I explain the problems with earlier forms of advertising: that advertisers were paying for the *display* of an ad — an ad *impression* — and not for any kind of action. Pay Per Click was an improvement because advertisers now paid for some kind of action, an actual click.

However, even this isn't perfect. A click isn't a sale, after all. And the PPC model introduces a huge new problem, *click fraud* (which I look at in Chapter 17). The basic PPC model *encourages* fraud, in fact, and fraud is now a huge problem.

So what's the next step? PPA — *Pay Per Action,* also known as CPA, *Cost Per Action.* This new system is being introduced by the same group that brought us Pay Per Click in the first place: Bill Gross's IdeaLab. In July 2005, Snap. com, an IdeaLab startup, announced a plan to provide "irrefutable ROI to advertisers." How? This is how Snap.com explains it:

> Snap.com offers advertisers the ability to pay for their desired business results, including sales, downloads, leads, subscriptions, or other actions important to the advertiser. With traditional Pay-Per-Click, advertisers pay the search engine whether or not a click leads to revenue. Snap's Cost-Per-Action ('CPA') system offers advertisers the ability to pay when a customer completes an action tied to revenue, eliminating this risk. Snap.com's CPA model eliminates the risk of click-fraud for the advertiser, a widely acknowledged problem in the industry.

I couldn't have said it better, which is why I quoted Snap.com verbatim (that and the fact that I've written a lot of books and I've begun to think I may be running out of words).

It's Not Just Google and Yahoo!

If this chapter has taught you anything, it's that PPC is not just about Google and Yahoo! (and, soon, MSN). You can use any number of other channels and other PPC methods that may work for you. If you're making money on Google or Yahoo!, why not experiment with some of the other channels. And if you're *not* making money with Google or Yahoo!, you may want to experiment with these other systems because they provide cheaper clicks.

Chapter 3

Calculating ROI (Return on Investment)

Surprisingly few companies spend much time, before beginning a PPC campaign, thinking about the primary purpose for the campaign — making money. And even after the PPC campaign has begun, many (most?) companies don't really track the numbers very well. This may come as a surprise to you, but my work in this field convinces me that it's so.

Just last week, I was talking to a company that spends $100,000 a year on clicks but admits that it isn't really tracking the effect of the clicks very well. The company can't tell you for sure how much money it's making from the purchased clicks and certainly can't tell you which keywords perform better than others — that is, which keywords drive traffic to its site result in more sales and which result in fewer. The company's pretty sure it's making money from PPC . . . it just doesn't know the details.

This chapter is not actually about tracking; I talk about tracking in Chapter 15. Rather, in this chapter, you find out about ROI — *return on investment* — and associated terms and concepts. This chapter gives you the foundation for understanding how PPC campaigns work, which is necessary for using the tracking data I discuss later.

Conversion Ratio, Click Value, ROI, and More

What is the basic idea behind PPC?

1. A PPC company presents your ads to people that are, hopefully, potential clients.

2. Some of those people click your ad, and you pay the PPC company for the click.

3. Some of the people who visit your site carry out some kind of desired action (desired on your part, that is). They buy from you, request more information, pick up a phone and call you, contact you via e-mail, or whatever.

One typically thinks of PPC as leading to sales, but that's not always the case, at least not directly. You want the PPC campaign to lead to some kind of action that is beneficial to your business, which *may* be an immediate sale but may be some other kind of action.

Now, this is all very well, but the devil, as they say, is in the details. A PPC campaign is not a success just because it achieves the above stated goal — buying clicks and converting them to a desired action. It's only successful if the *cost* of the desired action is reasonable and affordable.

Imagine you spend $2 for every click, and out of every 50 people who come to your site, 1 buys from you. That means the sale cost you $100. Is that a success? If, like one of my clients, you're selling a piece of equipment with an average price of $50,000, yes, that's successful. But if you're selling a $20 book, you just lost a lot of money.

So you have to understand the details. You have to understand costs and benefits. The following are a few basic terms and concepts related to how well a PPC campaign performs. (I connect the dots in a few moments.)

✔ **Conversion:** The process of changing a person from one state to another. You're primarily concerned with two processes: changing someone from a person viewing an ad into a person clicking the ad, and changing the person clicking the ad into a person carrying out the desired action. (There may be other conversions down the road. If the desired action is to provide you with lead information, then the person providing the information is a "prospect," and at some point you want to convert the prospect into a buyer.)

✔ **Conversion Ratio:** A measure of how well you "convert" someone. If one person out of 100 clicks your ad, you have a 1 percent conversion ratio. If one visitor to your site out of 200 buys from you, you have a 1:200, or 0.5 percent, conversion ratio. This number is critical; without knowing your conversion ratios, you can't figure out whether you're winning or losing the PPC game.

✔ **Cost Per Action:** How much it costs to get someone to carry out a particular action, such as filling in a lead form or making a purchase. For instance, if your average click price is 60 cents, and you need 100 clicks for every action, then your cost per action is $60.

✔ **Cost Per Sale:** If your action is actually a sale, the Cost Per Action is, of course, the same as the Cost Per Sale. If you're just gathering lead information, then there will be other calculations involved before you can ever get to the cost per sale — how much does it cost to convert your leads into sales? I won't consider these subsequent issues in this book; I take you up to the desired action on your Web site.

✔ **Breakeven Cost Per Sale/Per Action:** This is the maximum amount you can pay for a particular action, or a sale, without losing money. You don't *want* to spend this, of course, but you know that if you go above this number, you're losing money, and if you go below it, you're making money.

✔ **Click Value:** How much a click is worth to you — not how much you're paying for the click, but how much it would be worth paying. You may be paying way more than the click is really worth, or, if you're lucky, far less than you'd be willing to pay.

✔ **Breakeven Click Value:** Actually, how much a click is worth to you is really a range. A better way to think of click value is considering *breakeven click value* — the maximum you'd be willing to pay for a click. In other words, if you spend this sum on a click, you haven't made money, but you haven't lost money, either. Any more is too much (because you'll actually lose money) and any less is profitable; though again, you want to pay as little as possible for a click. Note that click values actually vary between systems, depending on conversion rates. And even within the same system, click values can vary between ads and between keywords. Clicks that convert more readily are worth more than clicks that don't convert so well.

✔ **Return on Investment (ROI):** This is the amount of money you make after investing in your PPC campaign. If you pay $1,000 for ads and make a profit of $300 (after subtracting the cost of your clicks), your ROI is 30 cents per $1 invested. ROI is expressed in different ways; you could see this example expressed as a 30percent ROI (30 cents profit for every $1 spent) or as an absolute sum — an ROI of $300 on a $1,000 investment.

- ✔ **Revenues:** The amount of money you get from selling your products. If you sell 20 books at $20 each, your total revenues are $400. You often hear people say things like, "I made $400 last week selling *x* online," but that's just shorthand for saying that they made $400 in revenues. Their revenues may have been $400, but their *profit* was less, because they had to pay for the items they sold.

- ✔ **Gross Profit:** The amount of money left over after subtracting the costs of goods, cost of clicks, and cost of fulfillment from the revenues. Gross profit is also known as *margin,* particularly in the retail business. I explain this in more detail a little later in this chapter.

Okay, so you've got a lot of concepts here, but they're really not that complicated, and I explain them in more detail throughout the chapter.

The PPC companies provide simple "ROI" calculation tools, and they're much simpler than all this jargon I've just thrown at you. But I'd caution against relying on these tools without understanding the big picture. Business is a numbers game, and if you don't understand the numbers, you really don't understand what's happening to your business. If you don't understand the above concepts, you don't fully understand what your PPC campaign is doing for you.

Calculating Gross Profit and Breakeven Cost Per Sale

Before you begin your PPC campaign, you can't accurately calculate all the things I have just explained; you don't know for sure how many clicks you'll need to make a sale and how much those clicks will cost. However, there are still various things you can calculate, and you can also estimate ROI. In fact, in this chapter, I work *backward* from the desired action — the sale or sales lead, for instance — to figure out a few numbers.

First, take a look at the *breakeven cost per sale.* How much can you afford to spend for a sale and not lose money?

To calculate the breakeven cost per sale, you essentially need to know how much a sale is worth and how much completing the sale costs. Companies that sell multiple products have different costs and revenues — different products sell for different prices and cost different sums to supply. Generally, companies average things out and figure out their average sales. If you have not yet sold a thing, all this is guesswork (but worth doing nonetheless because you're building a calculation you'll use later anyway).

Gather together the following information:

- ✔ **Average Sale Price:** How much is your average sale?

  For this example, imagine that, on average, buyers at your site purchase $132 worth of goods.

- ✔ **Shipping Charges:** How much will the buyer pay you to ship the products?

  For this example, the shipping charge on the average sale is $9.95.

- ✔ **Cost of Goods:** How much do these goods cost you to manufacture or purchase from the supplier? Include not just the direct cost of the goods, but any ancillary costs, such as the cost of shipping the goods to your warehouse, insurance, storage, and so on.

  For this example, the average cost of goods is $70.

- ✔ **Cost of Shipping:** How much does it cost to ship the average order? Include shipping fees, packing materials, insurance, the cost of labor to pack, and so on.

  An average shipping cost of $8 is good for this example.

- ✔ **Transaction Costs:** How much does it cost to process the online transaction? If you're selling online, you have some kind of transaction-processing fee — the sum you pay to the credit-card-processing company to take a credit-card transaction, the sum paid to PayPal for processing a PayPal transaction, perhaps a sum paid to the e-commerce hosting company for the transaction. (Yahoo! charges its Merchant Solutions customers a fee for every transaction that goes through Yahoo! Stores, for instance.)

  Assume the cost is 50 cents plus 2.9 percent of the transaction. (Transaction costs are typically expressed in this way, a fixed cost plus a percentage of the transaction.)

Now that you have some basic numbers, you're almost ready to calculate the breakeven cost. But what about fixed costs — the cost of your office and phone, your monthly Web-site hosting fee, your Internet access, and so on? Forget them. In these calculations, you're interested in whether a particular transaction is profitable or not, and if so, how profitable. You can't introduce fixed costs into the equation, or it gets way too complicated. Figuring out if your overall business is profitable is not part of what you're considering when you figure these sums.

In some cases, of course, you can omit the shipping charges and costs. If there's no delivery cost, for instance — if you're selling software and the buyer simply downloads it — or if the charges always equal the cost, you could omit these items. But many merchants actually make a little money on shipping, or perhaps lose money on shipping, so I've included it in these calculations.

Okay, here goes. Enter your numbers into Table 3-1 to figure your breakeven cost per sale:

Table 3-1 Calculating Breakeven Cost Per Sale	Example	Your Numbers
Sale price	$132	
+ Shipping charges	$9.95	
= Total revenues	$141.95	
Cost of goods	$70	
+ Cost of shipping	$8	
+ Fixed transaction cost	$0.50	
+ Variable transaction cost (2.9% × $141.95)	$4.12	
= Total costs	$82.62	
Total revenues	$141.95	
- Total costs	$82.62	
= Gross profit per sale	$59.33	

What about breakeven cost per action?

Many companies use the Internet to generate leads. One of my clients, for instance, doesn't sell his products online — his products cost anywhere from $8,000 to $100,000, so he knows he's not making that sort of sale without weeks of discussions. So his site is intended to generate leads, not direct sales.

Of course the breakeven cost per action is a more complicated calculation. Most companies in this situation, however, already know the value of a lead, or at least have enough information to figure it out. It's basically a matter of calculating how many leads result in a sale, how much it costs to follow the leads, and how much each sale is worth. Many companies already have an established "cost per lead"

that they are willing to pay. (Of course, different lead sources provide leads of different values; 100 leads from source A may result in a sale, while it might take 120 leads from source B, for instance.)

In such a case, you might not care so much about breakeven cost; rather, you're interested in getting leads at a particular cost — $50 per lead, $150 per lead, or whatever — that you already know is a viable lead cost . . . the *acceptable lead cost.*

I suspect, however — PPC mania being what it is — that many companies are gathering leads through PPC campaigns without actually knowing the true value of a lead.

You end up with the gross profit per sale (margin) that just so happens to be the breakeven cost per sale at this point. In other words, if it costs you this amount to make a sale — $59.33 in this example — you won't lose money; you'll "break even."

Note that the breakeven cost per sale is also the amount you can afford to spend on PPC advertising to generate the sale. In the example, you could spend $59.33 to generate a sale and still break even.

Breakeven Cost Per Click

The *breakeven cost per sale* is a solid figure; it should be pretty accurate because it's based on real numbers. The *breakeven cost per click* is based on a little guesswork when you start out.

First, you need to know the breakeven cost per sale (or *acceptable lead cost*). I show you how to calculate that in the previous section. In this chapter's example, it's $59.33.

You then need to know your *conversion ratio,* the percentage of visitors to the site who buy from you. More specifically, you need to know what percentage of visitors who come *through a PPC campaign* buy from you.

If you have already run a PPC campaign, maybe you have a number you can work with. (I assume you're tracking the numbers! See Chapter 15.) If not, do you have the more general conversion rate for your site? Use that. If you have a brand new site and have no idea what the conversion rate will be, you'll just have to guess!

But at least make an educated guess. Assume that you get a 0.5 percent conversion rate, which is a realistic estimate. This means that one visitor out of 200 will buy from you. If you wish, use 1 in 100. It may be more, but it could be less. Now, I'm not suggesting that online stores never have better conversion ratios than 1 in 200 — many have much higher conversion ratios — but in general, conversion ratios are small fractions.

Think about how *you* work online. You click here, browse for a few moments, click there, stay a few minutes . . . but you don't buy that often. Conversion ratios between a half percent and 1.5 percent are common, even for successful businesses.

Don't be misled by surveys claiming high conversion ratios in the online-retail field. It's true that there are sites with high conversion ratios, but they're way above average and are often large brand-name sites. More common are the tiny conversion ratios of half a percent to 1.5 percent or lower.

So, to figure out a breakeven cost per click, pick the best conversion ratio you've got or guess at a low one. Put your numbers into Table 3-2.

Table 3-2	Calculating the Breakeven Cost Per Click	
	Example	*Your Numbers*
Breakeven cost per sale (or acceptable lead cost)	$59.33	
× Conversion ratio	0.5%	
= Breakeven cost per click	$0.297	

This is a simple calculation; divide the breakeven cost per sale by the number of clicks it takes to get the sale (or multiply by the conversion ratio percentage, the same thing):

$59.33 × 0.5% = 29.7 cents per click

Or

$59.33 ÷ 200 = 29.7 cents per click

The breakeven cost per click (in this example, 29.7 cents), is the maximum you could spend on a click without losing money, assuming that the conversion ratio remains the same. Again, you're not actually making money, but you have an idea now of what a click could be worth.

In some cases, you may find that your breakeven cost per click is huge. Perhaps you're gathering leads, and you've been told by your company's sales department that it is willing to pay $150 per lead (your company sells very high-ticket items). Let's say that you were also very conservative, and decided to use a conversion ratio of 0.25% (one conversion in 400!). You've discovered that your breakeven cost per click (or, in this case, perhaps we should say *acceptable cost per click*) would be $37.50 cents. Based on this, you can be pretty sure you *can* make a PPC campaign work for you. You can almost certainly buy clicks at far less than $37.50 (even companies that are buying clicks are much higher prices have much lower-cost alternatives), and you can probably get a much higher conversion ratio than 1:400.

On the other hand, perhaps your breakeven cost per sale is $4 . . . well, I can tell you now that you probably won't make PPC work. But let's carry on with the calculation. Let's say that you were optimistic, and picked a 2 percent conversion ratio. That means, for every 50 visitors, one will buy; $4 / 50 = 8 cents . . . your breakeven click cost is 8 cents.

This is going to be tough to do, unless you can find a way to buy enough really low-cost clicks *and* can maintain that 2 percent conversion ratio (are you sure you're really going to get 2 percent?).

Mileage will vary

Of course, some of these numbers are merely guidelines when you get started, and they'll vary between keywords and between PPC systems. They're intended to give you a foundation to build on. You may discover that your breakeven cost per click is, for example, 45 cents on Google but 55 cents on Yahoo! because, for your particular products, you're "converting" Yahoo! visitors more often than Google visitors.

Different keywords will have different conversion ratios, and thus different breakeven click values. For instance, you may find that the term *rodent racing* is much more valuable than the term *rodent sports* because more people who click on the rodent racing ad turn into customers.

So at this stage in the game, you're getting a feel for the business; after you have real clicks, you'll have real numbers, and when you combine those numbers with continued tracking (Chapter 15), you'll be able to make out the real picture.

Figuring Out Return on Investment (ROI)

ROI is the flip side of the coin. In the previous section, you work back from a sale, trying to figure out what you can afford to spend on clicks. But after you are actually carrying out a PPC campaign, you'll want to calculate ROI, the *return on investment*. You want to know how much your investment in PPC advertising returns in profit. And generally, you calculate that for an entire PPC campaign, for a particular keyword, or for a particular ad, over a specific time period (rather than calculating ROI for an individual sale).

 It's even a good idea to run through an ROI calculation *before* you begin a PPC campaign. Most companies don't bother doing this, based on the idea that "we don't know the numbers anyway, so why bother trying to figure anything out?"

But you do know some of the numbers — or should, anyway — so it's a good idea to begin ROI calculations using some basic assumptions before your PPC campaign is launched. Later, you'll be able to plug in more accurate numbers, but in the meantime, you'll have a good picture of what may happen.

Calculating ROI is really very simple. You need just two numbers:

- ✔ **Total Click Price:** The total sum you spent on PPC in order to generate the sales you're looking at.

- ✔ **Gross Profit:** I show you how to calculate gross profit per sale earlier in this chapter. You need the gross profit for all sales derived from PPC during the period for which you want to calculate ROI.

After you have these numbers in hand, you can begin to calculate the ROI.

Calculating gross profit per campaign

I show you how to calculate gross profit per sale earlier in this chapter. But in order to calculate ROI, you need a slightly different gross-profit figure: the gross profit *per campaign*. You calculated the gross profit for the average sale on your site in the previous sections without considering advertising costs; for instance, for a sale generated by "free" traffic from the search engines. Of course, the cost of pushing visitors to your site is also part of the cost of making the sale, so you also have to subtract that cost.

In the earlier example, you had a gross profit of $59.33 for the average sale. Now, if the sale was generated by a PPC campaign and the clicks in that campaign cost an average of 20 cents, you might at first glance think that you must subtract 20 cents from the gross profit. But that wouldn't be correct.

Not everyone who visits the site buys. So the cost of advertising for this sale was not the cost of the click that sent the buyer to the site. You also have to include the cost of the clicks that sent people who *didn't* buy to the site.

Now, in the earlier example, you assumed a conversion rate of 0.5 percent. That means that for every visitor who buys, 199 *don't* buy. Or, another way to look at it, in order to find one buyer, you have to have 200 visitors. So the real cost of the sale is not the click from the one person who bought, but the entire block of 200 ad clicks.

Now, if the average cost per click is 20 cents, and you need 200 clicks to make the sale, the advertising cost of the sale is $40. So I've added another line to the earlier calculation in Table 3-1 to Table 3-3. (I indicate changes to the table in bold.) The gross profit for the campaign — after subtracting the advertising costs — after accounting for PPC costs, is now $19.33.

Table 3-3	Calculating Gross Profit for the Campaign	
	Example	*Your Numbers*
Sale price	$132	
+ Shipping charges	$9.95	
= Total revenues	$141.95	
Cost of goods	$70	
+ Cost of shipping	$8	
+ Fixed transaction cost	$0.50	
+ Variable transaction cost (2.9% × $141.95)	$4.12	

	Example	Your Numbers
+ Cost of PPC advertising	$40	
= Total costs	$122.62	
Total revenues	$141.95	
− Total costs	$122.62	
= Gross profit	$19.33	

Okay, so this shows how to calculate gross profit for a particular sale. When we're calculating ROI, you use the same principle, but this time you calculate for a particular block of sales.

When calculating for an entire PPC campaign, you figure out revenues for all sales generated by that campaign, then subtract all the costs for those sales, and then subtract the cost of all the PPC clicks during the campaign to end up with the gross profit for the campaign.

Calculating return on investment

Calculating return on investment is simple. Just divide the gross profit for the campaign by the cost of the campaign.

> Gross Profit Per Campaign ÷ Cost of All Clicks = ROI

For instance, imagine that your gross profit for all the sales generated by the PPC campaign is $11,959, and you spent $21,234 on clicks. No, you haven't lost money; remember, the $11,959 is the gross profit *after* paying for the cost of the advertising. (So, in fact, the gross profit for the campaign before subtracting PPC costs, is $33,193.)

> Gross Profit Per Sales ($33,193) – Cost of All Clicks ($21,234) = Gross Profit Per Campaign ($11,959)

Now you can calculate the ROI; divide $11,959 by $21,234, and you end up with 0.56, or 56 percent.

> Gross Profit Per Campaign ($11,959) ÷ Cost of All Clicks ($21,234) = ROI (0.56, or 56%)

I just want to clarify here. You must understand that you have actually made a profit. This ROI figure means that when you spent a dollar on advertising, you generated enough sales to give you the dollar back *and* another 56 cents. So an ROI of 56 percent means you spent a dollar, and got $1.56 *back*. Clear?

Of course, it doesn't always go this well. Look at these numbers:

Gross Profit Per Campaign (–$1,324.55) ÷ Cost of All Clicks ($15,234.14) = ROI (–0.087, or –8.7%)

In other words, you had a "negative return" of 8.7 percent. For every dollar you spent, you lost 8.7 cents.

Deferred Actions

Another value that you might want to consider when calculating your ROI, but that is very difficult to track, is *deferred actions*. Someone clicks your ad, arrives at your site, looks around for a while . . . and leaves. But that person returns later — perhaps a few hours later, perhaps a day or two later, maybe even weeks — and buys, or carries out whatever other action you're interested in.

It's very hard to track this kind of visit. You probably won't be able to do so, in fact. There *are* ways to track return visits to your site, and the more advanced tracking tools such as Yahoo! Search Optimizer (see Chapter 15) can help you do this, but it may be very difficult for many companies to not only identify return visits, but to actually match those visitors to an earlier click on one of your PPCads. Chances are, this number is small anyway, so you should probably be aware that your ROI may be *slightly* better than you have calculated, but probably not by much.

Offline Sales

There's another category of sales that are rather problematic; offline sales generated by your online PPC campaign. Many people research online, then purchase offline. In fact the offline component of e-commerce is actually greater than the online component. Consider some of these statistics.

ShopLocal.com commissioned a study of what it calls W2S sales — Web to Store sales, transactions that begin online but end in a brick-and-mortar store. (ShopLocal.com is owned by CrossMedia, a partnership of the newspaper giants Gannet, Knight Ridder, and the Tribune Company.) Here's what it found happened in the fourth quarter of 2004:

✔ 83 million people researched products online and then purchased offline.

✔ On average each of these people spent $250 on online purchases.

> ✔ On average each of these people spent $400 in a brick-and-mortar store, on products researched online.
>
> ✔ In addition, each of these people, on average, spent an *additional $200* in those brick-and-mortar stores on products *not* researched online.

According to these statistics, then, the average W2S buyer spends $250 online (29 percent), $400 offline on researched products (47 percent), and $200 offline on additional purchases (24 percent). That's 29 percent online, and 71 percent *offline!*

Hmmm, interesting. Well, that's just one bit of research, though. But how about this. Forrester Research studied what it called *off-channel shoppers* at about the same time; what are off-channel shoppers? They're the same as W2S shoppers, people who research online and shop offline based on the research. Here's what they found:

> ✔ Most Internet users are "off-channel" shoppers.
>
> ✔ They spend more money offline after online research, than they spend online.
>
> ✔ Almost half spend extra dollars once in the brick-and-store store, on products they didn't research.

Forrester Research believes that in 1994, off-channel shoppers spent over $100 billion in brick-and-mortar stores, based on its online research, of which perhaps 12 percent were incremental sales on products not researched.

Slightly different numbers, but the same overall conclusion; offline revenues based on online research are huge

Now, if you sell online only, you don't have this "problem." It's a good problem to have, of course, but the problem for companies that market online and make sales offline is . . . how do you measure it?

One of my clients owns 24 retail stores, and an online store. "We know the online store generates a lot of offline business," the VP of Marketing told me, "we just don't know how much." In the early days of Internet e-commerce, there was a lot of worry about "channel conflict." In particular the brick-and-mortar staff were worried that online sales would pull business away from its stores. The staff in my client's stores, however, have none of those concerns. They also realize that the online store pushes people into the brick-and-mortars. "We see a *lot* of people walking in with printouts from the Web site," one salesperson told me.

How do you measure this? It's really very difficult to do for most companies, especially large companies that, even if they can come up with some kind of mechanism to track sales, then have to integrate it into existing operations and Point of Sale software. You should be aware that there really can be such an effect, if you manage your Web site properly (some companies do better than others at pushing people to their offline stores).

Including Lifetime Value

There's another element you need to consider when calculating your ROI: the lifetime value of your customers. *Lifetime value* refers to the total income from a customer during the life of the relationship with that customer.

Say someone clicks one of your PPC ads today and spends $75 at your site right away and that it cost $30 in click costs. You've just made a $75 sale and, for example, a gross profit of $10. That's an ROI of around 33 cents for every dollar spent on advertising. Not too bad.

But now imagine that the customer returns a few weeks later and spends another $75. This time, your gross profit is actually higher because you didn't have to pay another $30 in click costs to get him there; the customer already knows about your business. So the gross profit on the second sale is, perhaps, $40. Now your ROI on the original click cost of $30 isn't $10, it's $50 ($10 + $40 = $50); as a percentage, it's 167 percent ($50 ÷ $30).

Perhaps the customer then returns every three months for the next three years — 12 more visits. And what if each time he returns, you make an average gross profit of $40? You now have a total gross profit of $530 for an initial click cost of $30, or an ROI of $17.67 for every dollar spent. (This is a simplified example; you should also consider the cost of maintaining the relationship with the customer, such as mailings, special offers, and so on.)

If you're already in business, you may already have an idea of the lifetime value of your customers and understand that your ROI grows over time.

There are dangers involved with using lifetime values, however. Much was made of lifetime values during the dotcom boom; but remember, the dotcom boom was followed by the dotcom bust, a very painful occurrence during which many companies discovered that their customer's lifetime value was actually a small fraction of what they'd assumed (and declared to investors).

Here are the two main dangers:

✔ **Businesses, in particular new ones, often grossly overestimate lifetime values.** They just *know* the value will be high, but it turns out to be almost nothing beyond the first sale.

✔ **Small businesses and new ventures often don't have the cash flow to finance the purchasing of new customers based on the lifetime value.** If you can spend $100 to buy customers who will, over the next five years, be worth $800 in gross profits to you, that's not a bad deal, except that you have to pay the $100 *today,* not over five years!

Lifetime values *online* are probably not as important as offline. Lifetime value is very important to Amazon.com, Expedia.com, and Buy.com. Many smaller, non-brand companies are making "hit-and-run" sales: The buyers have little or no loyalty; they bought simply because it was the right product at the right price. The buyer might never return, in fact, might not even remember *where* he purchased the product.

This is not to say that working to increase the lifetime value of your clients is not important; it's incredibly important, though beyond the scope of this book. All I'm saying is that you should be cautious of how you drop any lifetime value into your ROI calculations.

One more thing to consider: Just because a lifetime value justifies spending more money on clicks to get new customers doesn't mean you *should* spend more. The goal should be to get new customers at the lowest cost you can, not at any affordable cost. So in general, PPC campaigns should be managed with the intention of making a profit on the *first* sale, unless you are really on solid ground with your lifetime-value calculations *and* the business is willing to lose in the short run to make it up in the long run.

Forget the Value of Branding

Promoting PPC ads as a form of brand advertising is quite popular these days. But let me be really clear about this: For the vast majority of businesses, there is *no* brand-advertising value.

Why, then, do you hear so much about it? Well, if you were selling PPC ads, wouldn't you come up with every possible reason to use them? And if many companies found they weren't making money from PPC, wouldn't it be nice to have a reason to use PPC ads that wasn't related to silly factors such as actually *making money?* I'm not saying PPC ads *cannot* be used for brand advertising. I'm just saying that *you* probably can't use PPC ads for brand advertising. (I'm using the statistically average *you.* The average reader — the average you — is not in a position to use brand advertising; your mileage may vary.)

There are a few really good reasons why brand advertising won't work for most companies. But first, sit comfortably and let me explain what brand advertising *is*.

What are brands and branding?

A *brand* is a proper noun that identifies a company or product. IBM is a brand; Evian is a brand; Whopper is a brand; Microsoft is a brand. *For Dummies* is a brand. Everyone likes to think they have a brand, but a real brand is more than just a name that you wish everyone knew. A *real* brand is a name that everyone (or almost everyone) *does* know. Everyone's heard of IBM, Evian water, the Whopper burger, Microsoft, and *For Dummies* books. In fact, a good brand is a little more; not only do people know the name, when they think of the name, they think good things. They hold the name in respect in some way. (Enron is a brand, but few people these days would say it's a *good* brand.)

A real brand is a powerful thing. The name instantly conveys a concept of value to buyers that makes them more likely to buy and allows the brand owner to charge more.

So what's brand advertising? *Brand advertising* is advertising that is intended to keep the brand in the minds of potential customers, to maintain brand awareness, to maintain the power of the brand. It's not advertising that is intended to lead directly to a sale; it's intended to remind customers of the brand and to reinforce the brand in their minds. Then, when they're ready to buy, they'll remember the brand and may buy it. (Wiley, the publisher of this very book, advertises in libraries — where you can't buy books, of course. The company believes it's good brand advertising.)

Let me repeat: Brand advertising is *not* intended to lead directly to a sale. Yet Pay Per Click advertising has been used as a tool to lead directly to sales. Because it's possible to measure virtually every step of the advertising and sales process (you'll learn about this in Chapter 15), it's possible to measure whether or not you are making a sale from an individual ad placement and, if so, how much money you made. And by aggregating all the data, you can figure out if, overall, the advertising works, and how much money the advertising makes you (the subject of this chapter, of course).

PPC advertising is a wonderful thing, in part because you can actually find out whether you're making money from your ads. No longer do you have to place an ad and never really know whether it works, as businesses do every day with newspaper ads. But if you're clearly not making money from the ads, that's okay because you're building brand awareness, right?

Wrong. Finally, here's why.

Why brand advertising won't work in your PPC campaign

First, you don't own a brand. (Okay, maybe you do, but right now I'm talking to the average reader, and the average reader does not own a brand.) So you can't advertise your brand. But you could use advertising to *build* your brand, right? Wrong again.

There's a huge misconception that brands are built through advertising. They're virtually *never* built by advertising. Now, I'm not a branding guru, so let me quote a couple of 'em: "The birth of a brand is achieved with publicity, not advertising" (Al Ries and Laura Ries). In their book, *The 22 Immutable Laws of Branding,* the Rieses provide many examples of brands that were built not with advertising, but with publicity (and in some cases even today the brand owners spend very little money on advertising). Brands you've probably heard of, such as The Body Shop, Starbucks, Wal-Mart, Sam's Club, Band Aid, CNN, Domino's, Time, Xerox, Microsoft, Intel, Gateway . . .

I'll add one more to the list: Amazon.com. This company brand was built through publicity. It can't have been built through advertising because Amazon didn't spend much money on advertising, and even today doesn't spend much. Amazon even stopped running television ads a few years ago because the company decided they just weren't worth the money.

But companies do spend huge sums advertising their brands, don't they? Sure, many do (though when was the last time you saw an ad for Starbucks?). Even the brand experts accept that it may be necessary to spend large sums of money in order to maintain a brand: "Once born, a brand needs advertising to stay healthy," say Ries and Ries.

So, cool, if you have a major brand and want to use PPC as part of your brand-advertising strategy, go ahead. But if you don't own a brand

- ✔ Don't think that you can build one through PPC ads.
- ✔ Don't think that you can create "awareness" of your product through PPC ads and thus increase sales.

Awareness is sort of like *brand.* "Okay, so I don't own a well-known brand," people think, "but if I can build a little awareness about my business and products, that's a good thing isn't it?"

Sure it's a good thing, but the chance of doing it through PPC ads is pretty slim, and here's why: First, your ad budget, as big as you may think it is, is nothing compared to what's being spent online. Your PPC ads may appear now and then, but in most cases, in the larger scheme of things, they're a drop in the ocean.

But even if they weren't a drop in the ocean, you must remember that people still won't see them very often. People don't go online and carry out the same search every day. They search when they need to, not over and over again. So your PPC ads will not provide multiple impressions to potential customers. The big guys may be able to make it work; if you are doing print and radio and television *and* PPC ads, the PPC ads are just one part of a giant program to hit people over and over again with your brand. But if little ole' you are doing PPC ads plus a few ads in the paper, plus coupons in the mail . . . really, don't think your PPC ads are going to build awareness. They quite simply aren't!

Here's a rule of thumb for most readers:

If you're not getting the desired action (a sale, sales inquiry, lead, or whatever) *directly* from your ads, don't think there will be any "follow on" awareness or branding effect leading to sales at a later date. Assume that, after the ad has run, that's it; you'll see no future effect.

More reasons branding won't work

This whole idea of using PPC for branding is incredibly pervasive. One book about PPC that I saw recently spends an entire chapter discussing the merits of brand advertising for *any* online business; yet the chapter, if read carefully doesn't really hang together and provides no evidence that brand advertising can work for a small business (let alone for a large, well-funded one). And it completely ignores the fact that brands are not built through advertising, and often don't even require much advertising to maintain.

So, to help inoculate you against the PPC-for-branding virus, here are a few more reasons PP won't help you brand your company:

✔ Most PPC ads currently do not allow logos.

✔ PPC ads are very short; it's hard to get a strong branding message into a PPC ad.

✔ PPC ads are unobtrusive, a little block of text among 20 or 30 other little blocks of text.

✔ Editorial guidelines restrict many kinds of messages; the PPC companies want straightforward, nuts-and-bolts messages, not the sorts of messages often used for branding.

✔ Building a brand is far more than advertising, it's an all-encompassing process involving customer service, employee commitment, company philosophy . . . it's about building a reputation for quality in the minds of consumers.

✔ There's no effective way for you to measure ROI in a branding campaign. Do you really want to run and advertising campaign based purely on faith? "Sure, we're losing money, but don't worry . . . we're building our brand."

By the way, in 2005 *Business Week* published *Interbrand's* list of the world's most valuable brands. Guess what company is #38? Google, a 5-year-old company that spends *very little on advertising!* In 2002, in the middle of building its brand, the company spent $5.6 million on both promotional and advertising costs. In 2004, with revenues of over $3 billion, Google spent just $37.7 million in both promotional and advertising costs. But most of those costs are probably promotional — when was the last time you saw a Google ad?

Okay, so now I've upset plenty of people. But it's true, most people will see no branding effect or "awareness" effect from PPC ads.

So small businesses should forget awareness advertising?

If you don't have a large brand already, and you're just a small business, should you completely forget any kind of awareness advertising? Well, no, not exactly. In some cases, there *are* ways that small businesses can create awareness through online advertising, though generally not through PPC.

Brands vary in size. Some brands are global: Coca-Cola and McDonalds, for instance, are globally recognized brands. Other brands are national (though over time may become global). Gateway, for instance, is very well known in the United States and also does business in Japan, Great Britain, and Mexico . . . but most of the world has never heard of the company.

Some brands are much more limited; they are well known within a particular state or city, or even a particular industry. If your hobby is kayaking, for instance, you've probably heard of the *Dagger* brand; if it isn't, you haven't. It's easier to use advertising to build awareness through carefully placed ads in a *small* market than it is in a large one.

Consider an example. Imagine you own a company that makes exhibits for trade shows. It's a relatively small community; there are a handful of sites where company exhibit managers hang out. Placing banner ads on these sites could be a very good way to build awareness. (I'm on solid ground here; I know one company in the business that did just this.) Each time an exhibit manager comes to one of these sites, the manager sees your company name.

However, that doesn't mean PPC works in the same way; again, there's a big difference between people coming to a community site and seeing a banner over and over again, week after week, and seeing a PPC ad just once or twice.

Pulling It All Together

Now that you understand the various numbers — click values, ROI, gross profit, and so on — it's time to pull it all together and ask a very difficult question: Can you make money from PPC?

After reading all this, you might feel a bit despondent. First, you know the following:

- ✔ Clicks cost at least 5 or 10 cents apiece from major PPC systems but generally cost more, and often a lot more.
- ✔ Conversion ratios are low, perhaps 1:100 or 1:200.

"Wow," you're thinking, "how can I possibly make money with PPC!?" The unfortunate truth is that you might not be able to.

Look at an example of a failure in the making. Assume that your average sale has a gross profit — before paying the click costs — of $10. Assume also that you can convert 1 visitor in 50, not a bad rate. Finally, assume that you can buy clicks for 10 cents.

- ✔ One sale requires 50 clicks.
- ✔ You spend $5 to generate those 50 clicks (50 × 10 cents).
- ✔ You make $5 gross profit after paying $5 for the clicks, giving you an ROI of 100 percent. Pretty good.

Now you can change things and see what happens. You can change the conversion ratio, the click cost, and the gross profit per sale, one item at a time, and see the effect:

- ✔ **Drop the conversion ratio to 1:100.** Your click cost doubles to $10, and you just broke even.
- ✔ **Drop the conversion ratio to 1:200.** You spent $20 on clicks and lost $10.
- ✔ **Change the click cost to 30 cents.** Your clicks cost $15, so you lost $5.
- ✔ **Change the click cost to 50 cents.** Your click cost is $25, so you lost $15.
- ✔ **Change your gross profit, before PPC costs, to $6.** You only made $1.

As you can see, PPC doesn't work well in these circumstances:

- ✔ **Your sales have low gross profits.**
- ✔ **Your Web site has a low conversion ratio.**
- ✔ **Your click costs are high.**

Modifying the Essential Factors

Before moving on, I want to clarify what things affect your campaign and define whether you succeed or fail. These are the essential factors:

- ✔ **Gross profit (margin) per sale:** How much money you make per sale, after expenses
- ✔ **Conversion ratios:** How many visitors you can convert to buyers
- ✔ **Cost per click:** The price you pay for each click
- ✔ **Click-fraud rate:** This is actually part of the conversion rate

  I discuss this rate in detail in Chapter 17, but essentially, click fraud occurs when someone clicks a link for nefarious reasons. More fraudulent clicks means lower conversion rates, which means more expensive sales.

These things are Good Things:

- ✔ High gross profits
- ✔ High conversion ratios
- ✔ Low fraud rates
- ✔ Low click costs

These things, of course, are Bad Things:

- ✔ Low gross profits
- ✔ Low conversion ratios
- ✔ High fraud rates
- ✔ High click costs

If any one of these campaign characteristics is on the bad side, you could have a problem with your PPC campaign. But if all four are on the bad side, you're really in trouble. What can you do to fix the campaign? Well, just possibly, you can make one of these changes:

- ✔ Find a way to **increase gross profit.** Buy the products more cheaply, sell more to each buyer, reduce shipping costs, and so on.

- ✔ Find a way to **increase conversion rates** on your site. You may need to fix your Web site (most companies do!). See Chapter 5.

- ✔ Find a way to **reduce fraud rates.** See Chapter 17.

- ✔ Find a way to **reduce click prices.** You might target lower-cost keywords (Chapter 4) or use smaller PPC systems (Chapter 11).

I hope this discussion wasn't too tedious — but it was necessary. Don't make the same mistake many PPC advertisers make: not understanding the numbers. PPC advertising is a numbers game, so in order to win, you *have to* understand the numbers.

Chapter 4

Selecting Keywords

The foundation of all search-engine work is a keyword analysis. Whether you're doing natural search-engine work or planning a PPC campaign, you have to know the right keywords.

This is another area where most companies fall short. In their rush to bring visitors to the site, most companies jot down a few keywords and then quickly use the various keyword-analysis tools provided by the PPC company to pick a few more keywords. But they never fully understand their keywords. Without doing a full analysis, it's next to impossible to know which keywords you should be targeting.

Here's an example. A company I worked with recently was targeting the term *bsm,* which to them means *business system management* software. The problem is, it doesn't mean that to most people. When I did a quick analysis of this term with Wordtracker — which I discuss later in this chapter — I found that indeed the term *bsm* is used quite often; Wordtracker estimates around 114 searches every day, Internet-wide, on this term.

However, further analysis shows something else. When other words are combined with the term *bsm,* the searches are clearly not for *business management software.* I found searches such as the following:

- ✔ bsm treblebooster
- ✔ bsm fuzzbender
- ✔ bsm driving lessons
- ✔ bsm driving school

It turns out that a company called BSM creates electronic music devices. There's also a driving school in the United Kingdom called BSM. (When carrying out a PPC campaign, you could block the searches from the U.K. by using geo-targeting; see Chapter 12.)

Many, if not most, multi-word searches that include *bsm* include words that relate the searches to music or driving, which implies that many, if not most, of the searches done for the term *bsm* alone are probably related to music or driving. It turns out that *bsm* simply isn't a very good target term. I'm not suggesting that the company should not consider the term in its strategy; but it needed to understand that this term was not as popular with its target buyers as it thought, and that there are probably better keywords.

Understanding the Importance of Keywords

Why is understanding keywords so important? For a variety of reasons:

- ✔ **A good understanding of keywords helps you find keywords that other companies have missed,** letting you buy clicks at a lower price.

- ✔ **You can increase the number of visitors to your site by working with a large range of keywords rather than with just 10 or 20.** You may be able to work with hundreds, perhaps thousands, of different keywords.

- ✔ **You may find profitable keyword combinations that you hadn't considered.** In some cases, people search for keywords in combination with a location — *mortgage denver,* for instance, or *accident attorney houston.* Without a good analysis, companies often miss such combinations.

- ✔ **You can avoid ambiguous keywords** — terms that mean one thing to you and another to most other people.

Picking the right keywords is critical. As Woody Allen once said, "Eighty percent of success is showing up." If you don't play the game, you can't win. And if you don't choose the right keywords, you're not even showing up to play the game.

Selecting keywords for a PPC ad is a little different from doing so for a natural-search campaign. With natural search, you're interested in the frequency of searches on particular keywords because you don't want to spend a lot of time targeting keywords that are rarely used. With PPC, however, frequency of use is less important; you're interested in building large lists of keywords. If you can find hundreds of keywords that are used only infrequently, they'll probably provide low-cost clicks; each one will provide a few clicks, but in aggregate they may provide significant levels of traffic. You will also find keywords that are more finely targeted, and very targeted keywords tend to do well in PPC; that is, they have better conversion rates than more general terms.

Thinking Like Your Prey

It's an old concept: You should think like your prey. Companies often make mistakes with their keywords because they pick keywords based on how they — rather than their customers — think about their products or services. You have to stop thinking that you know what customers call your products. Do some research to find out what consumers really call your products.

I've learned from working with my clients that most firms don't do a good keyword analysis; even the ones that claim they have, it turns out, really haven't put much effort into it. And because of this, they have two significant problems. When I check to see what people are actually searching for on the Web, I discover that the words my client was positive people would use are rarely searched on. I also discover that the company has missed a lot of popular terms.

Sure, you may get some of the keywords right, but if you're spending time and energy targeting particular keywords, you might as well get 'em all right!

The term *keyword analysis* can have several meanings:

- ✔ When I use it, I'm referring to what I'm discussing in this chapter: analyzing the use of keywords by people searching for products, services, and information.

- ✔ Some people use the term to mean *keyword-density* analysis, finding out how often a keyword appears in a page, a characteristic of search engine optimization. (I'm not sure if I've mentioned this in the book thus far, but I wrote a tome you might be interested in checking out, *Search Engine Optimization For Dummies* [Wiley].) Some of the keyword-analysis tools that you run across are actually keyword-density analysis tools.

- ✔ The term also may be used to refer to the process of analyzing keywords in your Web site's traffic or "hit" logs.

Starting Your Keyword Analysis

Doing a keyword analysis is really not that complicated and can mean the difference between success and failure to your PPC campaign.

Identifying the obvious keywords

Begin by typing the obvious keywords into a text editor or word processor — the ones you've already thought of, or, if you haven't started yet, the ones that immediately come to mind. Then study the list for a few minutes. What else can you add? What similar terms come to mind? Add them, too. Later in your analysis, you'll find that some of these initial terms aren't searched for very often. But that's okay; this list is just a starting point.

Your company name

Include your company name on the list, in whatever permutations you can think of (Microsoft, MS, MSFT, and so on).

Trademarks and product names and terms

Think about all the product names and terms that people may be searching on, even your own trademarked terms if you have any. Don't assume that people will find you anyway, even without PPC; in many cases, the trademark owner does *not* rank well for the trademarked term. Experiment a little, typing common trademarks into the search engines, and you'll see this is the case. For instance, type in *balderdash,* the name of the popular board game by Mattel; when I tried this in Google, Mattel's Web site did not come up, even in the first 100 results.

Even if your company does rank near the top, consider whether you want to advertise in the sponsored results, too. Other companies may come above you in the sponsored results, perhaps your partners — agents, retailers, and so on — but also perhaps competitors.

Other companies' names and product names

If people will likely be searching for companies and products similar to yours, add those companies and products to your list for now. We'll discuss whether — and how — you can use these keywords later in this chapter.

Synonyms

Sometimes similar words are easily missed. If your business is a home-related business, for instance, have you thought about the term *house?* Americans may easily overlook this word, using *home* instead, but other English-speaking countries use the word *house* more frequently than *home.* Add it to the list because you may find quite a few searches related to it. There are even differences between terms within the United States — in some areas of the country people say *soda;* in other areas they say *pop,* for instance — so try to be aware of any differences pertinent to your business.

You might even use a thesaurus to find more synonyms. However, I show you some keyword tools that run these kinds of searches for you — see "Using a Keyword Tool," later in this chapter.

Split or merged words

You may find that although your product name is one word — RodentRacing, for instance — most people search for you using two words, *rodent* and *racing.* Remember to consider your customer's point of view.

Also, some words are employed in two ways. Some people, for instance, use the term *knowledgebase,* while others use *knowledge base.* Which is more important? Both should be on your list, but *knowledge base* is used four to five times more often than *knowledgebase.* (How do I know this? By using a keyword-analysis tool, which I describe a little later in this chapter.) If you only target *knowledgebase,* you're missing out on around 80 percent of the traffic!

Singulars and plurals

Go through your list and add singulars and plurals. Search engines treat singulars and plurals differently. For example, searching on *rodent* and *rodents* provides different results in both natural and paid search results.

A great example is to do a search on *book* (1,635 searches per day, according to Wordtracker, which I discuss later in this chapter) and books (16,475 searches per day) in Google. A search on *book* returns Barnes and Noble as the number-one result in the natural results, while *books* returns Amazon.com. And the results in the paid search are very different, too.

Common combinations

Consider common word combinations. For instance, many people combine the words *discount* and *coupon* with product and brand names, and perhaps other terms such as *low cost, cheap,* and so on.

Hyphenated words

Do you see any hyphenated words on your list that could be used without the hyphen, or vice versa? Some terms are commonly used both ways, so find out what your customers are using. Here are two examples:

- ✔ The terms *ecommerce* and *e-commerce* are fairly evenly split, with a little over 50 percent of searches using the latter term.
- ✔ The dash in *e-mail* is far less frequently used, with *email* being the most common term.

Find hyphenated words and add both forms to your list.

Geo-specific terms

Is geography important to your business? Are you selling shoes in Seattle or rodents in Rochester (or rodent shoes in Red Springs)? Don't forget to include terms that include your city, state, other nearby cities, and so on.

Obvious spelling mistakes

Scan through your list and see if you can think of any obvious spelling mistakes. Some spelling mistakes are incredibly important, with 10, 15, or 20 percent of all searches containing the misspelled word, sometimes even more! For example, about one-fifth of all Britney Spears–related searches are misspelled, spread out over a dozen misspellings — which might allow me to take a cheap shot about Britney Spears fans, but I feel that would be beneath me, and so I'll pass.

The word *calendar* is also frequently misspelled. Look at the following list, an estimate of how often the single word *calendar* is searched for each day in its various permutations:

> *calendar:* 10,605 times
> *calender:* 2,721
> *calander:* 1,549
> *calandar:* 256

Thirty percent of all searches on the word *calendar* are misspelled! Admittedly, the term *calender* has another meaning — it's an obscure term related to the use of rollers to smooth out paper — but I'll bet that's *not* what most people are searching for when they type that word into a search engine. (Where do I get these estimates of the number of times keywords are used? You find out later in this chapter, starting at "Using a Keyword Tool.")

One nice thing about misspellings is that competitors often miss them, so you can grab the traffic without much trouble. A keyword that costs several dollars when spelled correctly might cost only a few cents when misspelled.

Domain names

It's amazing how often people type domain names into search engines rather than into the browser's location or address bar. This is a very common mistake made by people who really aren't terribly adept at working with a computer. Here's just how common this is. I examined the Top 200 list from Wordtracker (a list of the 200 most popular search terms over the prior 130 days). I found the following entries, all of which were people attempting to find a particular Web site of which they already knew the domain name! The numbers represent the position in the list; thus the second most popular search term in Dogpile and Metacrawler (the search systems used by Wordtracker; more on this later) is *google!*

2	google
4	yahoo
5	ebay
22	yahoo.com
33	hotmail
61	hotmail.com
72	ebay.com
79	google.com
98	yahoo mail
118	www.yahoo.com
127	dogpile
135	amazon.com
168	aol mail

Admittedly, in most cases, people are not entering the full domain name — they're entering *google* or *yahoo* or *ebay* — but in a lot of cases they are entering the full dot-com domain name. So you may find it's worth including some domain names in your list — domain names of sites related to your business in some way, such as a competitor's domain names for instance.

Looking at your Web site's traffic stats

Take a quick look at your Web site's traffic statistics (often called *hit logs*). You may not realize it, but most logs show you the keywords that people used when they clicked a link to your site at a search engine. (If your logs don't contain this information, you probably need another traffic program!) Write down the terms that bring people to your site.

Examining competitors' keyword tags

You know who your competitors are. Go to their sites and open the source code of a few pages at each site — just choose View⟳Source from the browser's menu bar to get a peek. Look for the `<META NAME="keywords">` tag and see if you find any useful keywords there. Often, the keywords are garbage — useless keywords such as very vague or general terms — or simply not there, but if you look at enough sites, you're likely to come up with some useful terms you hadn't thought of.

Brainstorming with colleagues

Talk to friends and colleagues to see if they can come up with some possible keywords. Ask them something like, "If you were looking for a site at which you could find the latest scores for rodent races around the world, what terms would you search for?"

Give everyone a copy of your current keyword list and ask if they can think of anything to add to it. Usually, reading the terms sparks an idea or two, and you end up with a few more terms.

Using a Keyword Tool

After you've put together a decent-sized keyword list, the next step is to use a keyword tool. This tool helps you discover additional terms you haven't thought of and helps you determine which terms are most important — which terms are used most often by people looking for your products and services.

Both free and paid versions of keyword tools are available. I discuss the freebies first, but I might as well cut to the chase and tell you that I recommend that you fork over the dough and use Wordtracker, the world's top search-engine keyword tool. So you can skip to that section if you want, or read on.

The Yahoo! Keyword Selector Tool

Yahoo! Search Marketing provides a free tool that allows you to see how often a particular search term is used each month in Yahoo! and its PPC partners.

Unfortunately, since Yahoo! changed the Overture brand name to Yahoo! Search Marketing, it has been changing the look of its site every few days, it seems. Sometimes it's easy to find the free tools, sometimes it's hard. I think things have settled down for now, so the following instructions will probably work for you:

1. **Type** `http://SearchMarketing.Yahoo.com` **into your browser.**

   The Yahoo! Search Marketing home page appears.

2. **Click the Sponsored Search link.**

   This is the term Yahoo! now uses for its PPC program.

3. **On the Sponsored Search page that appears, click the Pricing link.**

4. **On the pricing page, click the Keyword Selector Tool link or button.**

   The Keyword Selector Tool page opens.

5. **Type a search term in the Get Suggestions For box and press Enter.**

   The tool tells you how often that term was searched for throughout the Yahoo! network during the previous month. Figure 4-1 shows the results for the search term *rodent.*

The absolute numbers often aren't terribly important; it's the relative levels that count. If one word was searched on 15,000 times last month, and another one was searched only 1,000 times, you can be pretty sure that, whether on the Yahoo! Search Marketing network or not, the first term is the more important one.

Yahoo! provides other search terms, too — related search terms that include the term you entered. If you search for *shoe,* it will also return the number of searches for *womens shoes, new balance shoes, man shoes,* and so on. You can click one of the additional terms, and Yahoo! searches on that term, too, bringing up similar and related terms.

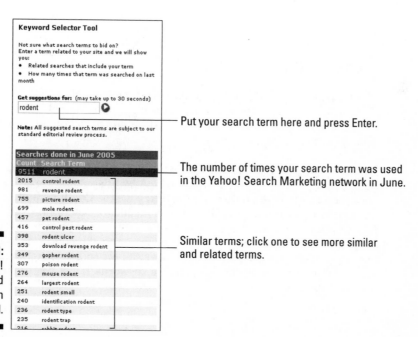

Figure 4-1:
The Yahoo!
Keyword
Selection
Tool.

Put your search term here and press Enter.

The number of times your search term was used in the Yahoo! Search Marketing network in June.

Similar terms; click one to see more similar and related terms.

For each term in your list, use the Search Term Suggestion Tool to find out how many times the term is used each month and to find related terms. Add to your list any related terms that look like they may be appropriate for you (and note the number of times they're searched for).

This process takes what is referred to in the search-engine-optimization business as *a bloody long time*. (Well, the business in England, anyway.) This is why I suggest that you use Wordtracker, which I discuss shortly.

Note, by the way, that Yahoo!'s Keyword Selector Tool has some problems. Significant problems. In fact, many in the PPC business feel that the numbers are significantly off for various reasons, such as the fact that the tool combines search results. For instance, search for *anti virus software program* and you get combined results for *anti virus software program, anti virus software programs, anti-virus software program,* . . . you get the point. It combines plurals and singulars, terms using filler words (the, a, and), and so on. And another problem with the tool: It doesn't look for related terms. Search on *shoe,* and it won't find any terms containing *boot* or *sandal.*

Anyway, as I've said once or twice before, you should use Wordtracker and not rely on this tool for more than cursory checks! The Yahoo! tool was never designed for careful keyword analysis, yet many marketers rely on this tool alone.

Other keyword tools

Several other keyword-analysis tools are available. Some of the other pay per click services provide tools, for instance, but, unlike Yahoo!, you generally can't get to the tool until you have already set up an account or gone through some preliminary sign-up process.

To use Google's tool, you have to jump through some hoops if you haven't yet set up a pay-per-click account with Google AdWords (`https://AdWords.com`). Click the **Click to begin** button; on the next page the **Continue** button; select a country and click Continue; enter an ad — Headline, Description, URL — and click **Continue**, and you'll find yourself on the **Choose keywords** page; see Chapter 9. You can also get to another keyword tool directly, using this URL: `https://adwords.google.com/select/KeywordSandbox`. But note that these tools don't show frequency of use of keywords, it just helps you find related keywords.

To find some of the other software tools and Web-based services, do a search on *keyword* or *keyword analysis.* The top tool is Wordtracker, which is discussed in the next section.

Note also that Yahoo! has a tool that shows you how much a click costs for a particular keyword, which can be very useful. Later, when you set up your PPC campaign, you'll see how to find prices for all your keywords en masse, but Yahoo!'s free tool is still a great system for quickly checking the odd keyword now and then. On the same page that you found the Keyword Selector Tool, you should find a link and a button leading to the View Bids tool (Figure 4-2).

In the View Bids tool, you enter the keyword you're interested in (and one of those little codes you see everywhere these days to make sure a real person is using the form) and then click Search. Yahoo! returns a page showing you the top 40 bids for the term (Figure 4-3). The very first entry shows you the maximum bid for the keyword; it's not necessarily the sum actually being paid, but it *is* the bid you have to beat if you want first position.

Figure 4-2:
Enter a keyword into the View Bids tool to find out how much it costs for a click.

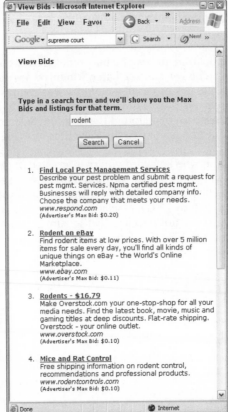

Figure 4-3:
Yahoo!
shows you
the top 40
bids for the
specified
keyword.

Using Wordtracker

Wordtracker (www.wordtracker.com) is the tool that virtually all SEO professionals use. (SEO professionals also like to throw the term SEO around, rather than use the more unwieldy but clearer term *search engine optimization*.) I know of no other tool that matches it or that is anywhere near as popular. It's the preeminent keyword tool throughout the SEO business. And it's cheap to use, so I recommend that you do so.

Wordtracker, owned by a company in London, has access to data from a couple of very large *metacrawlers*, Dogpile.com and Metacrawler.com. A metacrawler is a system that searches multiple search engines for you. For example, type a word into Dogpile's search box (www.dogpile.com), and the system searches at Google, Yahoo!, Ask Jeeves, and MSN.

Wordtracker gets the information about what people are searching for from Metacrawler.com and Dogpile.com, over 300 million searches during the prior 130 days (at the time of writing).

Wordtracker combines all this data and then allows its customers to search through it. Ask Wordtracker how often someone searched for the term *rodent,* and it will tell you that it had been searched for (at the time of writing) 101 times over the last 130 days, but that the term *rodents* is far more popular, with 462 searches over the last 130 days.

 Certain searches are seasonal — *pools* in the summer, *heaters* in the winter, and so on. Because Wordtracker has only the last 130 days of information, it may not be representative for a full year for some terms. And some searches may be influenced by the media. August 2005 saw quite a few searches for *john roberts.* (Remember him? He was nominated to the Supreme Court.) This number dropped after the confirmation hearings ended.

Here's what information Wordtracker can provide:

- ✔ The number of times in the last 130 days that the exact phrase you entered was searched for out of over 300 million searches
- ✔ An estimate of how many times each day the phrase is searched throughout all the Web's search engines
- ✔ Similar terms and synonyms and the usage statistics about these terms
- ✔ Terms used in hundreds of competing sites' KEYWORDS meta tags, ranked according to frequency
- ✔ Common misspellings
- ✔ A comparison of how often a term is searched on and the number of pages that appear for that term in the search results — a nice way to find terms with relatively little competition

Do metacrawlers provide better results? Here's what Wordtracker claims:

- ✔ **Search results at the big search engines are skewed.** Many Web site owners use big search engines to check their sites' rankings, sometimes several times a week. Thus, many searches are not true searches. Metacrawlers can't be used for this purpose, so they provide cleaner results.
- ✔ **Wordtracker analyzes searches to find what appear to be fake, automated searches.** Some companies carry out hundreds of searches an hour on particular keywords — company or product names, for instance — in an attempt to trick search engines into thinking these keywords generate a lot of interest.

Wordtracker is well worth the price. You can pay for access by the day (£4.20, around $7.40 currently), the week (£14/$24.60), the month (£28/$49.10), or the year (£140/$245.70). Most professionals in the SEO business have a regular account with Wordtracker, but for individual sites, it may be worth just getting a day or two of access. One strategy is to build your list first, as described in the earlier sections of this chapter, and then sign up for a day and run Wordtracker for that day. You may get enough done in a couple of hours; if not, you can always sign up for another day. (Of course these prices may change, so check the Wordtracker site.)

Creating a Wordtracker project

Wordtracker lets you create projects so you can store different groups of terms — perhaps one for each Web site or, if you're a consultant, one for each client. The first thing you should do — after plunking down your money and setting up the standard username and password stuff — is create a project. Here's how:

1. **Click the Projects button on the main navigation page (which you see after you log in).**

   The Projects page appears, as shown in Figure 4-4.

2. **Give your project a name and then click the Change Project Name button to save the new name.**

   Wordtracker allows you to have seven projects, each storing a different keyword list. You can empty old projects and rename them as you move on to new Web projects. This may be an important feature if you're an SEO professional or a Web designer working on multiple Web sites.

3. **To load your existing list (the one created as I explained earlier in this chapter) into the project, click the Import button, copy and paste the words from the list into the large text box (one entry per line, as shown in Figure 4-5), and click the Submit button.**

   I recommend that you leave the Compressed Import option button selected, in case you have duplicate entries with different cases. For instance, if you have *rodent racing* and *Rodent Racing,* and *RODENT RACING* in your list, with Compressed Import turned on, Wordtracker simply enters *rodent racing* into the database (and in fact any entries with uppercase are changed to lowercase for consistency).

You'll probably never use Precise Import, because you generally don't need to worry about case. Remember that Google and most other search systems are not case sensitive anyway, so *Rodent* is the same as *rodent*.

After the list is imported into the database, another page opens, which contains your list with a number in parentheses next to each keyword or keyword phrase; this is the count, the number of times the word or phrase appears in the database — the number of times that the keyword was searched upon over the last 130 days.

Type your new project name here.   Click here to set the new name.

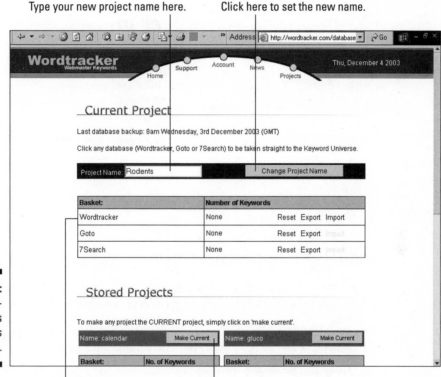

Figure 4-4:
Word-
tracker's
Projects
page.

Click here to view the words
stored in the project.
    Click here to load the selected project.

Paste your keyword list here.

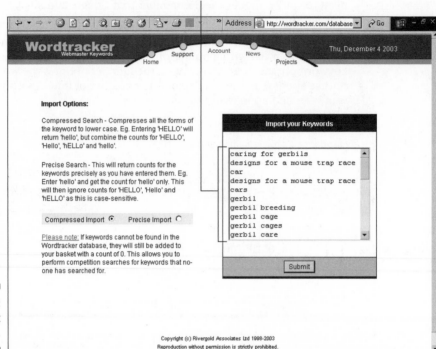

Figure 4-5:
The Import
page.

Adding keywords to your initial project list

To use Wordtracker to find more words that might be appropriate to add to your initial project list (created earlier in this chapter), follow these steps:

1. **Click the Home button in the navigation bar at the top of any Wordtracker page to go to the Wordtracker home page.**

2. **Click the Keyword Universe link.**

   You see the page shown in Figure 4-6.

3. **Type the first keyword in your list into the box on the left and then click the Proceed button.**

   Both the Lateral and Thesaurus check boxes are selected by default. Here's the lowdown on these options:

   • **Lateral:** Wordtracker searches the Internet using your keyword, goes to the first 200 Web sites it finds, and grabs keywords from their KEYWORDS meta tags. (This is a small piece of code near the top of a Web page containing keywords that are associated with the page content.)

Type a word here and click Proceed.

Type keywords here and click Go.

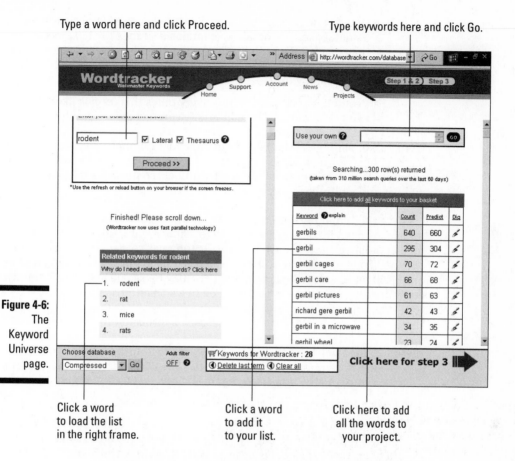

Figure 4-6:
The
Keyword
Universe
page.

Click a word
to load the list
in the right frame.

Click a word
to add it
to your list.

Click here to add
all the words to
your project.

- **Thesaurus:** Wordtracker looks up the word in a thesaurus and finds synonyms.

After clicking the Proceed button, wait a few minutes while Wordtracker builds a list. Then scroll down the left frame to see the list.

4. **Click a word in the list in the left frame to load it into the corresponding table in the right frame.**

The table shows you actual searches from the Wordtracker database that contain the word you clicked, as well as other keyword phrases containing that word. So, for instance, if you click *rodent,* you see search terms such as *rodents, rodent control, rodents revenge, rodent, rodent repellent, rodent pictures,* and so on.

Next to each term in the table, you see two numbers:

- **Count:** The number of times Wordtracker found the search term in its database. The database contains searches for 130 days — more than 300 million of them. So the count is the number of times the term was used in the last four months or so in the search engines from which Wordtracker builds its database.

- **Predict:** An estimate of how many times this term is likely to be used each day in all the Internet search engines combined.

Wordtracker simply extrapolates from the count number to arrive at the predict number. Wordtracker assumes that the search engines it's working with account for a certain percentage of all searches, so it simply takes the count number and multiplies accordingly.

I believe these numbers are too low. From what I've seen and heard, these terms may actually be searched for 50 to 100 percent more often than the predict number. However, what counts is the relative, rather than absolute, number. If one phrase has a predict value of 12,000 times a day, and another one 6,000 times a day, the actual numbers may be 24,000 and 12,000, but what really matters is that one is searched on twice as often as the other.

Here's what you can do with the list of search terms in the right frame:

✔ Click the Click Here to Add All Keywords to Your Basket link to add all the keyword phrases to your project. (The number next to the basket in the bottom frame increases as you add phrases to the project.)

✔ Click a term to add just that term to the project.

✔ Click the shovel icon in the Dig column to see similar terms. Click the shovel in the *rodents revenge* row, for example, to see a smaller list containing *download rodents revenge, rodents revenge download, download rodents revenge game,* and so on.

Should you add all the words in the list at once, or one by one? That depends. If the list contains mostly words that seem to you to be relevant keywords, click the All link at the top to add them all — you can remove the few that are no good later. If most of the list seems to be garbage, scroll down the list and add only the useful words.

After you've finished tweaking your project list, here are a couple of other things you can do:

✔ Click another keyword phrase in the left frame to load a new list in the right frame with search terms related to that phrase.

✔ Type another word from your original list into the box at the top of the left frame. Wordtracker then retrieves more terms related to it from the thesaurus and KEYWORDS meta tags.

✔ Type a term into the text box at the top of the right frame and click the Go button to create a list based on that term.

The left frame is handy because it runs your words through a thesaurus and grabs words from KEYWORD meta tags. But I also like to use the text box at the top of the right frame: I grab a few keyword phrases from my list and copy them into the box (each one needs to be on a separate line). This is a quick way to find matching phrases for the terms already in your list. Typing a word into the text box at the top of the right frame is the same thing as clicking a word in the left frame — Wordtracker looks for real search phrases that include the word. Type (or paste) multiple words into that text box, and Wordtracker looks for matches for each of those words.

Cleaning up the list

After you've worked through your list, checking for relevant terms, click the Click Here for Step 3 link at the bottom of the page. On the Step 3 page, you see the first 100 words in your project, with the most common appearing first (see Figure 4-7).

Scroll through this list carefully. Look for any keywords that really aren't appropriate. It's possible you'll find some, especially if you clicked the All link at the top of the previous page. To delete a term, select the check box to the right of the unwanted term and click the Delete button at the top. Then scroll to the bottom of the list and work your way up; if you delete 15 terms from the page, 15 more are pulled from the next page, so you need to check them as well. Use the right-pointing triangle at the top of the list to move to the next page.

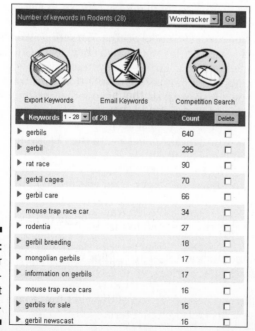

Figure 4-7:
Clean your
keyword-
phrase list
here.

Remove only those terms that are totally inappropriate. Don't worry too much at this point about terms that are not used much or terms that may be too general. I get to that topic in a moment.

Exporting the list

When you're satisfied with your list, you can export it from Wordtracker. At the top of the Step 3 page, click the Export Keywords button to open a window that contains your compiled list. The window contains a list of keyword phrases — a simple list with no numbers. To display the list with the count and predict numbers, click the Click Here to Get a Tab Delimited List of Keywords link.

You can highlight this list and copy and paste it into a word processor or text editor. You can also click the Email Keywords button at the top of the Step 3 page to e-mail the list to yourself or to a colleague.

Competitive analysis

By doing a competitive analysis, you can identify terms that are searched for frequently yet have low click costs. (Remember that Wordtracker is used for natural search campaigns, too, so not all these features are related to PPC.)

To do a competitive analysis, click the Competition Search button at the top of the Step 3 page. On the next page that appears (shown in Figure 4-8), you can check pricing in several PPC systems, two at a time. At present, the only major PPC system you can check is Yahoo! Search Marketing (Wordtracker stills shows the old name, Overture). You can also check with GoClick.com, a second-tier system, and Searchboss, a third-tier system. (Bay9, which is still listed at the time of writing, is out of business.) Note that Wordtracker *cannot* get information from Google AdWords; as you discover later (Chapter 9), Google makes finding keyword click prices a little tricky.

When you run the search, Wordtracker checks with the PPC system to find three types of information (see Figure 4-9):

✔ **Count:** The number of times the search term was found in the Wordtracker database.

✔ **24Hrs:** The number of times the search term is likely to be used each day in the selected PPC system.

✔ **Click prices:** If competitors are already bidding on the term, Wordtracker shows the click prices, up to 20 bids.

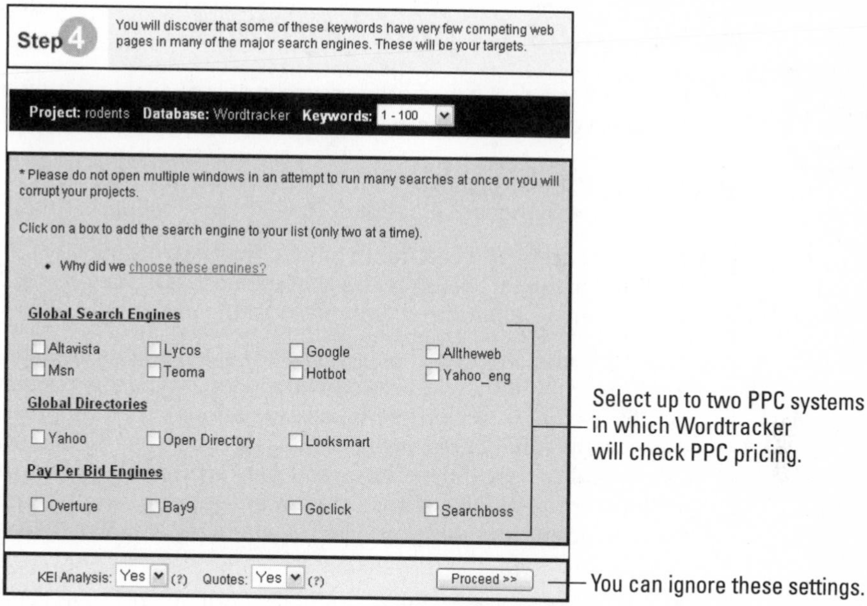

Figure 4-8: The Competition Search page.

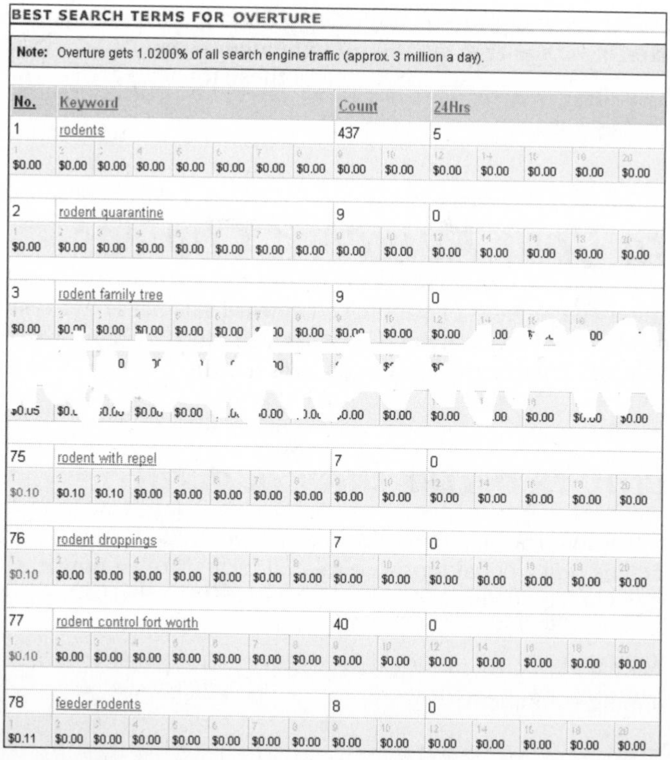

Select up to two PPC systems in which Wordtracker will check PPC pricing.

You can ignore these settings.

Figure 4-9: The Competition Report.

More ways to find keywords

Wordtracker has a number of other search tools available (although I mainly use the ones I discuss earlier in the chapter):

- **Full Search:** Wordtracker returns terms similar to the term you entered, in the same conceptual ballpark (a very large ballpark, though).

- **Simple Search:** You can dump a bunch of keyword phrases into a text box to find actual search terms that include those keywords. For example, *rat* turns up *rat terrier, pet rats, naked mole rat,* and so on.

- **Exact/Precise Search:** This is a mixture of several tools, including the Exact Search (shows you exactly how people type a particular search phrase — that is, the different case variations); the Compressed Exact Search (the number of times people search for a particular phrase, without regard to case differences); and the Precise Search (shows you results for the precise phrase you enter, ignoring search terms typed with different case — if you type *rodent racing,* you won't see results for *Rodent Raching*).

- **Compressed Search:** This is useful for finding plurals and singulars of words from a single list.

- **Comprehensive Search:** You can dig out a few useful related terms mixed in with a large number of unrelated terms.

- **Misspelling Search:** This is a good way to find common misspellings of your keywords.

Narrowing Your Keyword Choices

If you follow the process of building a keyword list that I have discussed in this chapter, you'll probably end up with thousands of keywords. But do you want them all? There are a few things to consider.

Specific is better than general

Specific search terms are generally better than broad terms. For example, if you're selling tents, consider these related terms; notice how they get more specific as you go down the list:

- camping
- camping equipment
- tents
- eureka tent

The first term is very general; if you're searching for *camping,* are you looking for campsites, information about camping vacations, camp stoves . . . ? *Camping equipment* is a bit more specific, but there are many different types of camping equipment — cooking gear, hiking gear, clothing, and so on. *Tents* is far more specific, of course, but even this covers a lot of ground (if you'll excuse the pun); people using the term may be looking for anything from tabletop tent signs to huge circus tents, which you probably don't sell. *Eureka tent* is more specific still: It's a particular brand of tent, so if someone searches on this, there's a very good chance he or she is interested in buying one.

Naturally, a general keyword is likely to have lower conversion rates overall:

✔ Most people searching on *camping* probably won't click your ad because they're not buying tents; in fact, you want to write the ad in such a manner to discourage them from clicking! (See Chapter 6.)

✔ It's possible that the people who do click the ad won't be as likely to buy because some people will click out of pure curiosity, not because they are looking for tents.

Look at your list for terms that are incredibly broad, too general to be of use. You may be tempted to go after high-ranking words, but watch the conversion ratios carefully (see Chapter 15) to ensure you're not paying for a lot of wasted clicks.

Suppose that your site is promoting *degrees in information technology.* You discover that around 40 people search for this term each day, but approximately 1,500 people a day search on the term *information technology.* Do you think that many people searching on the term *information technology* are really looking for a degree? Probably not. Although the term generates 40,000 to 50,000 searches a month, few of these people are your targets.

You can see an example of a really bad choice of keyword in Figure 4-10. In this case, the PPC ad is an IntelliTXT ad (we discuss these in Chapter 13). When someone points at the keyword *companies,* an ad for a "travel and permanent nursing job company" appears. Of course, this is an example of how "contextual" advertising often goes wrong — this ad is on a page related to the PPC business — but in addition, it shows poor keyword choice. Sure, the advertiser is a "company," but that doesn't mean it should have the ad placed on the word *companies!*

"Does it really matter?" you ask. "Nobody's going to click unless he or she is looking for a nursing job, right?" Well, for the most part, you're right. But some people are going to click this ad because of the "Oh, what's this?" factor. And now and then someone's going to click because he or she is drunk or not paying attention. This is, quite simply, the wrong place for this ad!

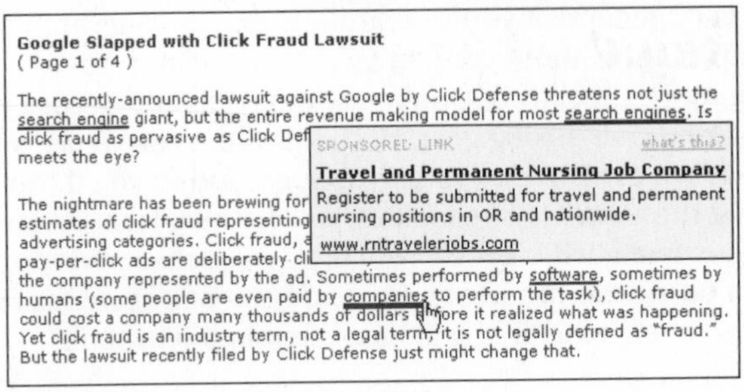

Figure 4-10:
This
keyword is a
terrible
choice for
the ad.

Different meanings

Take a look at your list to determine whether you have any words that may have different meanings to different people. Sometimes you can immediately spot such terms. One of my clients thought he should use the term *cam* on his site. To him, the term referred to *Complementary and Alternative Medicine*. But to the vast majority of searchers, *cam* means something different. Search Wordtracker on the term *cam,* and you come up with phrases such as *web cams, web cam, free web cams, live web cams, cam, cams, live cams, live web cams,* and so on. To most searchers, the term *cam* refers to Web cams, cameras used to place pictures and videos into Web sites. The phrases from this example generate a tremendous amount of competition, but few of them would be useful to my client.

Avoiding ambiguous terms

A client of mine wanted to promote a product designed to control fires. One common term he came up with was *fire control system.* However, he discovered that when he searched on that term, most sites that turned up don't promote products related to stopping fires. Rather, they're sites related to *fire control* in the military sense: weapons-fire control.

This kind of ambiguity is something you really can't determine from a system such as Wordtracker, which tells you how often people search on a term. In fact, it's often hard to spot such terms even by searching to see what turns up when you use the phrase. If a particular type of Web site turns up when you search for the phrase, does that mean people using the phrase are looking for that type of site? You can't say for sure. A detailed analysis of your Web site's access logs may give you an idea.

Building keyword phrases

You may want to extrapolate from what you've found and create phrases that you believe may be searched on now and then. This is often done in particular in relation to state names.

For instance, you've found that the following phrases are quite common:

✔ rodent racing

✔ rodent race track

✔ rodent sports

You also realize that people often search for these venues in combination with a location: *rodent racing colorado, rodent race track in dallas, georgia rodent sports,* and so on.

Now, you haven't actually found, for instance, *rodent racing texas,* but if such location combinations are common, then people probably are searching on the term now and then, or will in the future. So you could create more search terms — many, many more, in fact. You could combine the three search terms above with every city and state name in the United States, for instance. You'll end up with a huge list, which won't work well with Google — Google doesn't like large lists of keywords that are infrequently searched on, and may not let you use them (in fact Google makes it hard to work with very large lists, unless you have a very large budget). But you may be able to use these lists with other PPC systems.

Avoiding Trademark Problems

Can you bid on keywords that are also trademarked? *Coca-Cola, Nike, Pre-Paid Legal, NBC, AOL, HP,* and so on?

Yes, you can, in some circumstances. There's a lot of confusion about trademarked terms; many people seem to think they "belong" to the trademark holders.

They don't. The trademark holder has certain rights in relation to the term, but they don't have total control over its use. Thus, you can't sell a drink called Coca-Cola, but you *can* talk about Coca-Cola, put up a Web site discussing Coca-Cola — even saying how disgusting it is if you wish — or run PPC ads related to Coca-Cola.

In general, the PPC firms don't really want to get involved in trademark issues. As Google puts it in its Help Center, "we cannot arbitrate trademark disputes between advertisers and trademark owners."

Search on most well-known trademarks and you'll find PPC ads. (Except, for some reason, if you search at either Google or Yahoo! for the terms *google* or *yahoo,* you will *not* find PPC ads!) The only restrictions, in general, seem to be that those ads must still conform to the other requirements:

- If you say your product is better than Coca-Cola, you'd better have information on your site that proves it.
- If you say you sell the trademarked product, you'd better do so.
- If you claim to be an authorized reseller, you must be one.
- If you say you provide competitive comparison information, you must do so.

Of course, the devil is in the details, and some PPC companies have more detailed requirements. For instance, if you claim to have product comparisons, Yahoo! demands that they be detailed and "spanning multiple dimensions (for example, price, features, ingredients, third-party rankings, ratings or awards, etc.) and clearly help consumers to make an informed decision about the product or service." In other words, you can't simply compare your soda to Coca-Cola by discussing the color of the cans.

If your site offers a comparison to a trademarked item, Yahoo! also requires that you include the word *Compare* in the title: *Compare Us to [Trademark Term]* or *Compare Our Prices to [Trademark Owner]'s,* for example. Yahoo! also requires that advertisers agree that their ads and Web sites "do not violate the trademark rights of others."

There are actually two issues related to bidding on trademarks:

- Should an advertiser be able to bid on a trademarked keyword and run an ad that mentions the trademark?
- Should an advertiser be able to bid on a trademarked keyword, and run an ad that is not directly related to the keyword?

Sometimes companies run ads that are *not* directly related to the keywords. GameFly.com knows that if you type the name of a video game into a search engine, there's a good chance you're a potential customer, so it runs ads about renting video games, but not about the specific game for which you searched. So, should I be able to bid on *vuitton* if my ad is about handbags in general, and not specifically *Louis Vuitton* handbags?

Different PPC systems treat these issues differently. On the one hand, Google seems to accept both situations. I searched on *vuitton* and found the results shown in Figure 4-11. Nine ads, none of which mention *Louis Vuitton,* and most of which don't actually mention the brand on their landing pages.

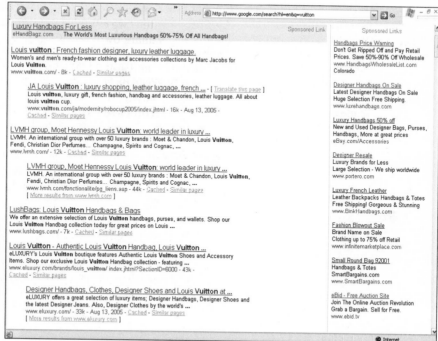

Figure 4-11:
Google is
pretty loose
with its
trademark
policies.

On the other hand, Yahoo! seems to be stricter. When I searched Yahoo!, I got the results shown in Figure 4-12. In this case, there are only three ads, and all of them mention Louis Vuitton products. Furthermore, all three link to landing pages that contain information about Louis Vuitton products. So Yahoo! allows the first situation, but not the second; you can bid on trademarked terms as long as you link to a page with information about that trademarked item.

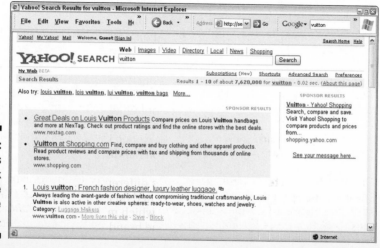

Figure 4-12:
Yahoo!'s
trademark
policies are
much more
strict.

Having said all that, it seems that this is somewhat of a "squeaky wheel" situation. Yahoo! doesn't allow bidding on *vuitton* if your ad is not directly related to *Louis Vuitton,* but what happens if you search Yahoo! for, say, *lord of the rings video game?* Two of the six ads are *not* related to *lord of the rings* specifically. It may be that the owner of the Louis Vuitton trademark has complained to Yahoo! about ads appearing as a result of a search on that trademark.

Trademark law comes down to honesty. If you use someone's trademark in order to mislead people — to lead them to think that you sell that product when you don't, for instance — then you are clearly infringing on someone's trademark. If you use it in an honest way — leading people to a product comparison, for instance — you are *not* infringing.

Chapter 5

Creating Landing Pages

. . . .

. . . .

Do *not* invest large sums of money into PPC advertising without first thinking about landing pages. A *landing page,* often referred to by PPC systems as the *target URL* or *destination URL,* is the page that people are sent to when they click a link to your site. In this context, of course, a landing page is a page that a PPC ad points to.

A good landing page helps sell; it's the first step in the process of convincing the visitor to your site to buy from you. Thus, when you point a PPC ad to your site, you don't, in most cases, want to simply point to your home page. If you sell 100 products, and your ad is pushing a particular product, pointing to your home page is going to lose a lot of people. Imagine Amazon.com running a PPC ad for video games and then landing people on the Amazon.com home page. That's not a great way to sell video games, is it? At the very least, Amazon would want you to land on a video-game category page, and in many cases, Amazon lands you on a very specific video-game page, as you see later in this chapter.

But there's another issue here that is also very important. Landing pages are all very well, but your entire site should be created with the idea of selling in mind. That's something we'll discuss under "Making Your Web Site Sell" later in this chapter.

Landing Pages That Work

A good way to begin figuring out what a good landing page looks like is to look at some examples of landing pages that work. I did a little test to see what would happen when I searched for a video game and then visited some of the sites linked from the PPC ads. I searched Google for a game called *Conker: Live and Reloaded.* (For those of you not fortunate enough to be British, *Conkers* is a kid's game in which the nut of the horse chestnut tree is dried, drilled, and threaded onto a string; the nuts are then battled against each other. The character *Conker,* from this British video game, is a squirrel.) In Figure 5-1, you can see the ads that appeared.

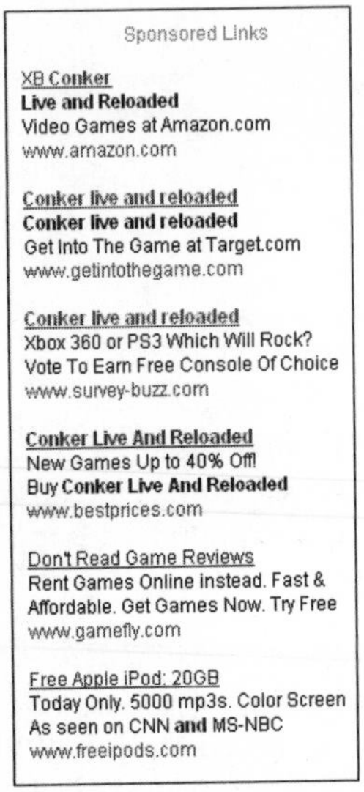

Figure 5-1: The PPC ads displayed when searching for *conker live and reloaded.*

Sponsored Links

XB Conker
Live and Reloaded
Video Games at Amazon.com
www.amazon.com

Conker live and reloaded
Conker live and reloaded
Get Into The Game at Target.com
www.getintothegame.com

Conker live and reloaded
Xbox 360 or PS3 Which Will Rock?
Vote To Earn Free Console Of Choice
www.survey-buzz.com

Conker Live And Reloaded
New Games Up to 40% Off!
Buy **Conker Live And Reloaded**
www.bestprices.com

Don't Read Game Reviews
Rent Games Online instead. Fast &
Affordable. Get Games Now. Try Free
www.gamefly.com

Free Apple iPod: 20GB
Today Only. 5000 mp3s. Color Screen
As seen on CNN and MS-NBC
www.freeipods.com

Now remember, these ads are not necessarily directly related to *Conker.* Rather, they're placed there because the advertisers feel that the people who are searching for Conker may be interested in what the advertiser is selling . . . even if the advertiser is *not* selling Conker.

If you click the very first ad, you land at Amazon.com, as shown in Figure 5-2. It's a direct hit: a page that has a picture of the game and all the associated information — the price, product description, reviews, and everything. If you'd landed on Amazon.com's home page, you would have had to search again for the game, and a lot of people wouldn't have bothered.

The next PPC ad on the list in Figure 5-1 points to a page at GetIntoTheGame. com, which is owned by Target. Again, it lands on a page directly related to the game I searched for (see Figure 5-3). Not too bad, though I do think there are some problems here. I had to look really carefully to discover that I can buy the game through this site; the BUY NOW button is pretty indistinct and well hidden. For a moment, I was almost convinced the site was an informa-tion site, rather than a sales site.

Figure 5-2:
Here's
Amazon's
Conker
landing
page.

Figure 5-3:
GetIntoThe
Game.com's
Conker
landing
page.

In Figure 5-4, you can see what appeared when I clicked the third ad, a page at Survey-Buzz.com. What is going on here? This site has nothing to do with *Conker.* Survey-Buzz.com doesn't sell it, and it has no information about the game on its site. But it's interested in people who are interested in *Conker.* In fact, Survey-Buzz.com is owned by Netblue, Inc., a company that delivers sales leads to Columbia House, Discover card, America Online, Video Professor, and others. These systems generally work like this: You sign up with a variety of offers, then get friends to sign up for a variety of offers, and then the company sends you a free item — in this case, a free game system.

By the way, you may be wondering if these free-this and free-that sites are for real? Well, yes, they are, at least many are. FreeiPods.com, for instance, really will send you a free iPod if you complete all the steps. The value of all the leads they sell to these various companies far exceeds the cost of the products they have to give away.

Next on the list is BestPrices.com, and again, it lands directly on the *Conker* page. After that, there's GameFly.com. This company rents video games, and the page you land on (Figure 5-5) has a very clear message, in large letters. It rents video games, it delivers the games to you, and you can have a 10-day free trial. A very clear, succinct message.

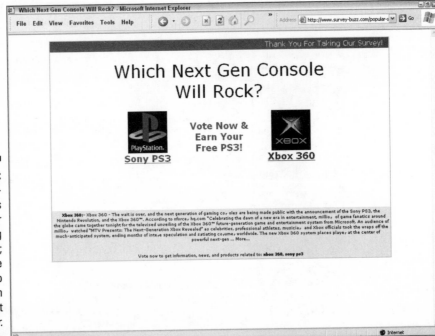

Figure 5-4:
Survey-Buzz.com's *Conker* landing page; though the site has no information about *Conker.*

Figure 5-5:
GameFly.
com's
Conker
landing
page.

If you scroll down, you find more information, very clearly portrayed. It's a very direct, clear offer that works well, I'm sure. Is there any way it could be improved? Perhaps if the page displayed the actual game that was searched for at the search engine, though I'll admit that starts to get a little complicated (definitely possible, however). It does display a few video game titles, as you can see in Figure 5-5. And although *Conker* isn't displayed here, when I returned to the site a few days later, *Conker* was displayed on the home page.

Finally, FreeIPods.com, another "giveaway" site similar to Survey-Buzz.com; no information about *Conker*. The site is looking for game players, not selling *Conker*.

Landing Pages That Could Be Better

Most PPC advertisers understand that the ads should link to something related to the ad, especially advertisers who are successful at what they're doing. But many advertisers, particularly small, unsophisticated businesses that are just beginning, do a pretty bad job. In fact, many companies have PPC ads that point to their home pages.

Here's an example. I searched Google for *dog coat.* Here's the first PPC ad that appeared:

> Summer Sale: Shop Now
> Puritan's Pride: Buy 1 Get 2 Free
> Quality, Discount-Priced Vitamins
> www.puritan.com

Huh? Well, accidents happen. It turns out that Puritan's Pride, a supplement company, had assigned the wrong ad to the keyword on Google; Puritan's Price was bidding on the same keywords on Yahoo! but using an ad that began with <u>Dog Coat Supplements: Buy 1 Get 2 Free.</u>

This ad was second:

> Clothes for Small Dogs
> Dog Clothes, Sweaters, Shirts, Coat
> Shoes, Boots, Harnesses, Collars.
> www.purecountry.net

When I clicked the second ad, I arrived at the page shown in Figure 5-6. This time, I landed on the home page. There are two problems with this landing page. First, why not take me directly to the dog coats page? This ad appears when someone searches for *dog coat,* and the site sells dog coats. In some of the example from the last section, the site doesn't actually have the product the searcher is looking for, which is okay — it's trying to attract the type of person who searches for *Conker.* But in this case, the site actually does have dog coats, so why not go right there?

The second problem is that, well, the page is downright ugly. "That dog won't hunt," as they say in Texas; it just won't work. Ugly doesn't sell, as I explain in a more detail in the "Ugly doesn't sell" section, later in this chapter. Okay, so maybe the site does make some sales, and in fact this sort of product has a bit of an exemption because people may assume the products are home-made. I believe when people are buying what they expect to be a hand-made, homemade product, they don't care so much about the professionalism of the Web site. But in general, ugly does not work well.

Here's another example. You figure out which is the best landing page. I searched Google for *ariakon paintball gun* and clicked three of the PPC ads. The corresponding landing pages appear in Figures 5-7, 5-8, and 5-9.

The best of the three is the last one, PaintBallPat.com; it takes me directly into the page matching my search keywords. With the other two, I have to start digging around looking for what I want. With Pat, I immediately get to view 11 different products matching exactly what I requested.

Figure 5-6:
This site should direct me to the dog coats page, not to the home page.

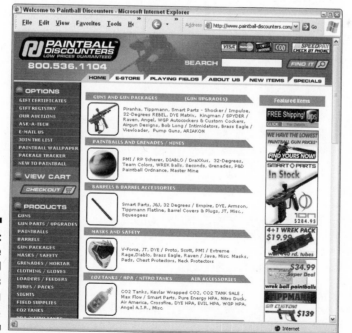

Figure 5-7:
The Paintball Discounters landing page.

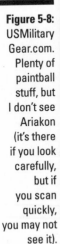

Figure 5-8:
USMilitary
Gear.com.
Plenty of
paintball
stuff, but
I don't see
Ariakon
(it's there
if you look
carefully,
but if
you scan
quickly,
you may not
see it).

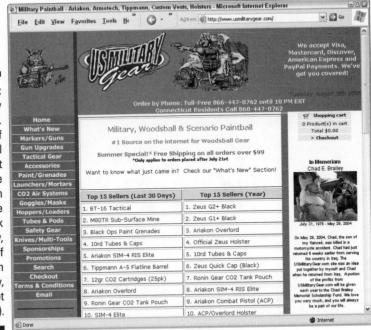

Figure 5-9:
The
PaintBall
Pat.com
landing
page.
Bingo!

Now, I don't want to be too critical here. What I'm recommending is an ideal, and it's difficult to do if you have hundreds, perhaps thousands, of keywords that you're bidding on. But consider your goal: to match as closely as possible the keywords people search on. Yes, it's work, and it may not be something that you'll ever do 100 percent perfectly. But it's your goal.

Remember all those *Conker* ads? Amazon.com, GetIntoTheGame.com, and BestPrices.com all used a landing page specific to the keywords entered into the search engine. It can be done, it just takes a little time and effort.

Picking a Landing Page

So where do you point ads to? You point an ad to the most effective page for that ad, the page that does the best job of "selling" the visitor based on what that person is looking for.

That page is often *not* the site's home page; Paintball Discounters would do better to redirect that ad to a category page for the particular products. On the other hand, for some companies — such as GameFly, which we looked at before — the home page probably *is* the best place to direct people because the home page has been built as the first step in the process of converting visitors to customers . . . and because in both cases these are one-product sites. They're selling one thing and one thing only.

In some cases you're bringing people to a site to sell a product to them, the product they searched for. In this case the product page is probably the best landing page.

What should the landing page do? Step into the visitors' shoes for a moment and consider what they're looking for. If a visitor searched on *ariakon paintball guns,* what do they want to know?

- ✔ **What products match the search:** If you have 20 different paintball guns, make sure the landing page makes this clear.
- ✔ **How much the product costs:** I discuss that in more detail in the next section.
- ✔ **Shipping costs**
- ✔ **Product information**

Perhaps most important, searchers want to know what they want to know without spending much time finding the information. Make it easy to get to everything.

In other cases, of course, you're trying to involve people in more of a sales process than just showing that you have the best price. Such a landing page would be different, more like the GameFly.com, Survey-Buzz.com, and Blockbuster.com pages discussed earlier.

By the way, do you *have to* create landing pages for your ads? Maybe not. If you're selling a product or service, trying to gather sales leads, or trying to get people to carry out some other kind of action, doesn't your Web site already have pages designed to do this? If so, point people to those existing pages. If not, you've got a problem. There's nothing "special" about landing pages; they should do what your site should be doing anyway: selling product. Often the reason a company builds special landing pages for PPC campaigns is because, on beginning the campaign, it's discovered that the site is a bad, bad site. Read "Making Your Web Site," later in this chapter.

On the other hand, sometimes there are reasons to create landing pages. Perhaps you're selling a limited-supply or seasonal product purely through a PPC campaign. You could then create a page purely for that campaign.

How do you ensure the page doesn't turn up in the natural search results, so you don't have an old page for a nonexistent product indexed months later? Create a text file named `robots.txt` in your Web site's root directory. Then add these lines to it:

```
User-agent: *
Disallow: /temp-products/product123.html
```

This tells the search engines not to index the file named `product123.html` in the directory named `temp-products`. Of course, you should substitute the name and directory of your limited-time landing page instead.

However, if you have a page indexed by the search engines, bringing traffic to your site, why not leave it there? Place text on the page explaining that the offer is no longer available, and lead the visitors into your main site.

It's Not Just about Pricing

This chapter is all about conversions; converting a visitor into a buyer, or into a sales lead. So we can't really discuss that subject without discussing *pricing*.

If your pricing is too high, there's *nothing* you can do. Regardless of how good your landing page is, you won't make sales. If you're selling a product for $100, and your competitors sell it for $20, any sales you make will be accidental and may not "stick" (the order will likely be cancelled or returned). But what if some competitors are selling for $20, and you're selling for $25? You still have a real problem.

Online buyers are very price-sensitive. In fact, over the last few years, the Internet itself has become far more price-sensitive. A few years ago, I wrote a book with the founders of CDnow.com; I recall Jason Olim telling me that CDnow.com's prices were good, but not the best. Selling online was far more than just giving a low price, he said. It was about selection and service.

Today, things have changed. Luckily, selling online is still not just about low prices; it's also about selection and service . . . but low prices are far more important now than they used to be, for two big reasons:

- ✔ **It's much easier to compare prices,** thanks to shopping directories and price-comparison services (see Chapter 14), such as Froogle and Yahoo! Shopping.

- ✔ **People are far less wary of buying online.** They know that whomever they buy from, they will probably get the product they ordered, so "comfort" is less important than price. Comfort is still important, just not as important as it used to be.

People shop prices now, to a degree they simply didn't do four or five years ago. So what do you do if your pricing isn't so great? You're going to have to find other reasons for people to buy from you. Here are a few ideas:

- ✔ **Bundle items together.** Although your price might be a little higher than competitors, it still seems reasonable because of the items that come with them. for example, include 200 paintballs with every paintball gun.

- ✔ **Provide free shipping.** This is often a real benefit because people don't like having to dig through sites trying to figure out how much shipping costs.

- ✔ **Work on the "comfort factor."** Find ways to make people feel more comfortable buying from you. Sure, people want a low price and aren't *too* worried about buying online, but still, they'd prefer to buy from someone reliable.

    Well-designed sites with pages that look professional increase the comfort factor. (See "Ugly doesn't sell," later in this chapter.)

- ✔ **Include a phone number.** Testing shows that the prominent display of a phone number on a Web site doesn't increase phone calls much, but does increase sales, all because of the comfort factor.

- ✔ **Don't look like you're hiding.** Provide background information that says who you are; if your Web site is the online component of a company that owns 20 brick-and-mortar stores, make sure people know that; it really helps build credibility. Sites that convey a personal feel — that convince the buyer there are real people behind the site — increase the comfort level.

Landing Page Tips

We've looked a few general concepts about landing pages, from making your landing page match the ad to making the offer competitive. But, of course, the devil's in the details, and there are a number of details you should be aware of . . . so let's consider a few specific tips related to your landing pages, from relevance to testing.

Make your landing pages relevant

Landing pages should be relevant. That is, they should be related as closely as possible to the keywords and ad. In fact, it's important to understand that there are two forms of relevance:

- Relevant to the keyword the searcher typed
- Relevant to your ad text

Your landing page must have some degree of relevance to both keyword and ad, though less to the keyword than to the ad, of course. Consider the ad for GameFly.com that appeared when I typed *conker: live and reloaded* into Google (refer to Figure 5-1):

> Don't Read Game Reviews
> Rent Games Online instead. Fast &
> Affordable. Get Games Now. Try Free
> www.gamefly.com

This ad is not directly relevant to the search keywords; it's only peripherally relevant, and the landing page that it leads to is also not particularly relevant to the keywords. It's not related to *Conker;* GameFly posted the ad because its marketers know that anyone searching for *Conker* is likely to be a potential customer for its game-rental business. The Amazon.com and GetIntoTheGame.com landing pages are more relevant to the keywords; they are about the specific game, *Conker.*

On the other hand, the GameFly.com landing page is very relevant to the *ad.* It brings the searcher directly to the page that begins the selling process for the game-rental service. If GameFly.com had landed the searcher on a more traditional "who we are and what we do" corporate-type page, that would have been less relevant and certainly less effective.

Of course, the GameFly.com landing page could also have been made more relevant to the keywords used; if GameFly.com had landed the searcher on a page that contained information about that particular game — *Don't Buy This Game, Rent It!*, for instance — the searcher might be more likely to sign up and rent that particular game.

The more relevant to both keyword and ad the better. But to some degree, your landing page *has* to be relevant to the ad, even if not to the keyword. The search engines want to provide relevant search results, so ads have to be at least peripherally relevant to the keywords . . . but they also don't want their results to be misleading, so they don't look kindly on *ads* that are not relevant; they want you to point to pages that provide the information promised in the ad.

Think of the landing page as an extension of the ad. Does the landing page seem to follow naturally from the ad, or is there a distinct break? If GameFly.com directed people from its ads to its corporate page, there would be a jarring disconnect. The way they have it set up now, you see an ad pitching the idea of renting games and then land on a page that explains the concept.

Design pages to be clear

Create a clear message on your landing pages. Don't throw too much clutter at the visitor — use large text, images, and a few simple ideas. Place all the important stuff near the top of the page; "above the fold" as it's known in both the newspaper and Web business. *Above the fold* in Web terms means the portion of a Web page that appears when the page is first loaded into a browser; the portion of the page visible if you scroll down is *below the fold*. Consider the GameFly.com page we saw earlier (Figure 5-5). All the important stuff is above the fold.

Of course, above and below depend on the screen resolution. You should assume that people are viewing your page with a resolution of 800 x 600 because many are. It's better to design pages for this lower resolution and have it work well in this and higher resolutions than to design it for higher resolutions and have it "fail" in the very common 800-x-600 resolution.

Call to action

If you've been involved in sales and marketing, you've probably heard the term *call to action.* You have to tell someone what you want him to do, tell him clearly, and tell him multiple times: *Buy, Buy Now!, Start 10-Day Free Trial, Try It Free Now, Learn More,* and so on. Use big, bright buttons, and use them more than once if necessary. It always amazes me how often site designers make me dig around to figure out what I'm supposed to do next. Make it easy for people to do what you need them to do, and they will be more likely to do it.

Compare the landing page in Figure 5-10 (from another game-rental company, Intelliflix.com) with the GameFly.com landing page you saw earlier (Figure 5-5). Which is clearer? Which is a clearer call to action?

Figure 5-10:
This landing
page simply
doesn't
work as
well as
GameFly's.

The Intelliflix landing page breaks all sorts of rules. It's cluttered, the design is bad — laying text over the photo makes it hard to read, for instance — and the call to action is weak. Why is the designer so ashamed of the Join Now button that he has to hide it down in the bottom right? Compare the Join Now button with GameFly's big, red, in-your-face Start 10-Day Free Trial button. GameFly knows how to ask for the action, Intelliflix simply doesn't. Of course this is a weaker offer, too — "give us your money now" as opposed to "try it free for ten days."

Make your calls to action prominent and clear, and make them multiple times.

Think about the message

Your landing page is a marketing piece; it contains a marketing message, whether you realize it or not. It might be a weak marketing message, like the one on the game-rental site in Figure 5-10, or it might be a strong one, like GameFly's (Figure 5-5).

Look at the GameFly landing page and you'll find a marketing message that contains these ideas:

✔ Rent video games (instead of buy)

✔ Unlimited rentals

- ✔ 2,500 titles — *plenty* of choice!
- ✔ A *free* trial of the service
- ✔ 12 *free* issues of a game magazine

The free trial is great; anything free is good, but it's easier to sell something to someone when it's free. Of course, they'll have to pay for it eventually, but it's easier to sell something to someone when they've already made the decision to use it. It's called the "puppy dog close." Let someone take home a puppy to see whether she'll like it and then see if she can bear to return it! She'll probably pay rather than lose the puppy.

If all that isn't enough, anyone who scrolls down below the fold sees more:

- ✔ No due date, no late fees
- ✔ Play (rent) two games at a time
- ✔ Prepaid mail both ways
- ✔ A simple diagram showing how the system works:
    1. Pick your games.
    2. Check your mailbox.
    3. Play and send back for more.
- ✔ Games for six different game systems

It's a nice, clean, succinct marketing message. And if it's still not enough, a Help/FAQ link and a Learn More link are available.

Here's something else to think about: When I e-mailed Intelliflix (refer to Figure 5-10) to ask whether it offered a free trial, it said no. But it did tell me that it had the lowest price in the business and also had a huge selection: 40,000 games and movies compared to GameFly's 2,500 games. (GameFly, by the way, is probably the "brand name" in this business, the one to beat.)

Does its landing page tell me this? It doesn't say anywhere that it's price is the lowest, and doesn't compare it's library size to Gamefly. Does its landing page give me any reason to buy from it? No.

Be careful not to lead them away

Make sure you don't lead your visitors away from your message. As an example, GameFly has a large image that says "Join now and receive 12 issues of PSM or OXM. See details." If you click the image, a small window pops up (see Figure 5-11).

Figure 5-11:
This
window
pops up
when you
click the
magazine
offer.

This window gets the message across — after your free trial, when you become a paying member, you get a free subscription to *Independent PlayStation 2 Magazine* or *Official Xbox Magazine* — but doesn't take you away from the landing page. Click the prominent Close Window button, and you're right back at the main message.

Most products need ancillary information; some people need to see it before they buy, others don't. If you have to provide additional information, use some kind of mechanism that

✔ Doesn't clutter your main message.

✔ Is available for those people who need an extra push before they buy.

✔ Doesn't take people away, but remains part of the main process.

Test your landing pages

There are real similarities between selling online and the direct-mail business and huge similarities between PPC campaigns and direct mail. What do successful direct-mail marketers do? They test, over and over again. You should do the same with your landing pages if at all possible. (Companies doing millions of dollars in sales online each year should constantly be testing. Companies doing a few bucks a week will have fewer resources to assign to such a task.)

Try different messages, different page layouts, different processes. There are even special software tools that will help you do what is known as *A/B testing* — they help you switch out pages and keep track of which ones do best.

Your Site's Part of the PPC Campaign

PPC is not just about placing ads. If it were, everyone would make money (and most people, as I may have mentioned before, probably don't). A PPC campaign contains two components:

- ✔ **Off-site:** The ad, placed on someone else's Web site, designed to push visitors to your site.
- ✔ **On-site:** Your Web site, designed to turn visitors into customers.

Now, before someone (such as you or my editor) complains that all this is not really related to PPC, I want to make the point that it most definitely *is*. I know of companies that are losing money with PPC by pointing PPC ads to poorly designed landing pages on poorly designed Web sites. It's not just about the landing page. If you have the best landing page in the world but then lead people into a cluttered, confusing, nasty little Web site, you're still going to lose the PPC game!

One of my clients, who hired me for a Search Engine Optimization project, complained that he couldn't get his PPC ads to work. "Your site is horrible," I told him (in a slightly more tactful way). There was *nothing* wrong with his ads; it was the site that had the problem.

So I spend a bit of time on this subject of good-looking Web sites in the following sections because it's really important. A PPC campaign isn't just a collection of keywords and ads; your Web site is a critical part of it. If your site stinks, so will your PPC campaign.

Making Your Web Site Sell

I spend a lot of time talking to Web site owners and managers, often during phone consultations in which we spend an hour or two looking at their sites and discussing problems and ways to fix them. And one of the most common problems I see is that sites are usually built without considering what they're supposed to do and how they're supposed to do it.

I recently spoke with a client who had recently spent $20,000 building a site. He called me because he knew something was wrong. People (though admittedly not enough) were arriving at the site, but they weren't calling. (This client sells very expensive software, in the tens of thousands of dollars, so sales are not completed online.) The problem was that the site simply did an awful job of selling. By *selling*, I mean the process of convincing someone to carry out some kind of action — to actually buy, or perhaps to call or e-mail.

He — and the two staff members on the conference call — "got it" as soon as I pointed out the problems. This isn't brain surgery. I asked what they wanted the home page to do, and someone said "get people to arrange a software demo." So I asked, "And does this home page do that?" And the reply came back . . . well, no reply came back for a few moments, just silence. They knew exactly what I meant. The page was cluttered, half the page was covered with a large image that said absolutely nothing about their business or software, there were no "calls to action," and so on.

So let's quickly look at the subject of making a site that sells . . . so you can avoid paying to push people to a site that *doesn't.*

Traditional Web site planning

Here's how Web sites are usually built; see if this sounds familiar (like your site, maybe?):

1. You or your company decides you need a Web site, or perhaps a replacement site.

2. Someone comes up with a list of things that the site must contain, such as

   • Contact information

   • An About Us page

   • Press releases

   • FAQs

   • Case studies

   • Products

3. You find a Web designer, any Web designer. (They're all the same, right?)

4. You tell the Web designer what goes on the site.

5. The Web designer creates a navigation structure that allows visitors to get to all these different things and creates some kind of pretty graphical design.

6. You take a look, change a few colors, shift things around on the navbar, and give the go-ahead.

7. The designer builds the site.

This, or something pretty similar, is how sites are generally built.

The right way to plan a Web site!

Before you can build a Web site, there are a few things you must understand.

First, you have to understand that a Web site is a piece of software. People click buttons, don't they? They make choices in drop-down list boxes, select option buttons, fill in forms, and so on. It's a piece of software, not a piece of graphic design. So the software design comes first, and graphic design comes second. In other words, if you are asking a designer to create an attractive Web site for you, you're doing things backward.

- ✔ *Function comes first!*
- ✔ *Graphic design comes second!*

When you first begin building a Web site, forget about graphic design; it's not important. An attractive site — such as the ones owned by a number of my clients — is worthless if the site doesn't accomplish anything, rather like an attractive façade on a building that's rotting inside.

Now, if a Web site is a piece of software, you have to think about what the software will *do.* A Web site, in the context considered here, is a piece of sales software. It's designed to sell — to sell a product, a service, an idea. It's designed to get someone to take some kind of action that moves them through the sales "funnel" — to place an order, to call you and talk about your products, to request more information, to schedule a software demo, and so on.

If you build your site by using the method I outlined in the previous section, you won't end up with a piece of sales software that does a good job of selling and getting visitors to take some kind of action. Instead, you'll end up with a really pretty site that people will look at just before they purchase products from your competitors.

Almost invariably, when I ask my clients whether they considered the following questions before building their sites, they say no. These are questions that often arise *after* they have built their sites — $20,000 later, $100,000 later, $250,000 later . . .

- ✔ What should the site achieve?
- ✔ What things must we make visitors to the site do in order to achieve our goals?
- ✔ Where will we lead visitors?
- ✔ How will we "convert" visitors into buyers or sales leads?
- ✔ How do we create the right impression (competence, experience, trustworthiness)?

This is a process that begins with the abstract — what is the site *for?* — and ends with the specific — how will the pages be laid out and how will those pages connect to each other in order to get the visitors to carry out the action you want them to carry out.

A Web site, being a piece of software, is all about *process.* The visitor must do this, then do that, then do another thing, and finally you end up with a sale or a sales lead. The traditional site-building method does not consider process; it's simply an information repository. Over here you have contact information; over there, press releases; in this area, the management team. Sites built like this don't get the job done. Sure, you need to present all this information, but it doesn't work as far as getting visitors involved in a process goes!

The Blockbuster Web site, shown in Figure 5-12, is a good example of a well-designed site. Blockbuster knows exactly what it wants you to do when you visit the site: sign up for its new, online DVD-rental service. But, you splutter,

- ✔ **What about existing members? They don't want to see this!** In most cases, they won't. After you sign up, when you arrive at the Web site, you see your account page instead.
- ✔ **What about visitors who are purely interested in corporate information?** Some companies actually have two domain names, one for purely corporate purposes and one for customers. (Dex Media, a large Yellow Pages publisher, does this; see www.DexMedia.com and www.Dex Online.com.) In Blockbuster's case, it's all one domain name, but there's an About Blockbuster link to a corporate "sub-site" at the bottom of the home page.
- ✔ **What about people who want all the other stuff — customer service, store locator, investor relations, and so on?** Yep, there are links to all these things, too, at the bottom of the page.

Now, I'm not saying that every site should look like this. But in this case, Blockbuster really has one main goal — to get you to sign up for a rental membership. Perhaps you have two, three, or four goals (going over this number gets difficult). Here's another example, a site that actually looks more traditional yet still does a good job of "channeling" people in the right direction. In Figure 5-13, you see HomeGain.com, a popular real-estate site.

Figure 5-12: The Blockbuster Web site, built with a process in mind.

Figure 5-13: HomeGain.com also does a great job of leading people in the right direction.

What is your eye drawn to when you look at the HomeGain page? It's pulled to four components: Find and Compare REALTORS, What's Your Home Worth?, View Homes for Sale, and Get a Mortgage.

What's the bet these are the choices HomeGain wants you to make? Note that there's plenty more information available. The main navigation and the links at the bottom allow a visitor to find all the usual, mundane stuff: press releases, their affiliate program, the corporate info, and so on. But the focus of the page remains on these four choices, the ones HomeGain makes money on.

Tips for an Effective Web Site

Once again, the devil's in the details. Let's consider a few quick tips — a few things to think about when planning your site — to help you build a Web site that sells.

Consider the marketing message

If a Web site is a piece of sales software, then the *message* is essential. Most Web sites have no real message beyond "here's some stuff for you; come and get it." Your site, to have the best chance of succeeding (not just in PPC campaigns but in all ways), needs to have some kind of message. We've seen a few good examples in this chapter, of course — GameFly's marketing message is clear and succinct.

Admittedly, the situation is not so clear when you have a site that sells large numbers of products; I discuss this situation in "Pure E-commerce Sites," later in this chapter.

Focusing your Web site

Don't throw a thousand different ideas and products at people on one page. Keep it to three or four main choices, with a number of other choices available if the visitor decides to look closer. With just one to four different choices, you can create a design that puts those choices front and center, drawing the eye to the choices and allowing the visitor to quickly read and understand the choices.

Remove clutter

Clutter is the enemy of clarity. You want a clear message, and if your page is full of extraneous information, you're confusing the message. Visit some sites and look carefully to see how much really isn't necessary. In particular, bloated, boring, self-congratulatory "who we are" text on home pages, and huge, pointless logs and graphics. I often run across Web sites with virtually the top half of the page taken up with a logo, navigation bar, or utterly meaningless graphic.

Get rid of this stuff; it just gets in the way of the message.

Use images and boxes to attract the eye

You want to attract the eye to the message; using boxes and images, combined with large, colored text, can often work well. For instance, the HomeGain.com home page (Figure 5-13) pulls your eye to the four main choices by using the four circular images next to the large headings. On the Amazon site, boxes are used to separate different messages and help the eye scan the page and pick out those different messages quickly.

Ugly doesn't sell

People occasionally e-mail me that they've had their site up "for months now, and haven't sold a thing; can you take a look and tell me why?" I type the URL into my browser, wait for the page to load, and then am knocked out of my chair by the unadulterated grotesqueness of the page! (I now keep a pair of very heavily shaded sunglasses — polarized, UV filtered, glare-protected glacier glasses — for these very cases. If I get a gut feeling that the site I'm about to see is one of these horrible things, on go the glasses.)

I don't get it. I know some people are colorblind, but are some ugly blind? Can't they see?

Here's the fact: Ugly doesn't sell. By *ugly,* I mean a range of problems:

- ✔ Awful color combinations that just don't work
- ✔ Terrible typeface choices, making the pages close to unreadable
- ✔ Combinations of fonts and colors that make the text close to unreadable — such as white text on black backgrounds (no, it's *not* cool)
- ✔ Cutesy backgrounds that look . . . cutesy, not professional
- ✔ Incredibly clunky images that look like they were created by an amateur in front of the TV one evening
- ✔ Messy page layouts that look amateurish

I sometimes help clients build Web sites, but I know my limitations. I'm not a graphic designer, and I don't pretend to be one; I'll build sites, but find an expert to do the graphic design. Way too many people out there have decided to "play" graphic designer. If you're not one, don't try to act like one.

Having said that, be careful with graphic designers. Too many people in the Web business build beautiful pages that are not particularly functional, and some of them like to use every graphic design tool in the box, making your site beautiful but unusable.

Remember that your Web pages are your face to the world. Ugly, clunky, amateurish pages send a message: "We're clunky, ugly amateurs."

Think about our discussions of ROI in Chapter 3 and then remember this:

- ✔ *Ugly = Low Conversions*
- ✔ *Amateurish = Low Conversions*

Would you buy from a horrible little site that looks like it was built by one-handed gnomes? Well, if you wouldn't, why would anyone else? They don't.

By the way, I do understand that many small businesses have money issues; they can't afford a top professional designer. But there is actually no direct correlation between good Web design and dollars. It's possible to pay very little and get a decent site or to pay a lot and get garbage.

If, thanks to budgetary considerations — you're stone cold broke and plan to pay the designer with food — you have to use Cousin Joe the fireman to create your site, or perhaps your sophomore daughter, Jenny. (I've seen both situations.) If both Joe and Jenny have, let's say, less-than-adequate design skills, what do you do? Buy some templates! Search online for *web page templates* and then spend a few hours looking for something nice. Even if you you've got the slimmest of budgets and have to use a non-designer to create your site, you still don't settle for a lousy design.

There's a level below which you must not go. Remember the phrase "the kingdom was lost for the want of a nail"? Or "penny smart, pound foolish"? Saving money short-term by creating a bad Web site will cost you long-term by increasing your click costs.

Pure E-commerce Sites

It's true that pure e-commerce sites that sell more than a handful of products — in particular, Web sites that sell thousands of products in dozens or even hundreds of categories — present a special challenge when trying to create a site that sells. How do you "lead" people in one or two directions when you actually have thousands of stories to tell?

Amazon doesn't focus on a small number of marketing messages overall, but the site definitely does use clear marketing messages throughout. In Figure 5-14, you see that the Amazon.com home page tries to lead you into the Sony Audio area, that it's pushing its new Free Shipping program (Amazon Prime), and that it's promoting an Outdoor Furniture Clearance. Down the right side, Amazon uses several little boxes to pull you to other promotions.

Of course, some observers say that Amazon is not the epitome of well-designed sites, anyway, and that it's way too cluttered. Take a look at AllAboardToys.com (Figure 5-15), a good example of a site that prides itself on being easier to use than Amazon. You can see that the buttons at the top clearly lead people into various product categories — Sesame Street, Madeline, Winnie the Pooh, and so on — while there's also a prominent Search box in the middle of the page. Of course, AllAboardToys focuses on far fewer products than Amazon does, too.

Figure 5-14: The Amazon.com home page.

Figure 5-15:
AllAboard
Toys is
a good
example of
a clear site
that leads
people into
different
product
areas.

PPC Rules of Landing Pages

By the way, you should also be aware that the PPC firms themselves have
their own landing-page requirements. You've already learned that the PPC
firms require that the landing pages are relevant to the ads. In addition there
are other regulations, in particular these two:

✔ The Back button must work properly — the visitor must be able to click
the button and return to the search engine.

✔ The page should not display pop-ups when the page loads.

Chapter 6

Finding the Right Words for Your Ad

*Y*ou may think I wrote this book backward. In the preceding chapter, I look at how to create landing pages, and now I'm going to look at how to write the ads that bring people to those landing pages. But creating landing pages is a much more complex issue than creating the ads, so you may be able to put off the ad-writing process for a while.

I assume, however, that you've figured out the landing-page thing, and you're ready to roll. It's time to consider those ads.

Note that each PPC system is a little different. They have different allowable ad widths, a different number of lines, and different regulations. But many of the concepts are similar, so I discuss them in general terms here.

PPC ads are a little different from television, newspaper, and radio ads and other types of advertisements. In most cases, you want as many people as possible to get involved in your ad — to spend time thinking about your products and services.

With PPC, you actually have two aims:

- Ensure that your prospects — potential buyers — click on the ad.
- Ensure that people who are *not* your prospects do *not* click on the ad.

Avoiding attention is a big part of the game — every click costs, so you want to avoid the clicks that are not worth paying for. In this chapter, I help you maximize the good clicks and minimize the bad clicks.

Small Changes = Huge Benefits

A combination of a good ad and a good landing page can make all the difference to your PPC campaign — the difference between failure and success or average success and mind-blowing success.

Small changes in the results from an ad make a huge difference to your campaign's profitability. Here is an example: Imagine that you're selling a product that has a gross profit of $75 (see Chapter 3 for a discussion of *gross profit*) and running an ad with these numbers:

Number of times ad is displayed	100,000
Conversion (click-through) rate	1%
Number of times clicked	1,000
Cost per click	$0.35
Total cost of clicks	$350
Conversion (buy) rate	1%
Number of sales	10
Click cost per sale	$35
Gross Profit per sale (before click costs)	$75
Gross Profit for all sales (before click costs)	$750
Gross Profit for all sales (after click costs)	$400
Campaign ROI	114%

It's time to tweak. First, look at what happens if you replace a mediocre ad with one on which 5 percent of the people who see the ad click it. (The italicized numbers show the changes.)

	Original	Now
Number of times ad is displayed	100,000	100,000
Conversion (click-through) rate	1%	*5%*
Number of times clicked	1,000	*5,000*
Cost per click	$0.35	$0.35
Total cost of clicks	$350	*$1,750*
Conversion (buy) rate	1%	1%
Number of sales	10	*50*
Click cost per sale	$35	$35
Gross Profit per sale (before click costs)	$75	$75
Gross Profit for all sales (before click costs)	$750	*$3,750*
Gross Profit for all sales (after click costs)	$400	*$2,000*
Campaign ROI	114%	114%

This is, in effect, a comparison between an ad that people sometimes click on, and one that they frequently click on. In this case, a profit of $3,750 instead of $400. The ROI remains the same — you'll have to spend the same amount to generate each dollar of profit — but your volume is much higher.

Now look at what can happen if you can convince just one more person out of 100 to buy from you. (Of course, this is not caused by just the ad; the combination of both the ad and the landing page affects conversions.) In this example, I set the ad conversion rate back to 1 percent and increase the sales-conversion rate. Again, italicized numbers indicate changes.

	Original	Now
Number of times ad is displayed	100,000	100,000
Conversion (click-through) rate	1%	1%
Number of times clicked	1,000	1,000
Cost per click	$0.35	$0.35
Total cost of clicks	$350	$350
Conversion (buy) rate	1%	*2%*
Number of sales	10	*20*
Click cost per sale	$35	*$17.50*
Gross Profit per sale (before click costs)	$75	$75
Gross Profit for all sales (before click costs)	$750	*$1,500*
Gross Profit for all sales (after click costs)	$400	*$1,150*
Campaign ROI	114%	*329%*

The same number of people arrive at your site this time, so the total click costs are the same. But your total sales and ROI are much higher. In this case, convincing just one extra person out of 100 to take the desired action on your site nearly triples the return on investment and profits.

Of course, if you combine the two components — a higher click-through rate and a higher sales-conversion rate — then the effects are spectacular.

	Original	*Now*
Number of times ad is displayed	100,000	100,000
Conversion (click-through) rate	1%	5%
Number of times clicked	1,000	5,000
Cost per click	$0.35	$0.35
Total cost of clicks	$350	$1,750
Conversion (buy) rate	1%	2%
Number of sales	10	100
Click cost per sale	$35	$17.50
Gross Profit per sale (before click costs)	$75	$75
Gross Profit for all sales (before click costs)	$750	$7,500
Gross Profit for all sales (after click costs)	$400	$5,750
Campaign ROI	114%	329%

As you can see, the combination creates a huge jump in gross profit. Now, here's what's important to understand. These numbers are in the realm of the possible. It *is* possible to greatly increase the number of people clicking your ads, and it *is* possible, through a combination of good ads and good landing pages, to add a percentage to your conversion rates. Sure, if you're already doing a great job, making another jump is tough. But most advertisers are not doing a great job, so these large improvements are quite possible.

Different Systems, Different Ads

In general, PPC ads are small, which is both good and bad. Good because, hey, how long can it take to create a 12-word ad? I'm not talking about 12 *pages* here, just 12 words. Bad because, well, writing an effective 12-word ad can be tricky!

No PPC ad is huge, but different PPC systems give you different amounts of space to play with. Google is particularly stingy. Some of the third-tier systems provide far more room; they're trying to be more competitive, after all. (But even Yahoo! provides a lot more space.) Google has the brand name, and the folks there figure you'll take what it gives you, so Po-Dunk Pay Per Click needs to work a little harder to please you.

Table 6-1 shows a few ad sizes, the number of lines, and the number of characters on each line for a few of the more popular PPC systems. See Figure 6-1 for an example of a PPC ad.

Table 6-1	Ad Field Lengths for Popular PPC Systems				
PPC System	*Headline Length (Characters)*	*No. of Lines*	*Line Length (Characters)*	*Display URL Length (Characters)*	*Target URL Length (Characters)*
Google	25	2	35	35	1,024
Yahoo! Top	40	1	190	120	1,024
Yahoo! Side	40	3	~80 characters, wrapped onto 3 lines	27	1,024
MSN	25	1	70	35	1,022

Note that Yahoo! doesn't really have a Display URL field; it grabs the domain portion from your Target URL and uses that. The Display URL numbers shown in the table are how much space is available in those positions.

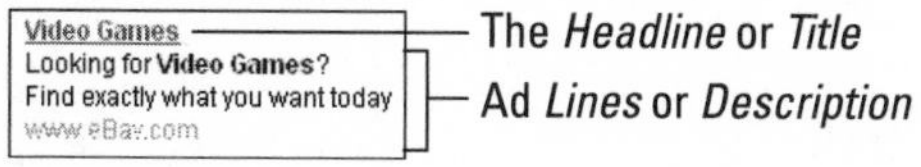

Figure 6-1:
An example
PPC ad from
Google
AdWords.

Video Games ———— The *Headline* or *Title*
Looking for **Video Games**?
Find exactly what you want today ┐— Ad *Lines* or *Description*
www.eBay.com

Note that the ad has both a *Display URL* and *Target URL*. Virtually all PPC ads end with the URL of the site that the ad points to — www.eBay.com, www.GameFly.com, and so on — but that's usually the URL of the home page and not really the page that the ad actually points to. Clicking the ad takes you to a landing page, which is deeper into the Web site than just the home page. So when you create your ad, you provide a *target* or *destination* URL, the URL of the landing page associated with the ad (see Chapter 5 for information on landing pages).

Also note that, in some cases, lines will wrap or even be truncated. Google's ads have two lines (in addition to the description or title line). If an ad is placed on the right side of the search-results page, the two lines are displayed one above the other; if the ad is placed along the top of the search results, the lines are placed together on a single line. Regardless of whether the ad is on top or the right, the entire ad is displayed, all words and characters.

On the other hand, Yahoo!'s ads have a single, very long line (up to 190 characters long) that are sometimes truncated when the ads appear on the right side of the results page. You can see in Figure 6-2 that the last lines of some of the ads on the right side trail off with an ellipsis at the end of the description.

The first ad at the top of the page is truncated. Here's what the full ad looks like:

> Video Game Design School
> Prepare for an exciting new career by learning valuable game design skills at Collins College in Tempe, Arizona. Request official school info today.
> videogame.career-edu.org

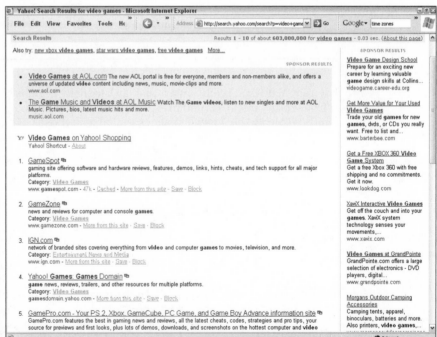

Figure 6-2:
Look carefully at the ads on the right side; they've been truncated.

Of course, this really means that if you're creating ads for Yahoo!, you need to consider placement; if you're planning to place your ads in one of the top two positions, create a larger ad, but if you are targeting position number three or lower, create a smaller ad.

Viewing the Editorial Guidelines

Pretty much every PPC system has documents that explain how to create ads that work and what you can and cannot say in the ads. You should check with the PPC system for which you're creating ads to see what their guidelines say. Both Google and Yahoo! are pretty strict about the different terms you can use, while many of the smaller systems are nowhere near as picky.

Remember, the PPC systems have two basic concerns. They want you to create ads that

- **Work well.** The more people click the ad, the more money the PPC system makes; the more you sell, the more ads you'll place.

- **Are good search results.** The PPC system wants to provide good search results to searchers to keep them coming back. So ads have to provide search results that searchers will feel are relevant. They don't want gimmicky or misleading results, they want relevance.

I recommend that you check the guidelines *before* you start writing the ads; after all, there's no point spending time figuring out the perfect ad, only to discover that the PPC system doesn't think it's so perfect. It *will* reject your ad if it doesn't match its guidelines; Yahoo! Search Marketing claims that it rejects around 30 percent of all the ads submitted.

You can find the editorial guidelines for the three major PPC systems at the following URLs:

- **Google:** https://adwords.google.com/select/guidelines.html

- **Yahoo!:** http://searchmarketing.yahoo.com/rc/srch/lg.php

- **MSN:** http://advertising.msn.com/msnadcenter/

Encouraging Clicks

The primary purpose of a PPC ad is to get people to click on the ad, of course. There are various ways to do that, from placing the keywords in the ads to using "action words," from including benefits in the ad to including calls to action.

Include keywords

Ideally, every ad you create would be optimized for a particular keyword. If you're working with thousands of keywords, that can be difficult to do, but you should understand that placing the keywords into the ad can help encourage people to click the ad.

You see elsewhere (starting in Chapter 8) that when you work with a PPC system, you create an ad and then associate the ad with the keywords for which you want the ad to appear. You can associate an ad with hundreds of different keywords or just a handful.

In Chapter 5, I searched for the video game *Conker* by searching on *conker: live and reloaded.* I found this ad:

> Don't Read Game Reviews
> Rent Games Online instead. Fast &
> Affordable. Get Games Now. Try Free
> www.gamefly.com

As you can see, this ad is not directly related to the game Conker. Imagine, however, that the ad said this:

> Rent **Conker**, Don't Buy
> Rent **Conker** Online instead. Fast &
> Affordable. Get Games Now. Try Free
> www.gamefly.com

Notice that *Conker* is boldfaced in this ad. Do any search on Google, Yahoo!, or MSN, and you'll notice that the search engine boldfaces words you search on that appear in the PPC ad titles and descriptions. (MSN boldfaces in the title, but actually colors the word in the description rather than boldfacing it.)

So placing the keywords into your ads does two things:

✔ **It makes the ad stand out.** As the searcher scans the list of search results, the bold words make the ads more noticeable.

✔ **It makes the ad more relevant to the searcher.** In effect, it tells the searcher, "Hey, you were searching for these keywords."

Placing the keywords into an ad does have a significant effect. Even better than simply placing the keyword somewhere in the ad is placing it at the beginning of the title.

According to Yahoo! Search Marketing, having the keyword in the ad increases click-through rates by 50 percent; the company also claims that searchers perceive the "quality" of the Web site as 60 percent higher if they reach the site through an ad that matched the term for which they searched (I'm not sure how it quantifies quality, but that's what it claims).

Combining an ad that matches the keyword with a landing page that matches the keyword can be very effective and can make a big difference to your results. If you're working with thousands of keywords, yes, this can be difficult. A good first step is to match ads with groups of keywords that have common elements. For instance, we could create a single ad that matches this group of keywords:

> *conker: live and reloaded*
> *conker video game*
> *conkers video game*
> *buy conker game*
> *conker game*

We could have other ads to match similar keywords for different games.

Matching keywords like this can have a huge effect. One client told me that working with hundreds of thousands of keywords, carefully matching keywords, ads, and landing pages so that as much as possible searchers saw, in the ad and on the landing pages, the keywords they typed, "made a huge difference to conversion rates." Placing the relevant keywords in the ad really does make a big difference.

Selling the sizzle — Think benefits

If you've spent any time learning about sales and marketing, you've probably heard the phrase, "sell the sizzle, not the steak." It means that nobody wants the object you are selling, they want the benefits of the object . . . they don't want the steak, they want the "sizzle": the taste, smell, and satisfaction of eating the steak.

Look at these ads on the Google search-results page for the word *candles:*

Buy **Candles** for Less
Free Candles with any purchase
Tealight, Votives, Pillars,
Wedding
www.candle4less.com

Great Scents-Great Price
Hand Poured, Maximum Scented
Clean Burning **Candles** in Jars
www.welcomehomescents.
com

DiscountCandle.com
Free Shipping on orders over
$50.00 great discounts on
Over 5,000 items
www.discountcandle.com

Candle, Soap, Tea & More.
Hand Made in San Francisco CA
Check out this month Prices
Gmoora.com

Candles
Bargain Prices.
See the difference.
BizRate.com

If you read through these, you can really see that some are stronger than others. For instance, this one is pretty weak:

Candle, Soap, Tea & More.
Hand Made in San Francisco CA
Check out this month Prices
Gmoora.com

First, it's not focused on candles; it's a bit of this and a bit of that (candles, soap, tea, and other stuff). "Hand made in San Francisco CA"; is that really a benefit? "Check out this month Prices"? Apart from the fact that it's not grammatically correct, it's also not a benefit. Are the prices good or bad?

This one seems better in a couple of ways, but it's still not great:

Candles
Bargain Prices.
See the difference.
BizRate.com

It does have *Candles* in the title, which is good. It also has the term *Bargain Prices,* which is a benefit. *See the difference* doesn't say much, though.

How about this one:

DiscountCandle.com
Free Shipping on orders over
$50.00 great discounts on
Over 5,000 items
www.discountcandle.com

It would have been better not to use the site name in the title. Nobody cares about the site name (and, besides, it's repeated in the last line). The title should have been used for a benefit, and because we don't have the word *candles* in the title, there's no bold text. The word *Candles* would have been bolded had they written the title in one of the following ways, and a stronger message would have been conveyed (though admittedly the company name itself does include a benefit):

Discount **Candles**
Great Prices on **Candles**
Low Prices on **Candles**
Save Money on **Candles**

The ad does a decent job, though; it quickly gets across the idea of three benefits:

✔ Free shipping

✔ Great discounts

✔ Large selection

It could be cleaned up a little:

<u>Save Money on</u> **Candles**
Free Shipping over $50.
Deep discounts on over
5,000 **candles** & votives
www.DiscountCandle.com

Now we have a stronger title, with *Candles* bolded. Free shipping is clearly stated and in fewer words. The superfluous *.00* on the end of $50.00 has been removed, and the punctuation problem (*$50.00 great discounts*) has been fixed. We have the word *candles* in there again — so now the ad has *two* bold words in it. And we've "mixed-cased" the URL, making it easier to read (see "Use mixed-case domain names," a little later in this chapter).

So, when writing your ads, think about benefits. Why should someone care about your product or service? What can you do for them? *Check out this month Prices* is not a benefit; *Deep discounts* is.

Think competitive advantage

Stating benefits is all well and good, but think about the benefits that make you stand apart. In Chapter 5, I show you a couple of companies that rent video games. You may recall that Intelliflix claims two competitive advantages: a huge selection of both games and movies, and the lowest price.

When you search on the term *rent video games,* you see lots of ads claiming things like this:

✔ Rent games online

✔ Free trial

✔ No due dates

✔ No late fees

✔ Free delivery

And what does Intelliflix say?

> Unlimited Games $14.75
> 3 at a time includes movies too!
> Intelliflix delivers free to you!
> www.intelliflix.com

Is there anything in this ad to make Intelliflix stand apart? Not much; it's just another game-rental company. Sure, $14.75 is a low price, but many people don't know that it's the lowest price. Free delivery? Doesn't everyone have that? As for *movies too,* that seems to be hidden away.

How about this for an ad?

> **Rent Video Games**
> Lowest price, huge selection
> 40,000 Game & Video titles
> www.Intelliflix.com

Benefits are good, but think about what benefits you have that others don't — think about your competitive advantage. (And if you can't think of one, you may be in trouble!)

By the way, there is one problem with the ad; the PPC editors are probably going to block it the first time it's submitted, because of the phrase "Lowest price." However, if you can prove that you really do have the lowest price in the business, they should accept it. (This wouldn't be possible in most businesses, but in the game-rental business, with very few companies competing, it could be done.) I explain more about this later in this chapter.

Be clear and direct

Why, to paraphrase Mark Twain, would you use the word *metropolis* when you can say *city.* Not only is *city* more direct, it uses fewer characters, allowing you to get more information into the ad.

Google claims that short, non-repetitive sentences work well, and I'm sure it's right. Clarity allows people to quickly scan your ad and figure out what it's about . . . and make a quick decision to click.

Use "power words"

Some words convey more than others. Use terms that have a strong effect on the reader, words sometimes known as *power words* or *trigger words,* such as

✔ 100% Guaranteed	✔ Latest
✔ Absolutely Free	✔ Limited
✔ Affordable	✔ Low Price
✔ Amazing	✔ One-Day Sale
✔ Bargain Price	✔ Proven
✔ Breakthrough	✔ Relax
✔ Convenient	✔ Results Fast
✔ Delivers	✔ Safe
✔ Discover	✔ Sale
✔ Easy	✔ Secrets
✔ Effective	✔ Stop
✔ Extraordinary	✔ Stunning
✔ Fast-Acting	✔ Superior
✔ Free	✔ Useful
✔ Half Price	✔ Wealth
✔ Increases	✔ You

Many marketers believe questions are very powerful, too. Asking a question engages the reader in the process:

✔ Looking for Video Games?

✔ Want to lose weight?

✔ Looking for work?

✔ Need new shoes?

Try calls to action

You might try specific *calls to action.* Your ad already has an implied call to action: *click.* So there's no need to say *Click here,* for instance.

However, you could try a call to action that gets the searcher ready for what you want him or her to do on your site. In effect, you use verbs to tell searchers what they can do on your site:

- ✔ Register now
- ✔ Join now
- ✔ Buy at wholesale
- ✔ Save money

- ✔ Save 50%
- ✔ Get started
- ✔ Start your free trial
- ✔ View a live demo

Add some urgency

Another old marketing technique is to add a sense of urgency to your ad. Experiment with ad copy that stresses limited time availability. Give people a reason to click *immediately.* Try special pricing for 24 hours or some kind of special limited-time offer — free shipping or some kind of free gift.

Use phrases like *introductory pricing, while supplies last, limited inventory,* and so on, assuming they are correct. These are all things that you can test to see how they affect your click-through rate.

Use mixed-case domain names

You should mix-case your domain name in your ads whenever you can (Yahoo! and MSN won't let you do this for some reason, which seems to me rather unenlightened.) Don't use `www.discountcandles.com`, use `www.DiscountCandles.com`; don't use `www.candlesjustonline.com`, enter `www.CandlesJustOnline.com`.

Why? Because it makes the domain name easier to read. For some reason, many people think domain names and URLs *have to be* written in lowercase. Domain names *never* have to be in lowercase (URLs that include directory and filenames sometimes do). If you have a domain name with useful key-words in it, why not mix-case it so the words are clearly read?

Also, in some cases, a domain name is close to unintelligible when lower-cased, such as this: `www.horanandmcconaty.com`. Wouldn't it be better as `www.HoranAndMcConaty.com`?

Check spelling, grammar, and punctuation

Two of the *candles* ads we looked at had grammatical or punctuation errors (three if you count a missing hyphen, but people just don't care about hyphens anymore!), which looks sloppy. Look, you're not writing 20-page sales letters here; these ads are around 15 to 20 *words!* Spend a few moments checking your work.

Bad spelling, grammar, and punctuation may reduce your click-through rates . . . or maybe not. But why take the risk?

Discouraging People from Clicking

As I mention earlier, you have two aims when you create your ad: To get people to click your ad, and to discourage people from clicking your ad. You want the *right* people to click the ad — and you're willing to pay for them — but you don't want people to click if there's no way they will buy from you.

How do you do that? One way to avoid useless clickers is *clarity.* If it's clear what your ad is about, you'll avoid accidental clickers. For instance, look at these two ads:

Video Games
Looking for Video Games?
We have thousands to choose from
www.gamesource.com

Rent Video Games
Don't buy, rent. Save $1,000s
Free shipping, huge selection
www.GameSource.com

The first is almost certainly going to get clicks from people who simply aren't interested in renting, so if GameSource.com were a game-rental company, the second ad is clearly more appropriate than the first.

A more complicated issue is one of price. If you're selling products that cost thousands of dollars, but a similar class of products sells for hundreds, you don't want the people who are only willing to spend hundreds to click your ad. This is a problem for companies that sell enterprise-level software. For instance, you can pay tens or hundreds of dollars for e-commerce software, or you can pay tens of thousands of dollars.

For instance, this ad, I'm sure, gets a lot of wasted clicks:

> Ecommerce Software
> Versatile & Robust-Manages Web,
> order mgmt, fulfillment & forecast
> www.ecometry.com

The problem is that most people are searching for e-commerce software that costs tens or hundreds of dollars, not the many thousands of dollars charged by this company.

In this case, you somehow want to discourage the small businesses from clicking, so you want to imply in the message — in the few words you've got — that this product is more than they need. To do so, perhaps the ad could be written this way:

> Ecommerce Software
> Order mgmt for medium to large firms
> Robust tools for major retailers
> www.ecometry.com

If you're selling a product that competes with freebies — often the case in the software business — you may want to get some mention of price into the ad in order to discourage people who are looking for free products. For instance, if you sell Web utilities, you're in competition with all the sites giving away free Web scripts. Here are some real ads that have dealt with this problem, mentioning price in order to stop people from clicking if they are not willing to pay:

> Buy Web Templates
> Save time & money! Choose
> from thousands of quality designs.
> www.pixelmill.com

> Web Templates
> Download 1000's of web templates
> Unlimited access for only $49.95
> www.boxedart.com

> Web and Flash Templates
> Website templates, Flash templates
> Unlimited downloads for only
> $35.00
> www.artwebtemplates.us

> Web Templates Package
> Instant Access to 10,000+ Templates
> PSD, Flash, HTML for Only $19.95
> www.templatesguys.net

Another way to discourage clicking is location. If you are selling shoes in your shoe store in, say, Denver, and do not ship product, you probably don't want people from New York clicking your ad. You'll want to mention your location in the ad.

Avoiding Rejection

As I mention earlier, you must check the PPC system's guidelines before you begin writing. If you don't, you will almost certainly do something it doesn't like and have your ad rejected. Remember, the PPC systems want to provide relevant search results, not high-pressure ads, to searchers.

Here are a few common problems to watch out for.

Check the banned list

Most, if not all, PPC systems have certain products that you simply cannot advertise. For instance, here's a sample from Google's list (`https://adwords.google.com/select/contentpolicy.html`) of types of ads that Google will not run:

- Aids for passing drugs tests
- Alcohol
- Ads advocating against any person or organization (except political candidates and parties)
- Cable descramblers
- Counterfeit designer goods
- Gambling
- Miracle cures
- Prostitution
- Radar jammers
- Weapons

Having said all that, clearly Google's list is either out of date or not applied religiously. You *can* find gambling ads, for instance, and apparently the proscription against prostitution doesn't apply to escort agencies. Are these just "slipping through," or is Google just "ignoring" the rules? I don't know.

Watch your superlatives!!!!!

Google doesn't like 'em, nor does Yahoo!. For instance, you shouldn't do something like this:

Great Web Templates!!!
Cheapest templates on the Web!!!!
Save time & $$$! Thousands designs
www.CoolTemplates.com

This ad is pretty much guaranteed an editorial rejection. You can't say *cheapest templates on the Web* because you almost certainly can't prove that.

You can't use *!!!*. It's a non-standard repetition of a punctuation mark that is, in effect, a superlative. And the same goes for *$$$!*. Google bans the use of an exclamation mark on a title line, and in fact allows only a single exclamation mark in the entire ad.

You really have to be careful here. You may think your product is the best, but you may not be able to say it in an ad. Google, for instance, flags all ads that contain the word *best*, even, as I've noticed, if the ad refers to a "best-selling author."

If it's not demonstrably true, you can't say it, and even if it is, you may find yourself going around in circles trying to explain to the PPC editors, via e-mail, why it's a fact and not a superlative. You may get away with it if the landing page contains third-party verification of your claims.

Avoid, avoid, avoid repetitions

The previous section shows a couple of repetitions that are, in effect, superlatives, so they're banned by PPC systems' editorial boards. But unnecessary repetitions of any kind are generally banned by the PPC systems. For example,

Templates, Templates, Templates
Cheapest templates on the Web!
Save time and money
www.CoolTemplates.com

Or

<u>How to Win Any Lottery</u>
Win, win, win!
Win any lottery today.
www.lotterywinners.com

Sorry, this is a rejection waiting to happen.

DON'T OVER-CAPITALIZE

UNLESS THERE'S A GOOD REASON TO DO SO, AVOID CAPITALIZING EVERY-THING IN YOUR ADS. YOU MAY NOT HAVE NOTICED, BUT CAPITALIZED TEXT IS VERY HARD TO READ. GOOGLE *REALLY* DOESN'T LIKE IT, AND YOU'LL PROBABLY FIND THAT MOST OTHER PPC SYSTEMS DON'T EITHER.

Use symbols appropriately

While some say that you should avoid all symbols, in general, you *can* use symbols in your ads if you use them properly. Perhaps the most common symbol is the ampersand — & — used in place of *and*. It's a very useful symbol when you're watching every single character you type, and both Google and Yahoo! allow its use.

Some other symbols may not be approved. Google, for instance, doesn't like the use of @ to mean *at*. Nor does it allow "texting" — the abbreviated writing used on cell-phone text messages, such as `the bst prices 4 u`.

Be relevant and honest

Your ad must be related to the landing page it points to, and it must be honest — you can't mislead people about your offer.

The ad must be accurate; you can't promise a free trial, for instance, then make it next-to-impossible to find the free trial on your site. And if your business is local, the PPC company may require that you put this in the ad, which isn't a bad idea anyway, for reasons mentioned earlier (to discourage clicks from non-local searchers).

Different PPC systems regard *relevance* differently. In Chapter 5, I show you how GameFly was advertising based on the search term *conker: live and reloaded,* despite the fact that the ad is not directly related to the keywords.

So there are two forms of relevance:

- ✔ Is the ad relevant to the keywords
- ✔ Is the landing page relevant to the ad

The landing page *must* be relevant to the ad. The degree of the relevance of the ad to the keyword will vary, though.

No phone numbers

You can't put your phone number into a PPC ad! The PPC firm gets paid when someone clicks, not when he or she picks up the phone to call (see Chapter 14 for information on Pay Per Call services). And in general, you should avoid putting your URL into the ad description; the URL goes in the bottom line, the *Display Link* field.

Appealing rejection

You can, of course appeal an ad rejection, though some PPC companies don't make it very easy. Google has a very quick review process, that automatically checks your ad during the creation process, and so it also has a built-in appeal tool that you'll see if your ad is rejected. You can appeal, and continue the process, and let a live editor make the final decision before your ads go live.

Quite frankly, one of the biggest problems working with the PPC firms are their editors — just about anyone who's spent more than a few bucks on PPC can tell you frustrating stories of trying to get honest, reasonable claims past editors who seem to apply the rules with no common sense or flexibility.

Testing your ads

As I mention in the previous chapter, online selling and the direct-mail business are similar. What do successful direct-mail marketers do? That's right: they test, over and over again. They test the wording of their ads very carefully — in fact, they test everything about their ads; the envelope size, envelope text and illustrations, letter text, letter layout, and so on. It can be a very complex job, but you're in luck: Testing PPC ads is much simpler. After all, you have no envelope, and you have only three or four lines to play with.

I ran a few different searches on Google that I knew would bring up GameFly. com ads (*rent games*, *game rental*, and so on). Here's what I found.

Don't Read Game Reviews
Rent Games Online instead. Fast &
Affordable. Get Games Now. Try
Free
www.gamefly.com

Don't Buy another Game
Save Cash. Play Every Game You
Want
by Renting. Fast, Free Trial
www.gamefly.com

Want Video games?
Over 2500 Titles, No Due
Dates
Free 10-Day Trial,
Discounts & more
GameFly.com

Rent or Buy Games Online
Over 2,500 Titles Delivered To You
Pre-paid Mail Both Ways!
www.gamefly.com

Rent Video Games Online
PS2, Xbox, GameCube & PSP. No Risk
Free Trial - Sign Up Now!
www.GameFly.com

On Yahoo! I found this one, though only this one:

Unlimited Video Game
Rental - Free Trial
Choose from over 2,500
PlayStation 2, Xbox,
GameCube, PSP, GBA and DS
titles. Free delivery both
ways. No late fees – try
GameFly for free.
www.gamefly.com

GameFly has basically one service, one marketing pitch: rent video games through the mail. Yet it has all these different ads, and quite likely many others, too. GameFly is clearly testing its ads; they're saying the same thing in different ways.

✔ Some ads highlight the selection — 2,500 titles

✔ Some highlight the free trial

✔ One mention the free, prepaid mailing, while one mentions the different game systems

Of course, testing does you no good if you're not tracking. You need to look at how each ad works — how well it *converts*.

Actually, you're interested in several things:

- ✔ **How well does the ad convert impressions to clicks?**
- ✔ **How well does the ad convert clicks to sales?** People clicking on ad A may be more likely to buy than people who click on ad B.
- ✔ **What is the ROI?** I talk about Return on Investment in detail in Chapter 3.
- ✔ **What is the total sales volume?** It's great if you can run an ad and get a 100 percent conversion rate, but if your volume drops from, say, 1,000 sales a week down to 10 sales a week, you probably won't be happy.

So tracking, which I discuss in Chapter 15, is essential. You have to follow the traffic and see what it does. And the overall picture is what counts. There's no point dramatically increasing clicks, for instance, if you don't increase sales; you'll just pay more for the same business.

If you've been running ad A and then introduce ad B, and B does better, then drop A and use B instead. But what is it about B that works? Do you think it's the fact that you added the phrase *Free Trial,* for instance?

You really have two ways to test: Create completely different ads, or change existing ads and then try again. For example, imagine you're running this ad:

> Don't Buy Another Game
> Save Cash. Play Every Game You Want
> by Renting. Huge selection
> www.Gamefly.com

You could now change one thing and see what happens:

> Don't Buy Another Game
> Save Cash. Play Every Game You Want
> by Renting. Free Trial
> www.GameFly.com

You've removed mention of the selection and replaced it with *Free Trial.* Which "pulls" best (to use direct-mail parlance)? Which *converts* best? I don't know, but testing will show you.

Chapter 7

Bidding on Keywords

. . . .

In This Chapter

▶ Understanding basic bidding concepts

▶ Learning bidding strategies

▶ Mastering the method in the matching madness

▶ Finding cheaper clicks

. . . .

The foundation of the PPC system is *bidding*. You bid against other advertisers for how much you're willing to pay per click for a particular keyword. In other words, you are saying, in effect, this:

> *For this particular keyword, show my ad, and if someone clicks the ad,*
> *I'm willing to pay as much as $x.xx.*

If someone else bids more than you, he or she appears higher in the search results. If nobody is interested in bidding on a keyword, the clicks are cheap; if everyone in the world wants to bid on a keyword, the clicks are expensive.

Bids start low — the minimum bid on Google is a penny (though Google has a more complicated bidding mechanism, and click prices usually really begin higher than this; you learn about Google's bidding in Chapter 9); on Yahoo!, 10 cents. Other systems often start low, perhaps as low as a penny. (By the way, sometimes you see people paying 5 cents on Yahoo!; these are people who have been advertising through Yahoo! for some time, since before Yahoo! increased its minimum to 10 cents a few years ago; their bids have been "grandfathered in" at a lower rate.)

There's more to bidding than meets the eye. You have to understand a little about bidding strategies in order to avoid paying too much for your clicks. And that's just what this chapter is all about.

Understanding Basic Bidding

We're going to look at how bidding functions in its most basic form. I use Yahoo! as an example, because Yahoo! is the largest system to use this basic form of bidding; as you learn later, Google's bidding mechanism does *not* use this basic bidding system.

Let's begin by taking a quick look at a few bids. Yahoo! provides a nice little bid checker that makes checking bid prices very easy, so PPC marketers often use it as a quick research tool.

To find the tool, go to `http://SearchMarketing.Yahoo.com`. Click the Sponsored Search link, then click the Pricing link, and finally click the View Bids Tool link or button. (Alternatively, go directly to `http://uv.bidtool.overture.com/d/search/tools/bidtool`.) You see the page shown in Figure 7-1.

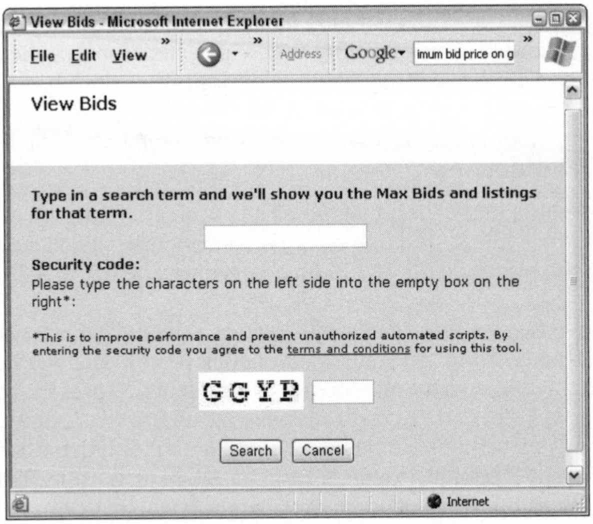

Figure 7-1:
The Yahoo!
Search
Marketing
View Bids
tool.

Type a keyword into the text box. Here's an expensive one to try (at least, at the time of writing): *vioxx attorney*. Then type the Security Code in the lower box and press Enter. After a few moments, you see something like the information shown in Figure 7-2.

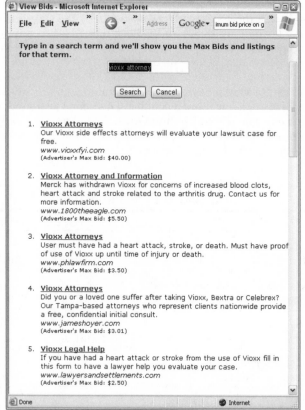

Figure 7-2:
The View
Bids tool
shows you
how much
people are
bidding on
various
keywords.

The View Bids tool now shows you the ads related to the keywords you entered and the bids. (Yahoo! actually shows up to the first 40 bids.)

You see the exact ad that will appear in Yahoo!'s search results. In addition, there's an extra line showing the advertisers' maximum bids, in this case, $40.00 and $5.50.

What exactly are these numbers? They are *not* necessarily the amount being paid by the advertiser. In this case, in fact, the first advertiser is *not* paying $40 for a click. These days, most search engines charge 1 cent above the next lower bid. These bids are actually *maximum bids,* and in fact that's just what Yahoo! calls them. When you bid, you're saying you're willing to pay *up to* that much, but as long as nobody is bidding right below you, you won't actually pay it. You'll pay a penny more than the maximum bid of the bidder right below you.

When someone clicks the first ad in our example, the advertiser actually pays $5.51, *not* $40. Now, if the second advertiser (who, by the way, is not paying $5.50, because #3 is bidding $3.50), raises his bid to $6.00, #1 pays $6.01. If #2 bids $7.50, #1 pays $7.51, and so on. And the whole time, #2 continues paying only $3.51.

So the Max Bid is just what it says; it's the maximum sum the advertiser is willing to pay. Here are a few more examples. This time I searched on the term *colorado real estate*. Table 7-1 shows the ad title, the URL, and the maximum bid. But there's some extra information: The Actual Paid column shows what each advertiser actually pays for a click.

Table 7-1	**Example Bids and Actual Click Costs**	
Advertiser	*Max Bid*	*Actual Paid*
1. **Free New Colorado Home Listings,** www.justlisted.com	$2.05	$2.04
2. **Denver Colorado Area Woodcrest Homes,** www.woodcresthomes.com	$2.03	$1.07
3. **Colorado Real Estate,** www.automatedhomefinder.com	$1.06	$1.06
4. **Colorado Real Estate: Colorado Acreage,** www.coloradoacreage.com	$1.05	$1.05
5. **Real Estate Agents Serving Colorado,** www.realtorsreferrals.net	$1.05	$1.01
6. **Ken Gold - RE/MAX Steamboat Springs, CO,** www.skitownrealtor.com	$1.00	$1.00
7. **Southwest Colorado Real Estate Services,** www.donricedorff.com	$0.99	$0.99
8. **Colorado Real Estate,** www.catsman.com	$0.98	$0.91
9. **Colorado Real Estate,** www.stevescheer.com	$0.90	$0.86
10. **Four Seasons Private Residences - Denver,** www.teatroresidences.com	$0.85	$0.85
11. **Sell Your Colorado Home Fast,** www.sell-your-place.com	$0.85	$0.85
12. **Aspen, Colorado Real Estate,** www.friasproperties.com	$0.84	$0.81

Bidding with Google

When bidding on Yahoo!, or most other PPC systems, you can see exactly what you're bidding for. You can see the current bid on a position and then bid above it to grab the position.

Google, on the other hand, makes bidding rather difficult. You can't bid for a particular position. Rather, you bid a price, and Google decides what that price gets you.

Thus, some of the bidding strategies I discuss in this chapter are tricky when using Google — when you adjust your bid, you don't see exactly what position you'll get. The bidding discussion in this chapter is primarily for a simple, bid-for-position type system; I discuss the vagaries of Google bidding in Chapter 9.

Note, by the way, that positions 10 and 11 are bidding and paying the same price. Who gets position 10? The first person who bid that sum. And how about positions 4 and 5? They're both bidding the same, but the lower one is paying a penny above position 6.

Look at #1. The top bid is $2.05, but #1 only pays $2.04; why? Because the #2 maximum bid is $2.03, so #1 pays just 1 cent more.

What does #2 pay? $1.07, because the #3 maximum bid is $1.06. What is #3 paying? That advertiser pays exactly what he bid, because #4 bids just one penny less.

You can go down the list reviewing these numbers and see what people are really paying. In some cases, click costs are close to the bid. In other cases there's a big gap between click cost and bid price. #37, for instance, bid $.20 but pays only $.11 per click, 55 percent of the actual bid. #2 pays just 53 percent of the bid price. As you review this list, a few bidding strategies may come to mind.

The "one penny above the lower bid" adjustment is the norm in PPC these days. In the early days, you paid what you bid, which could get incredibly expensive if you weren't careful. Imagine the scenario above with bid-equals-price costs:

#1 Bids (and pays) $2.05

#2 Bids (and pays) $2.03

#3 Bids (and pays) $1.06

Bidder #2 pays almost double the $1.07 he needs to pay in order to place in position #2. Combine this sort of pricing with a fixed maximum bid and inattention, and you get an unnecessarily expensive PPC campaign. So, while Yahoo!, Google, and many, if not most, other PPC systems currently have one-penny-above pricing, make sure when you start working with a new PPC system that this is the case; if not, watch your bids carefully to ensure you're not wasting money.

Using Bidding Strategies

You might think that there's not much to bidding; everyone places their bids, and the highest bid wins; what more can there be? There's nothing new about bidding — auctions have been around for years.

Ah, but PPC systems are not really auctions. With an auction, you bid for the first position; in general there is no second position. (Okay, so there are some unusual auction types, such as Dutch auctions, but in general, there's one winner and a bunch of losers.) With PPC bidding, you're bidding for a position in relation to other bidders. So, as you'll see, there are different bidding strategies.

I'm not saying you have to use all these strategies, but you do need to understand them. At the least, understanding these strategies will make you think about bidding and its effects on your budget more methodically. Often you can drop your ad spending by 50 percent or so by merely dropping one position, often without a large drop in the click rate and with a comparable, and perhaps even a higher, conversion rate. So a good understanding of bidding can make a huge difference to your return on investment (ROI), which I explain in Chapter 3.

Remembering your breakeven click value

The first "strategy" is to know your breakeven click value, something I go over in Chapter 3. Understanding this value is critical because, without it, you're bidding blind; you don't really know for sure if it makes sense to bid at all.

Imagine, for example, that you're bidding on *colorado real estate*. The first 12 bids are $2.04, $1.07, $1.06, $1.05, $1.01, $1.00, $0.99, $0.91, $0.86, $0.85, $0.85, and $0.81.

Now, let's say you've figured out that the breakeven value of a click to you is $.50; on average, buying clicks at 50 cents allows you to make sales without making money, but without losing money. Well, you know that there's absolutely no point bidding anywhere in the first 12 positions. In fact, there's no point bidding anywhere above position #24 (the maximum bid price for position #24 is $.49, which is what the advertiser is actually paying). And if you bid at position #24, you won't make money, you'll just break even.

But perhaps your breakeven click value is $2.00. You're well in the game. For that price, you could have any position from #2 down and still make money.

Remember, click values vary depending on conversions, which are related to keywords (among other things) — thus the maximum value of a click from one keyword could be twice as much or half as much as the maximum value for a click from another keyword. But you'll often know, in general terms, that certain click prices are simply way too high. So all the following strategies in this chapter depend on this concept: Don't bid for top position if it means paying $10 per click if your maximum click value is somewhere around 50 cents!

As I discuss in Chapter 3, although you can estimate click values, you don't know for sure until you track your campaigns. See Chapter 15 for more information about tracking your PPC ads.

Bidding too high to be matched

One strategy some people use when they want to stay in the top position is to bid way above everyone else. Look back for a moment at the *vioxx attorney* maximum bids in Figure 7-2:

#1 $40.00

#2 $5.50

#3 $3.50

#4 $3.01

#5 $2.50

At $40, the #1 bid is more than seven times the next lowest bid. It's 16 times bid #5. What's this guy thinking? He wants to be in the #1 position, so he's bidding so high to try to scare people off competing with him. He *may* even be willing to pay $40 a click; on the other hand, he may just be bluffing, betting on the fact that nobody will try to beat him.

Sometimes people bet in this manner as a way to reduce the time invested in managing bidding. They figure they'll simply bid the maximum they're willing to pay (as, in fact, the PPC systems encourage you to do), and then let the bid sit. They know that they only pay a penny above the next highest maximum bid, so why worry? If nobody else is willing to bid high, they'll always pay just a penny above those lower bids. This, as you'll see, is a dangerous thing to assume.

Forcing competitors to pay too much

Look back at the first three *vioxx attorney* bids (Figure 7-2). Here's what they're bidding and what they're paying:

Bid Position	Max Bid	Actual Paid
#1	$40.00	$5.51
#2	$5.50	$3.51
#3	$3.50	$3.01

Now, watch what happens when #2 ups her bid:

Bid Position	Max Bid	Actual Paid
#1	$40.00	$40.00
#2	$39.99	$3.51
#3	$3.50	$3.01

If #2 bids just below #1, she still pays the same — $3.51. But bidder #2 called bidder #1's bluff, and #1 is now forced to pay $40 a click. If #1 is not paying attention, he's going to run through his advertising budget seven times faster than he expected! This is sometimes known as *jamming* your competitor, though I'm sure other terms have been used by those being jammed!

Does anyone really play this game? Sure. This, in fact, is exactly what's going on in the real-estate list we looked at in Table 7-1:

Bid Position	Max Bid	Actual Paid
#1	$2.05	$2.04
#2	$2.03	$1.07
#3	$1.06	$1.06

As you can see, #2 is bidding 2 cents below #1, yet pays almost a dollar less. Either this person is intentionally pushing up #1's budget or perhaps is playing the same game as #1, bidding much higher than #3 in order to keep position #2.

Here's another example that shows bids and actual paid prices for the keywords *chocolate fountain*:

Bid Position	Max Bid	Actual Paid
#1	$3.25	$3.25
#2	$3.24	$0.86
#3	$0.85	$0.70

In this case, bidder #2, by bidding a maximum of $3.24, above a bidder who is bidding a maximum of $0.85, is forcing bidder #1 to pay almost four times the position #2 click price.

Sometimes bidding like this is actually not intentional, it's coincidental. Someone may be bidding to a price or bidding to a position (see "Bidding to position or bidding to price," later in this chapter), which just happens to be right below a very high bid and a long way above a much lower one. But often such bids are intentional.

Bidder #1 in this example could drop down to $3.23, almost quadrupling bidder #2's click price, to see if he can get #2's attention! #2 may decide he doesn't *really* want to pay that much and drop his bid, allowing #1 to come back in at the #1 position for a much lower bid price.

You can also use this strategy to force someone out of a position. Let's say you want position #1 for *vioxx attorney* (do you really want it?; we discuss that question in the next section). You decide to bid just below position #1 and force him to pay $40 a click. If he just sits there, either he's not paying attention, or he really is willing to spend that much to keep position #1. If you really want #1, you then know what you'll have to spend!

On the other hand, the spend might be more than he's willing to pay, so he might drop his bid below yours; in which case you drop yours below his. If he drops below you again, you drop below him. In this way you'll eventually come down to the point at which he's really willing to spend to keep position #1 . . . and you can then bounce back above that level (if you want to).

Do you really want position #1?

Why bother fighting for the top position? The PPC systems encourage you to do so, but is it really worth it? Many PPC experts will tell you that it isn't, that you're better off bidding somewhere on or between positions 3 to 6.

Why? Because position #1

✔ is often far more expensive.

✔ has a higher click-through rate but often a lower conversion rate.

✔ has a lower ROI (see Chapter 3).

Yes, you'll get more clicks from position #1 than from any other position, but those clicks will be expensive and may not convert as well as clicks on some lower positions. This is probably because a lot of people simply click the first result they see on the page but then return to the search results and click the next ad, then on the next, and so on. Many people won't buy until they've "looked around a little." Thus, many in the PPC business feel that conversion rates on ads in positions 3 to 6 are often comparable and sometimes higher than for position 1. And because of the lower price, the ROI is much higher.

Click prices often drop dramatically from positions 1 to 6. For instance, look at the click prices for *chocolate fountain* (these are click prices, not bid prices):

#1	$3.25	#4	$0.57
#2	$0.86	#5	$0.51
#3	$0.70	#6	$0.43

The click price for position #6 is about an eighth of position #1.

Or how about *buy home in seattle?*

#1	$0.53	#4	$0.36
#2	$0.52	#5	$0.31
#3	$0.37	#6	$0.17

The click price for position #6 is about a third of position #1.

Admittedly, this isn't always the case. In particular, for very competitive keywords, it's often not. The following list shows bids for the keyword *mortgage:*

#1	$4.16	#4	$4.07
#2	$4.10	#5	$4.07
#3	$4.08	#6	$4.06

There's very little difference between the click prices; #6 is 98 percent of #1 in this case. In fact, prices don't even drop below $3 per click until position #30. But with less-competitive phrases, you often find the rapid-drop situation, as in *mortgage rates denver:*

#1	$4.37	#4	$3.00
#2	$4.01	#5	$2.46
#3	$3.01	#6	$2.45

The click price for position #6 is just 56 percent of that for position #1.

Now, consider the effect on your ROI of being at position #6 instead of position #1. True, you get fewer clicks, but those clicks will quite likely convert as well as, and perhaps better than, the #1 position clicks. And your click cost is dramatically lower; in one of these examples, as low as one-eighth of the position #1 click price. That could be the difference between failure and a blockbuster PPC campaign.

Bidding above the fold

Even if you pick a lower position, you'll probably want to bid so that your ads appear "above the fold." *Above the fold* is an old newspaper term meaning the top half of the paper, the part you see when the paper is folded in half. In Web terms, it's the area of a page that appears when you first load it, before scrolling down.

What's above the fold depends on how the browser window has been sized and how many toolbars the browser has loaded. But in general, assume that "above the fold" measurements are for maximized browsers with little more than the standard toolbars displayed. However, there's another huge factor, screen resolution, as you can see from Figures 7-3 to 7-5.

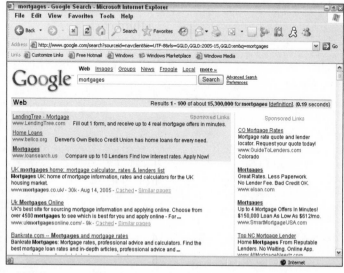

Figure 7-3: A search-results page displayed on a screen with an 800 x 600 resolution.

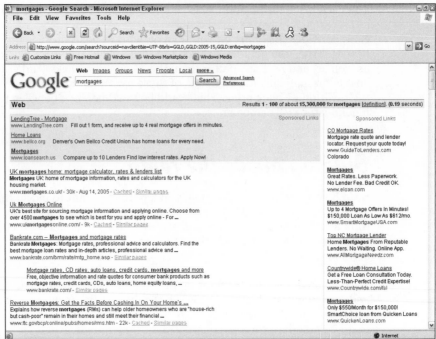

Figure 7-4:
A search-
results page
displayed on
a screen
with a
1024 x 768
resolution.

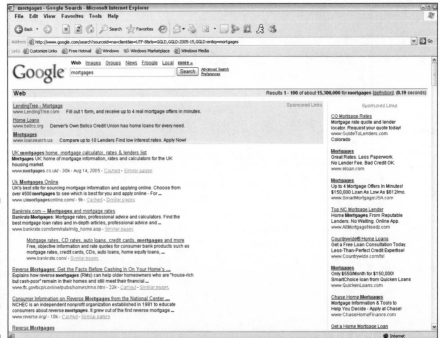

Figure 7-5:
A search-
results page
displayed on
a screen
with a
1152 x 864
resolution.

These images were taken with different screen resolutions, and as you can see, there's a big difference between the number of ads displayed.

800 x 600 = 7 ads

1024 x 768 = 9 ads

1152 x 864 = 10 ads, plus a title from the eleventh

In order to be "above the fold" on an 1152-x-864 resolution screen, you just need to be in position 10 or above. But for an 800-x-600 resolution screen, you need position 7 or above.

Different people use different screen resolutions, of course, but right now the breakdown is probably something like this (these statistics are from Browser News at www.upsdell.com/BrowserNews/stat_trends.htm):

| 640 x 480 | 0.75% | 1024 x 768 | 70% |
| 800 x 600 | 27% | 1152 x 864 and higher | 2.75% |

The bottom line is this: Few people are using 1152 x 864 or above, so forget that resolution for "above the fold" purposes. Very, very few people use 640 x 480, which is why I didn't take a snapshot of that resolution (combined with the fact that I can't get my computer to display in that resolution, and you probably can't get yours to do so either!). Most are using 1024 x 768, with a very large minority using 800 x 600.

Also, consider that many people actually display more toolbars than just the standard ones, reducing space in the browser, and they may not have their browsers maximized. In general, then, keeping your ad in position #6 or above keeps the ad "above the fold" in the greatest number of browsers.

Bidding for distribution

The major PPC systems, and many of the minor ones, distribute their PPC ads to other search systems. For example, Google's ads appear on Netscape.com, AOL.com, Earthlink.com, Amazon.com's A9.com system, and many others. Yahoo!'s ads go to MSN.com, CNN.com, InfoSpace.com, AltaVista.com, and others (though as I discuss in Chapter 1, by the summer of 2006 Yahoo! will no longer feed ads to MSN).

Unfortunately, different systems display ads in different locations on the page. For instance, Table 7-2 shows the placement of ads when I search different Google partner systems.

Table 7-2	Where Ads Are Placed on Google Sites		
Search System	**Ads on Top**	**Ads on the Side**	**Ads on the Bottom**
Google	3	8	0
A9.com	2	0	3
Netscape.com	4		4
AOL.com	5		4
Earthlink.com	6		2

As you can see, when the ads are distributed to other systems, they often don't get displayed as prominently. On Google itself position #6 will get you above the fold, but on A9.com you need position #2 at least; on AOL.com you need to be at least position #5. For this reason, the higher you rank, the more likely you are to be seen widely, and the more clicks you get.

I also searched at a few Yahoo! partner sites, but as you see in Table 7-3, the problem is not as serious with Yahoo!. Still, keeping in position #5 or above would be good — it will keep you above the fold on all these sites:

Table 7-3	Where Ads Are Placed on Yahoo! Sites		
Search System	**Ads on Top**	**Ads on the Side**	**Ads on the Bottom**
Yahoo!	3	8	2
MSN.com	3	5	3
CNN.com	5	0	0
AltaVista.com	5	0	4
InfoSpace.com	5	Another 10 ads sprinkled through the next 15 search results . . . a mix of paid and natural results	

Note, by the way, that Yahoo! places the ads for bid #4 and #5 in two places; the ads appear at the top of the column down the side, *and* at the bottom of the page.

Some smaller PPC systems encourage high bidding by distributing only the top few ads throughout their networks. Luckily, this isn't done with Yahoo!, and even with Google, you can get good distribution on positions 4 through 6 and in many cases pay a much lower price than positions 1 through 3. As for the smaller systems, clicks are often much cheaper, so bidding high is more practical.

Look for bid gaps

A bid gap is, of course, a gap between bids. Rather than a neat one-cent progression up the list — as indeed you do see sometimes with very competitive keywords — you find large gaps in the bidding. Let's look at a possible scenario. In the list below, I've bolded the text where there's a gap greater than 20 cents; the smallest of the bolded gaps is 23 cents.

#1 2.05		**#6**	**0.75**
#2 2.03		#7	0.74
#3 1.06		**#8**	**0.73**
#4 1.05		**#9**	**0.50**
#5 1.05		#10	0.49

There are three large gaps here, between positions #2 and #3, #5 and #6, and #8 and #9. These gaps are useful because they allow you to save a lot of money for a small compromise. Let's say you'd love to have position #2; that will cost you $2.04 a click. If you're willing to compromise, though, you could have position #3 for $1.07, almost halving your click spend.

Or perhaps you're looking at position #5, which costs $1.06. Maybe it's worth taking #6, and saving 30 cents.

Adjusting based on CTR

If your CTR — click-through rate — is good on an ad, and you can see an opportunity to drop your click price significantly by dropping one or two positions, you may want to experiment to see whether it's worth it. A position just one lower may have the same click-through rate, after all. With a lower click price, your ROI increases (see Chapter 3).

Remember, of course, that it's not all about ROI; it's also about sales volume, as I discuss in Chapter 3. If you increase your ROI dramatically at the expense of the majority of your traffic, you'll still end up worse off than when you started. A single sale with a huge ROI won't keep you in business . . . many sales with more modest ROIs will.

Bidding to position or bidding to price

PPC systems generally provide a couple of basic ways to bid; you can *bid to position* or you can *bid to price*.

Bid to position means you tell the system what position you want, and the maximum you're willing to pay, and the system tries to keep you in that position, adjusting your bid as necessary to do so.

Bid to price means that you tell the search engine what price you're willing to pay, and it always bids that sum; you get the highest position for the price you bid.

Bidding to price seems to be a weak strategy, and bidding to position without careful monitoring is dangerous. Bidding to price is certainly easier; just set it and leave. But you may end up paying more for your clicks than you really need to, missing beneficial bid gaps. Still, it's okay for advertisers who are lucky enough to be competing in an area with low bids.

With more competitive areas, though, bidding to position seems the better strategy . . . but you have to watch the campaign carefully to get the best click prices.

Bidding from different accounts

Once you've played in the PPC arena a little while, a simple trick to push your traffic out of the bidding might occur to you. If you really wanted to edge out your competition, perhaps you could create multiple ads for a single keyword, each one using slightly different wording. You would be able to dominate the listings for the keyword, bidding different prices for each, *and* see which one works best. Of course, it would get expensive because you might get several clicks instead of just one. But you might be able to block out other advertisers, and of course some advertisers have tried this strategy.

However, the PPC systems won't let you run multiple ads for a single keyword; as you learn in the chapters on particular PPC systems, starting at Chapter 8, you can assign multiple ads to a single keyword, but the PPC system will only run one of your ads at a time for any keyword.

But how about this? Set up five different accounts with a PPC system. Then, in each account, bid for the same keywords using different ads. Sorry again. You're too late; it's been tried before. While PPC companies have slightly different rules, most run only a single ad on a search-results page pointing to a particular Web site. Yahoo! demands that you own the site you point to, while Google and others allow you to point to someone else's site (which you might wish to do if you are an affiliate of that site, earning commissions on all sales). Either way, only one ad in the results will point to a particular site.

Does that mean nobody does this any more? I suspect, as competitive as online commerce is, some companies are still playing the game, setting up not just multiple Web sites, but multiple business "fronts," allowing them to get most of the traffic. Of course a company would need a product or service with very high margins to make this trick work.

Use Auto-Bidding Software

Managing thousands of different keywords, combined with dozens or even hundreds of different ads, can be a real challenge. That's why many PPC advertisers use automated bidding software.

You have a wide range of options, and if you're a large-enough advertiser, the PPC system may even provide you with some kind of über-bidding interface not available to the mere mortals working with the basic system. For more information on automating your bidding, see Chapter 16.

Finding Cheaper Clicks

All this talk of $40 bids might be a little off-putting. Perhaps you find that many of your keywords are simply not viable, or you get into the bidding and discover that the prices are way too high.

What can you do?

- **Try buying clicks on second- or third-tier search engines or elsewhere (see Chapters 11 through 14).** You may get much cheaper clicks.

- **Find less-competitive keywords (see Chapter 4).** Often, useful keywords are available at lower prices, even on the first-tier systems.

- **Increase conversion rates (see Chapter 5) in order to make your breakeven click value higher.**

Keyword Matching Methods

You might think keyword matching is easy. If you bid on the term *video game,* and someone searches on the term *video game,* your ad comes up, right?

But what happens if someone searches for *video games?* How about *games video* or *buy video games?* What do you want to happen?

Each PPC system has a different method for handling keyword matching. Yahoo!, for instance, allows you to use three different matching techniques, while Google provides four methods. Other PPC systems have different, though likely similar, matching choices. And note that a keyword matching method can generally be set to apply to all your keywords, or you can use different methods for different keywords.

Understanding the search tail

To a great degree, this talk of different matching methods is all about the *search tail* — the fact that if you match a keyword too closely, you miss most of the traffic.

Look at the following list of search terms taken from Wordtracker (see Chapter 4). I searched for *video games,* and Wordtracker returned a list of 300 results that contained the term *video games* (I don't have room for 300, so I've shown the first few):

		Searches per Day	**Cumulative Searches**
1	video games	9,132	9,132
2	music video games	859	9,991
3	adult video games	621	10,612
4	used video games	269	10,881
5	video games xbox	240	11,121
6	video games playstation 2	237	11,358
7	violent video games	230	11,588
8	online video games	229	11,817

Look at the Searches per Day column. It starts at 9,132 searches a day, drops immediately to 859, then 621, and by the eighth search term, it's down to just 229 searches a day. The 300th position gets only seven searches a day. So as you can see, there's this big "tail" . . . the searches tail off, as you can see in the chart in Figure 7-6.

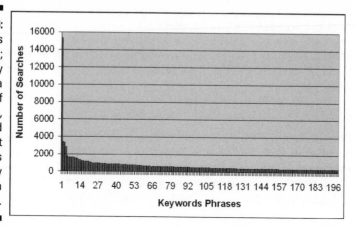

Figure 7-6: Searches "tail off"; the primary term has a lot of searches, and subsequent searches quickly decline in importance.

Wordtracker gave me only the first 300 search phrases; there are probably hundreds more containing the phrase *video games*. For each phrase, Wordtracker gives me an estimate of how often the phrase is searched upon every day. (The Cumulative Searches column, of course shows the total number of searches for all positions from #1 through the current position.). And even in this first 300 searches, *most* of the searches are *not* for the term *video games,* they are for phrases containing the term *video games:*

> ✔ The **combined daily total for all 300** search terms is 18,557.

> ✔ The daily total for the top search term is 9,132.

Thus, if your keywords get matched only with the exact phrase *video games*, you're missing 51 percent of the first 300 phrases, many of which — perhaps most — would be useful to you.

A crude PPC system could exactly match the keywords you're bidding on with the keywords people search for, and indeed the major PPC systems let you do just that if you wish. But the PPC-system designers know that an exact-match means you'll miss many other useful matches . . . and they'll miss the money they would earn by matching you with other searches. So the PPC systems provide different matching systems to help you place your ad on search results pages that you might otherwise miss. Broadening the search match can, in some cases, dramatically increase the number of times your ad is displayed . . . though it can also reduce ROI (see Chapter 3).

Using Google's matching choices

Google has four different ways to match keywords; the Broad match method is used by default unless you choose another one:

✔ **Broad match:** With this default method, Google looks for searches that *include* the keywords you specified. If you are bidding on *video games* and someone searches for *buy video games, games video,* or even *stop kids playing video games,* your ad will be matched. Broad match also includes something known as *expanded match;* Google matches the singular and plural versions of the keywords (in this case, *video game*), synonyms, misspellings, and related terms. (Expanded match is *not* used with Phrase match and Exact match, below.)

✔ **Phrase match:** With the Phrase match method, Google displays your ad if someone searches for your keywords in the same sequence, although other words may be included in the search before or after your keywords. If you bid on *video games,* your ad appears for searches on *buy video games* or *video games shop,* but not *buy games video.*

✔ **Exact match:** With Exact match, your ad is displayed only if the exact keywords are searched for; your ad will not appear, in these examples, for anything but *video games.* The searched-for words must be exactly the same (with the exception of capitalization) and in the same order.

✔ **Negative match:** A Negative match is one in which Google will *not* display your ad in the results if the specified negative word is included in a search. For example, if you sell most game systems but not PS2, you could make *ps2* the negative term, so if someone searches for, say, *ps2 video games,* your ad is not displayed. (Of course, negative matches have no effect on exact match keywords.)

By the way, capitalization is never taken into consideration with these matching techniques. It doesn't matter whether the person searches using lowercase, uppercase, or mixed-case, the matching is based on the words and spelling, not capitalization.

Table 7-4 shows how you can enter keywords into the Google PPC control panel (see Chapter 9) to specify what matching technique to use.

Table 7-4		Google's Keyword Matching Systems
Match Type	*Keyword*	*Search Result*
Broad match	*video games*	Display ad for any search that includes these words, in any order and any combination.
Phrase match	*"video games"*	Display ad only if the search includes this phrase.
Exact match	*[video games]*	Display ad only for this specific search.
Negative match	*-ps2*	If using broad or phrase match, exclude searches that include this term.

By the way, Google's ranking algorithm is really quite complex, and some of the intricacies add a little complexity to how these matching types work. For instance, Google may decide to Broad match your keywords with some terms but not others. If you are bidding on *video games* using a Broad match, Google may decide that your particular ad works well when Broad matched with *ps2 video game* but not when matched with *xbox video game;* thus, it will continue to match with the former but not with the latter.

As we discuss in Chapter 9, Google evaluates how successful your ad is (to Google, a successful ad is one that gets clicked frequently), and gives more weight to successful ads and less weight to less successful ads, and pulls very bad ads entirely. Google creates a *Quality Score* to determine if and where your ad will be placed into search results, and the company claims that the Quality Score requirements are stricter for Broad and Phrase matches than for Exact matches; in other words, even if you select Broad or Phrase match, your ad might appear only for Exact matches.

Using Yahoo!'s matching choices

Yahoo! provides three matching choices, but unfortunately it's not entirely clear how these work. (I can guarantee that the vast majority of Yahoo! Sponsored Search users do not know how these choices work because there's no way to figure it out from the current Yahoo! documentation.) Yahoo! currently has these three match types (it does not have the equivalent of Google's Phrase or Exact matches):

- ✔ **Standard match:** This is similar to Google's Broad match. It looks for any search that includes all the words, in any order, and also looks for common misspellings (*viddeo games*) and singular and plural versions (*video game, video games*). It's not quite the same as Google's Broad match, though, because while Broad match allows other words to be included in the search query, Standard match allows only for your keywords and no others. They can be in any order, but they can't be mixed with other terms.

- ✔ **Advanced match:** This default matching type is closer to Google's Broad match. It works like the Standard match, but other words can be mixed in with your search terms. If you're bidding on the keywords *running shoes,* then your ad is also matched with *nike running shoe.* Also, if you use Advanced match, your ads are likely to be placed onto more pages when using the Yahoo! Content Match service (explained in Chapter 13); Yahoo! uses a much broader matching system when deciding what pages relate to your ads.

- ✔ **Excluded words:** Just like with Google's Negative match, you can tell Yahoo! to exclude words from searches; you can exclude them from a particular ad, a category of ads, or all the ads in your account.

There's one very important thing to remember about Yahoo! Advanced matching; at least at the time of writing, *Advanced match is not used by Yahoo! itself;* it's only used on (some) of the Yahoo! partner sites. I recently tested this, and found it working on AltaVista, CNN, InfoSpace, and MSN, but I'm told that some partner sites may choose not to use it. So your ads will be standard matched when placed onto search-results pages on Yahoo.com itself, but *may* be advance matched when placed onto other sites.

There's real confusion surrounding Advanced match amongst some people, including some of Yahoo!'s support staff. Some say it's only on partner sites, others that it's network-wide. Certainly, at the time of writing, though, it's working only on partner sites . . . by the time you read this, maybe Yahoo! will be using it on Yahoo.com, too.

By the way, the difference between Advanced and Standard matching is hard to check for yourself because the changes are made to the database once a day; thus, you can't just change the setting and go to, say, AltaVista.com and test it, you have to wait up to 24 hours.

Picking the best matching method

With all these matching methods, which do you pick? Consider what might happen if you bid on very specific terms — the equivalent of Google's Exact match:

- ✔ You get far fewer ad displays and, therefore, fewer clicks.
- ✔ The displays and clicks you do get are very targeted.

In general, you don't want to use Exact match or similar with very general phrases. You might use it for *george bush,* but not for *president,* because in the second case, you get an exact match with a very vague term.

Now take a look at what happens when you bid on a very specific term combined with other words, the equivalent of Google's Phrase match:

- ✔ Use this if you know the exact phrase you're interested in and believe the phrase is likely to be combined with other words. Use Phrase match for *george bush,* for instance, and you'll be matched with terms such as *george bush approval ratings,* but not *george w bush approval ratings* or *george herbert bush family tree.*
- ✔ You'll get more ad displays, so potentially more clicks.
- ✔ You may find that you have a lower click-through rate; the more exact the matching, the better the click-through rate.
- ✔ You may find that you get a lower conversion rate, too.

The Broad match–type search creates more searches, of course. In effect, while Google has one type of broad match, Yahoo! has two. Here's a closer look at Yahoo!'s Standard and Advanced match.

Advanced match is the broader match of the two (Standard is broader than Google's Exact and Phrase matches, but not quite as broad as Google's Broad match.) Yahoo! recommends that you use Advanced match for searches in which you are using specific longer phrases, such as *tony lama cowboy boots.* If you use Advanced Match with the term *boots,* your ad is matched with all sorts of worthless phrases — *ugg boots, these boots are made for walking,* and so on. Use Advanced match with *tony lama cowboy boots,* and your ad is matched only with searches that include the words *tony lama cowboy boots,* such as *tony lama women's cowboy boots, vintage tony lama cowboy boots,* and so on.

Broad searches are, in a sense, a way to take a very specific phrase that won't be matched very often with a more exact search type, and broadening it so that you do, in fact, get more matches.

Don't forget, of course, what Google calls the *Negative match* — *Excluded Words* in Yahoo! parlance. These nonmatches can be useful if you find that many of your matches are inappropriate. Imagine you're selling antivirus software. Research tells you that more people search on the phrase *free antivirus software* than on *antivirus software,* and that the people who see your ad after searching for *free antivirus software,* not surprisingly, don't convert well, so you simply don't want your ad to appear for those people. You can use a Broad match — so you'll still appear for phrases such as *computer antivirus software* and *windows antivirus software* — but if you set *free* as a Negative match or Excluded Word, you won't appear for *free computer antivirus software* or *free windows antivirus software.*

Keep an eye on your Web-site traffic logs for words that you should exclude.

All of this raises another question. Why not go with a few keyword phrases and Broad match them to be sure to get everything? A few reasons. Some phrases are not suitable for Broad matching; you get way too many matches. Also, you won't always be sure to get everything. For example, as I mention above, Google won't Broad match with every phrase anyway. And, depending on the PPC system's rules, a bid on a particular phrase probably gets priority over a bid on another phrase that is being Broad matched. Also, Google's Broad match may be *too* broad; Broad matching the term *rodent racing* may match you with *horse racing* and *rodent extermination.* You may be better off going with a larger list of keywords and Phrase matching them (or using Negative words, though it's hard to anticipate all the terms with which you don't want to match your ad).

Where will you be ranked?

If, thanks to the wonders of Broad matching, you're not directly bidding on a keyword phrase with which you're matched, how does the PPC system rank you?

Each system has different rules, but there are a few general principles. First, you may have double matches in a sense. If you bid on the term *antivirus software* (and it's Broad matched), and you also bid on *windows antivirus software,* then you have two matches when someone searches for *windows antivirus software.* Of course, as I discuss earlier, the PPC system won't place two if the ad that is the specific match has precedence, and you'll rank according to the normal bid rules.

But if you didn't bid on *windows antivirus software,* and your *antivirus software* bid is broad matched to *windows antivirus software,* now the system has to decide what to do. You haven't bid on *windows antivirus software,* after all. So where will you be ranked, and how much will you be paid? On the Yahoo! system, for instance, the Standard match listings appear first, followed by the Advanced match listings. On Google the decision is more complicated because you don't directly bid for position in Google, as you find out in Chapter 9.

Part II
Using the PPC Systems

The 5th Wave   By Rich Tennant

"Guess who found a KISS Merchandise blowout at eBay while you were gone?"

In this part . . .

*N*ow you're ready. If you read through the preceding part and applied what you learned, you're way ahead of the competition, and you're now ready to begin your PPC campaign. But where do you start?

In this part, I show you the two big systems: Google AdWords, Yahoo! Search Marketing. These services are the two monsters, the dominant PPC systems that are responsible for over 95 percent of all paid clicks. They can bring huge amounts of traffic to your Web site . . . if you're willing to pay, and pay well. Still, you should be able to figure out whether you can make money on those clicks (and with what I show you in Part III, you'll be able to confirm it, one way or the other). We'll also look at MSN Keywords, which will be joining Google and Yahoo! in their bigness status.

Of course, these three systems aren't all there is to PPC; and, in fact, traditional PPC isn't all there is to paid clicks. So in this part, I point out other advertising systems that can often provide much cheaper clicks. I show you second-tier PPC systems, paid inclusion and Yahoo!'s trusted feed, Local Search, and alternative PPC systems, such as shopping directories and the Yellow Pages.

Chapter 8

Working with Yahoo! Sponsored Search

I start the discussion about specific PPC systems by looking at Yahoo! Search Marketing's Sponsored Search PPC system for a couple of reasons. Sponsored Search is the descendant of the first PPC system — IdeaLab's GoTo.com — and it's also fairly straightforward to use. (As you discover in Chapter 9, bidding on Google AdWords is a little more complicated.)

Furthermore, if you're planning to use both Yahoo! and Google, starting with Yahoo! is a good idea, not just because it's easier to get started, but because you'll be able to figure out click costs and bid positions more easily on Yahoo! and then apply that knowledge to your Google AdWords campaign.

Picking a Membership Level

Yahoo! Search Marketing offers three membership levels: *Premier, Gold,* and *Platinum. Premier* is the basic level. (Have you noticed that you can't buy a small soda at many places any more, that the smallest is called *medium?* This is the same principle; we all want to feel special, even if we're not.)

Everyone starts off with the Gold membership for at least 90 days, at the end of which most companies are either dropped back to Premium or, if the advertising spend warrants it, stay in Gold. If you want to jump right into Platinum, you have to call Yahoo! and convince them that you're going to spend at least $80,000 a year.

By the way, Yahoo! doesn't clearly state that you get Gold membership for the first 90 days (it's in the small print, at least at the time of writing), and you might actually have to remind Yahoo!'s support staff of this fact in order to use some of the benefits. And what are those benefits? Table 8-1 shows you.

Table 8-1	Yahoo! Sponsored Search Membership Levels		
Benefit	*Premier*	*Gold**	*Platinum*
Fast editorial review of your ad listings		✓	✓
Spreadsheet upload of your listings		✓	✓
Telephone and e-mail support	✓	✓	✓
Priority telephone service		✓	✓
Priority e-mail service		✓	✓
Personal service from Yahoo!'s more-experienced customer service professionals			✓
Personal consultation on editorial guidelines			✓
Personal assistance with ad-listing optimization, including keywords, titles, and descriptions			✓
Spending requirements per year	$0–$5.9K	$6–$79.9K	$80K+

In practice, what does this mean to the average company? It means that for the first 90 days, you should be getting more-rapid review of your ads, and faster phone and e-mail support than for a standard "Premier" account. It also means you can upload keywords with a spreadsheet, something I discuss later, in the "Uploading a spreadsheet" section.

Creating Your Yahoo! Account

In the summer of 2005, Yahoo! began rebranding; the division name was changed from *Overture* (originally an independent company purchased by Yahoo! in 2003) to *Yahoo! Search Marketing*. This division has a number of advertising products:

- ✔ **Sponsored Search:** The PPC system I show you in this chapter. The Sponsored Search service incorporates the Content Match service in which ads are placed on content, rather than search-result, pages.

- ✔ **Local Advertising:** Two services designed for brick-and-mortar businesses. *Local Sponsored Search* is simply localized PPC, which you find out more about in Chapter 12, and *Local Listing* is a way to enter your business into the Yahoo! Local Search (for free or for $9.95 per month for enhanced features).

- ✔ **Search Submit:** A service for submitting your Web pages to the "natural" search results through a paid-inclusion service (*Search Submit Express*) and a trusted-feed service (*Search Submit Pro*). I explain these in Chapter 14.

- ✔ **Product Submit:** A way to feed data into the Yahoo! Shopping price-comparison directory.

- ✔ **Travel Submit:** A way to feed data into the Yahoo! Travel directory. See Chapter 14.

- ✔ **Directory Submit:** A system for entering information about your Web site into Yahoo! Directory (`http://dir.yahoo.com`).

During the rebranding, Yahoo! has been renaming and moving things; *Sponsored Search* is the most recent name for the PPC system; it used to be known as *Precision Match*. Thus, you may, while viewing information about Yahoo!'s PPC services, hear the old names, in particular *Overture* and *Precision Match*.

If you *know* you're going to be spending over $10,000 a month on PPC ads, call Yahoo! directly; don't bother with the following sign-up procedure. It wants to talk to you! It'll assign a representative to help you . . . Otherwise, read on and get started.

You can go directly to the Yahoo! Search Marketing site if you wish; point your browser to `http://SponsoredSearch.Yahoo.com/`, then look for the Sign Up link. Better still, though, follow this procedure to get a special $50 discount offered to readers of this book.

1. **Point your browser to PPCBulletin.com. I've posted a page that contains details, and a link to the appropriate page to take advantage of the offer.**

2. **On the page that appears, click the SIGN UP button.**

3. **Choose one of the sign-up plans. You can select the Self Serve plan, and do the work yourself, or pay for the Fast Track plan and get a little help from Yahoo!**

Whichever sign-up plan you choose, you still get the same system to work with — the same Web system to control your campaigns. However, if you pay $199 (this fee is not returned in clicks) for the Fast Track program, Yahoo! helps you in various ways by

- Setting up the software for you

- Helping you pick the best keywords

- Writing your ads

- Recommending a budget for your campaign

- Providing a proposal document, showing an estimate of clicks and prices, keywords, bid amounts, and the recommended ads

- Providing account review 60 to 180 days after you've begun your campaign, to recommend changes

- Adding tracking URLs to all your ads (see Chapter 15)

Note that all ads have to be approved before they can be run; if you sign up for Fast Track and use the recommended ads, they are, in effect, preapproved.

The Fast Track program really is a good deal for many companies. If you're in the mom-and-pop-business-learn-everything-and-save-money mode of thinking, sure, go ahead and use the *Self Serve* option. If you're independent and value your time in terms of tens or hundreds of dollars per hour, or if you work for a company that spends a couple hundred bucks on the office pizza day, go ahead and use Fast Track.

Serving Yourself

From here on, I assume that you're the mom-and-pop-do-it-yourself type and show you the Self Serve option for creating your account.

1. **Click the SIGN UP button under the Self Serve option, in the page you arrived at earlier.**

   The page shown in Figure 8-1 opens. Notice that this page refers to setting up a Content Match account, as if it is something different. It's really the same thing; after you have a Sponsored Search account set up, you can choose to turn Content Match on or off, which I discuss later in this chapter, in the "Adjusting Account Settings" section.

2. **From the Select Country drop-down list, choose the country in which your business is based.**

3. **If you wish, select the check boxes for other countries in which you are interested in advertising services.**

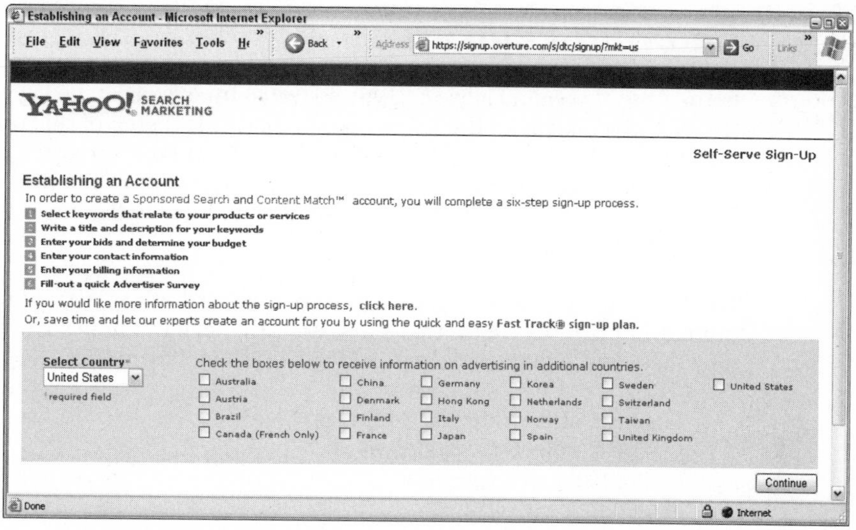

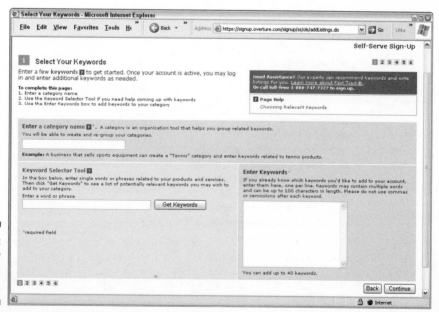

Figure 8-1:
The first
step in
setting up
Yahoo!
Sponsored
Search.

This has no effect on where your ad runs, it's purely to help Yahoo! know where you are marketing.

4. **Click the Continue button.**

The page shown in Figure 8-2 opens, and you're ready to begin entering keywords.

Figure 8-2:
Start by
entering
keywords.

Entering keywords

In the page shown in Figure 8-2, you enter your keywords; the keywords that "trigger" the display of the ad you create in the next step of this process. Ideally, you should already know the keywords you want to work with and have them broken down into groups, as recommended in Chapter 4. In Chapter 6, you discover that it's a good idea to include the keywords in your title and description.

The absolute ideal situation is to have one ad for each keyword or keyword phrase, but in most cases, that's just not practical. But here's a way you can play the game. Imagine you're working with the following list:

> business web strategies examples
> business web strategies plans
> content site strategy web
> developing web strategy
> successful web strategies
> web design strategies
> web marketing strategies
> web marketing strategy
> web search strategies
> web site design strategies
> web site marketing strategies
> web site marketing strategy
> web site positioning strategy
> web site promotion strategy
> web site strategies
> web site strategy
> web strategies
> web strategy

You could split this into two lists, one for each ad, like this:

> web strategy
> web site strategy
> web site promotion strategy
> web site positioning strategy
> web site marketing strategy
> web marketing strategy
> developing web strategy
> content site strategy web

> web strategies
> web site strategies
> web site marketing strategies
> web search strategies
> web site design strategies
> web marketing strategies
> web design strategies
> successful web strategies
> business web strategies plans
> business web strategies examples

The first list has the words *web strategy* in every keyword phrase; the second has *web strategies*. Thus, you can create one ad using the keywords *web strategy* and one using *web strategies*.

By the way, Yahoo! allows you to enter only 40 keyword phrases into the Enter Keywords text box on this page.

To enter keywords, you need to do the following:

1. **In the Enter a Category Name text box, type a reference name for the group of keywords you're about to enter (up to 20 characters, with no spaces).**

   You might use the chosen keywords as the category name.

   A *category* can be defined as a collection of related keywords and their associated ads; a category includes at least one keyword and one ad, but may contain multiple keywords associated with a single ad or multiple keywords associated with multiple ads.

2. **Copy the first keyword group from your list and paste it into the Enter Keywords text box.**

3. **If you want to play with Yahoo!'s Keyword Selector Tool, type a keyword into the Keyword Selector Tool text box and then click the Get Keywords button.**

   You'll see a list of keywords derived from the one you entered (see Figure 8-3) and how often each keyword is searched on. (The Est. Clicks column actually shows 5 percent of the Monthly Search Volume figures.)

4. **If you want to add keywords from the list to the Enter Keywords text box, simply click the check boxes next to the keywords.**

Note, by the way, that when you get down on the keywords list to where the monthly search volume is in the tens, rather than hundreds or thousands, the chances are those searches are one or two people searching on a number of occasions; those keywords might never be searched again. For instance, how many people, really, are searching on, say, *beyond border globalization strategy web.*

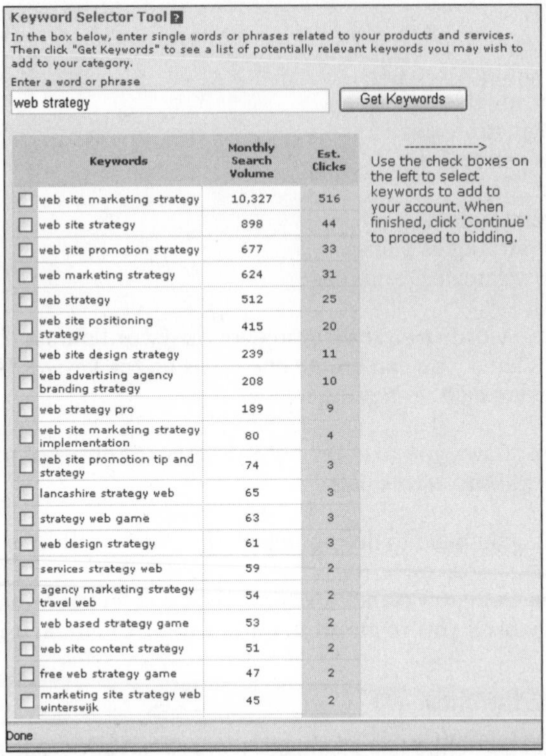

Keyword Selector Tool [?]

In the box below, enter single words or phrases related to your products and services. Then click "Get Keywords" to see a list of potentially relevant keywords you may wish to add to your category.

Enter a word or phrase

web strategy [Get Keywords]

Keywords	Monthly Search Volume	Est. Clicks
web site marketing strategy	10,327	516
web site strategy	898	44
web site promotion strategy	677	33
web marketing strategy	624	31
web strategy	512	25
web site positioning strategy	415	20
web site design strategy	239	11
web advertising agency branding strategy	208	10
web strategy pro	189	9
web site marketing strategy implementation	80	4
web site promotion tip and strategy	74	3
lancashire strategy web	65	3
strategy web game	63	3
web design strategy	61	3
services strategy web	59	2
agency marketing strategy travel web	54	2
web based strategy game	53	2
web site content strategy	51	2
free web strategy game	47	2
marketing site strategy web winterswijk	45	2

---------------->
Use the check boxes on the left to select keywords to add to your account. When finished, click 'Continue' to proceed to bidding.

Done

Figure 8-3: The Keyword Selector Tool.

5. **When you have finished entering your keywords, click the Continue button, and you'll see the page in Figure 8-4.**

You are now ready to create your ad.

Creating your ad

On the page shown in Figure 8-4, you enter your actual ad: the title, description, and the URL the ad points to on your Web site. Notice the big Yahoo! Search box on the right side; as you enter your information into the boxes on the left, the text you type appears in the sample layout on the right.

Remember, though, this is only a sample layout for a top placement. If your ad appears on the right side of the page, it will be different. Although you can enter up to 190 characters into the Description, only around 85 characters are displayed if the ad appears on the right side, so if you know you'll be bidding on positions #4 and lower, you may want to limit yourself to 85 characters. As for the Title, you can still enter 40 characters, and it will wrap onto two lines if the ad appears on the right side.

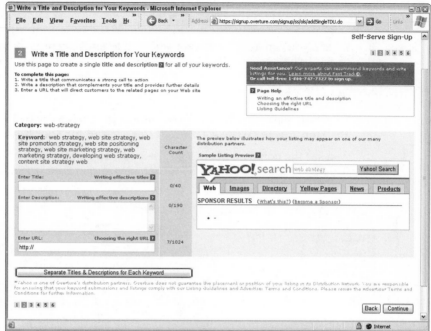

Figure 8-4:
You'll create
the ad in
this page.

Follow these steps to create your ad:

1. **Type a title for the ad, up to 40 characters long, into the Enter Title box.**

   Remember to include keywords if possible.

2. **In the Enter Description text box, um, enter your description.**

   You can enter up to 190 characters or limit it to 85 if you know the ad will appear on the side of the search results.

3. **Type the full URL of the ad's landing page in the Enter URL box.**

   By the way, Yahoo! automatically extracts the domain-name portion of the URL to create a "Display URL." When the ad is displayed at the top of the page, in the first two or three positions, there's no practical limit. On the side, though, only 28 or 30 characters will be displayed, so if you have a very long domain name, you may want to drop the www. piece; use *veryverylooongdomainname.com* rather than *www.veryverylooong domainname.com,* for instance. Also, although you can use mixed-case domain names if you wish, as I explain in Chapter 6, Yahoo! changes it all to lowercase.

4. **When you finish, you can click Continue to move to the next step. But first, let me explain how you can use the current page to create multiple ads.**

Creating multiple ads

If you wish, you can assign different ads to different keywords. Remember, the ideal is to have one customized ad for every keyword. (You don't have to do this right now; you can always create other ads later, after setting up the account.) Here's how:

1. **Click the Separate Titles & Descriptions for Each Keyword button, in the Step 2 page (Write a Title and Description for Your Keywords).**

   You see the components in Figure 8-5. Notice that there's now one set of Title/Description/URL boxes for each keyword in your original list.

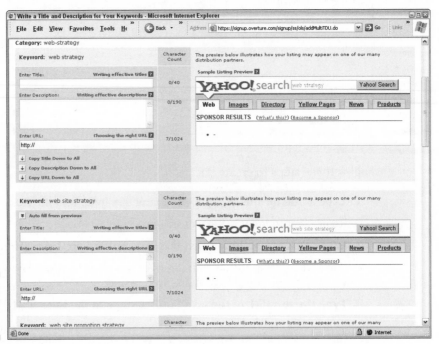

Figure 8-5:
Creating
multiple ads.

2. **Enter the first ad in the first box.**

3. **Create ads for subsequent keywords:**

   • Click the Copy Title Down to All, Copy Description Down to All, and Copy URL Down to All links, and Yahoo! duplicates your ad into each set of Title/Description/URL boxes. You can then go into each keyword's ad and modify the information.

   • If you wish, don't click the links mentioned above; simply enter the information for each ad separately.

4. **If you change your mind and decide you don't want multiple ads, click the Single Title & Description for All Keywords button at the bottom of the page to remove the multiple-ad components.**

5. **When you finish, click Continue to move to the next step, where you'll bid on keywords.**

Bidding on your keywords

After you have created your ads and clicked Continue, you'll see the page in which you bid on your keywords (Figure 8-6). As you can see, a table lists the keywords you entered in the instructions in the previous sections of this chapter. For each keyword, you can find this information:

- **Category:** This is the category name you entered on the Select Your Keywords page.

- **Monthly Search Volume:** This shows the number of times the keyword is searched for per month on the Yahoo! network of search engines.

- **Your Max Bid ($):** In this column, you enter the amount you're going to bid on the keyword. As I mention in Chapter 7 — which you *must* read before bidding! — the bid price is not necessarily what you pay; you pay just 1 cent above the bid below yours. Note that Yahoo! automatically enters the bid that would be required to, at the current time, take the top position. As I explain in Chapter 7, you probably won't want to keep this bid.

- **Pos.:** This column shows the position in the paid-search results that will result from your Max Bid. When you first enter this page, it shows 1 for each keyword because Yahoo! recommends that you bid for first position (don't blindly take that advice!).

- **Top 5 Max Bids:** This shows the bids from the current top five advertisers. If you want to see more bids, click the Bid Tool link to open the Bid Tool, which I show you in Chapter 7.

- **Est. Clicks:** This column shows the estimated number of clicks from the currently selected position. Don't worry too much about this number; run your PPC campaign and see what the results actually are.

- **Est. CPC:** This column shows the estimated cost per click from the currently selected position.

- **Est. Cost:** the last column shows the estimated total cost from those clicks.

Your first step should be to bid on your keywords based on what you find out in Chapter 7 — the bidding strategies you have decided to use. As an example, look at the current bids for *web strategy*. Here are each advertiser's maximum bid and actual click price paid:

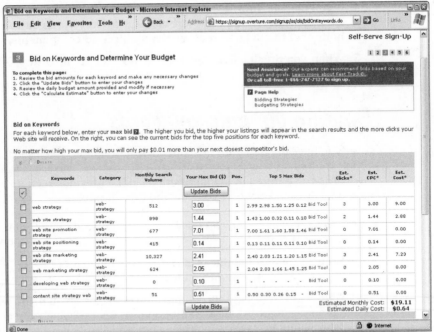

Figure 8-6:
Bid on the
keywords
you're inter-
ested in.

Bid Position	Max Bid	Actual Paid
#1	$2.99	$2.99
#2	$2.98	$1.51
#3	$1.50	$1.26
#4	$1.25	$0.13
#5	$0.12	$0.12
#6	$0.12	$0.11
#7	$0.10	$0.10
#8	$0.10	$0.10
#9	$0.10	$0.10

Consider some options:

✔ If you bid Yahoo!'s minimum bid amount, 10 cents, you'll be at position #9, below the other people already bidding 10 cents (they get priority because when multiple advertisers bid the same, they are ranked according to who bid first).

✔ Taking position #1 will cost you $3 per click.

✔ Taking position #2 will cost about the same, $2.99 per click.

✔ You can take position #3 for $1.51 per click, 50 percent of the #1 and #2 click prices.

✔ You can have position #5, a pretty good position, for just 13 cents, just 4 percent of the position #1 price!

Hmmm, position #5 looks pretty good!

How about the pricing on *web site positioning strategy?*

Bid Position	Max Bid	Actual Paid
#1	$0.13	$0.12
#2	$0.11	$0.11
#3	$0.11	$0.11
#4	$0.11	$0.11
#5	$0.10	$0.10

In this case, bidding 10 cents gets me position #6, which is not too bad. But these are such low prices anyway, I might consider bidding 14 cents for that top position (assuming it makes sense considering my breakeven click value, see Chapter 3).

When you've figured out where you want to bid, enter the numbers into the text boxes in the Your Max Bid ($) column and then click the Update Bids button. Yahoo! updates all the bid-related information for you.

Now scroll down the page and you'll find the Daily Budget information (Figure 8-7).

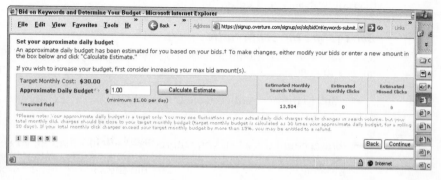

Figure 8-7: Here's where you calculate your costs.

This area simply helps you calculate your costs. Yahoo! enters a daily budget and shows you how many clicks you'll get for that payment. If you adjust the daily budget and click Calculate Estimate, Yahoo! recalculates; for instance, it will estimate whether you are likely to miss clicks because you don't have enough money in your budget to buy them all.

When you've finished in the bidding area, click the Continue button to proceed to the Contact Information page, where you will finalize your account setup.

Completing the account setup

After you've finished bidding on your keywords and setting your budget, the last phase of account setup is the Contact Information page, where you'll enter the usual contact and billing information.

Entering contact information

This is the normal contact info rigmarole, so I'm sure you don't need help with it. Name, address, blah, blah, blah. Oh, and the Terms and Conditions blurb: I know you'll read it *very* carefully. It's only 18,447 words long (yes, I counted), so it shouldn't take more than a minute or two.

Entering billing info

The next step is the usual billing info stuff, but with a slight twist. Yahoo! takes your estimated monthly budget and recommends that you deposit this amount, though you can deposit less if you wish (there's a $30 minimum). You have to enter credit card information to complete your application.

Completing the advertiser survey

It's required, so you'd better fill it in.

Don't forget the confirmation page

Make sure you save the information on the confirmation page for future reference. You need

- ✔ A link to the account console (currently `http://dtc.overture.com`)
- ✔ A link to basic information about working with Yahoo!
- ✔ Your account ID (when you entered contact information, you entered a User Name, but Yahoo! also assigns an account ID number to you)

Okay, you're done; you've created your account. Though actually it's not yet running. So let's move on and look at the account console.

Adjusting Account Settings

Your account has been set up, but there's more to do, both before you begin running your advertising campaign and throughout the campaign, to keep track of what's happening. So let's log in to the account console. Go the main Yahoo! Search Marketing page (http://searchmarketing.yahoo.com) and click the Manage My Accounts button. Log in using your username and password. You'll see something like Figure 8-8.

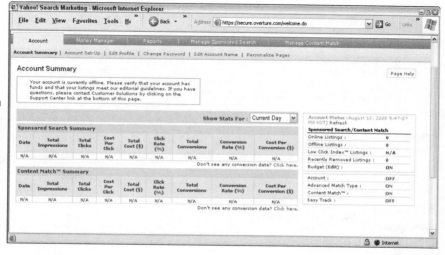

Figure 8-8: The management console's main page, the Account Summary.

You'll notice that the account is not yet running. You can see a "Your account is currently offline" message in the top-left corner of the page. Until your ad has been reviewed by the editorial staff, your ads won't run.

But there's something else you should do before you begin your campaign, anyway (no need to wait for editorial approval, you can continue setting up the account before you hear from the editors). You should turn off content match. As I discuss in Chapter 2, content match ads — ads placed on content sites rather than on search sites — are likely to have a lower return on investment (ROI) than normal Sponsored Search ads. Luckily, you can manage both campaigns separately (note the Manage Sponsored Search and Manage Content Match tabs at the top of the page). You could bid less for content-match ads than for sponsored-search ads.

However, I recommend that when you start, you turn off content-match ads. After you have everything running well — and making money — and you are comfortable with the whole process, then you can turn on content match and experiment.

Apart from content match, there are a number of other account settings you should be aware of. Click the Account Set-Up option (under the Account tab) to see the Account Set-Up area (see Figure 8-9), which offers these four settings (again, no need to wait for the editors, you can make these changes at any time):

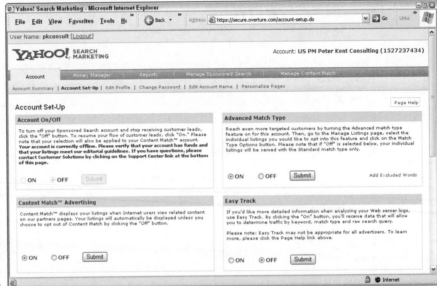

Figure 8-9:
The Account Set-Up page.

- ✔ **Account On/Off:** This pauses your campaign. When you first set up your account, it's probably already turned off. When the editors approve your ad(s), they turn it on. (Turning this off turns off both Sponsored Search and Content Match; if you turn it on, Content Match is not on unless the Content Match Advertising option buttons are also set to On.)

- ✔ **Advanced Match Type:** By default Advanced Match Type is turned off. See "Setting Match Type Options," later in this chapter, for more information.

- ✔ **Content Match Advertising:** This is where you can turn off content-match ads; by default, it's turned on.

- ✔ **Easy Track:** This is a tool that you can use to add information to your Web server's traffic logs; you can find out more in Chapter 15. (It's turned off by default.)

Further down on this page, you find information about Conversion Counter, a tool to help you figure out your conversion rates; I discuss conversion rates in Chapter 15.

You can also remove a specific ad category from content match, rather than turning it off completely. Use the Category On/Off button in the Manage Categories page (click the Manage Content Match tab at the top of the page). Individual ad listings can be turned off, too.

Checking Editorial Status

Your ads must be reviewed by Yahoo!'s editors before they'll run. Want to see the status of your ads? Click the Manage Sponsored Search tab at the top of the page and then the Editorial Status option. You see a table with three more tabs: Declined Listings, Pending Listings, and Removed Listings; you'll probably find your ads listed under Pending Listings, at least to begin with. (A listing is a keyword/ad combination.)

Yahoo! has four basic listing statuses:

- **Approved:** The ad is running and can be found in the Manage Sponsored Search or Manage Content Match pages.
- **Pending:** The ad has been submitted for editorial approval.
- **Declined:** Ads have been rejected because they don't meet the guidelines. You'll find them on the Editorial Status page, under the Declined Listings tab.
- **Removed:** Ads that have been running but were removed for underperforming or for not meeting editorial guidelines; you'll find them on the Editorial Status page, under the Removed Listings tab. You can modify and resubmit these ads.

 Note that even if Yahoo!'s editors approve an ad, they may actually change it before they accept it! So once approved, check your ads carefully to make sure they say what they are supposed to.

 As soon as your ads are approved by the editors, they go live. You may not always want that to happen, though. If you prefer to have the ads go live when you're ready, turn off the ads' category:

1. **Click the Manage Sponsored Search tab at the top of the page.**

2. **Click the option button next to the category you want to turn off.**

3. **Click the Category On/Off button.**

When the editors approve your ads, they'll be placed into the category, but won't go live until you turn the category back on.

If your listing appears on the Declined Listings, it was rejected by the editors. Editors can reject your ads for many reasons, and many, many ads do indeed get rejected. Not all rejections are directly related to your ad, but may be a problem with the Web site or landing page. Click the Decline and Remove Reasons link to see details. You may see one of the following reasons, or something similar:

- ✔ **Adult URL – Escort:** No ads related to prostitution allowed.
- ✔ **Back Button:** Clicking the back button after arriving at the landing page does not return the visitor to the search results.
- ✔ **Blocked Term:** The ad relates to one of Yahoo!'s banned products.
- ✔ **Content Not Found:** The landing page or site does not contain information related to the keyword.
- ✔ **Insufficient Content:** There's insufficient content on the landing page matching the keyword.
- ✔ **Job:** Your ad uses the term *job* or *employment,* yet the site is not directly related to an "employee/employer relationship."
- ✔ **Prescription Drugs:** You can run prescription-drug ads only if you have been through a special approval process first. (You'll have to talk with Yahoo! about this.)
- ✔ **Recreational Drug URL:** Yahoo! doesn't run ads for "recreational mind alteration."
- ✔ **Spawning:** The landing page "spawns" more than one pop-up window.
- ✔ **T/D: Clarity:** The Title or Description is unclear.
- ✔ **T/D: Contact Info:** You added contact information to your ad, such as phone number, address, e-mail address, fax, or full URL.
- ✔ **T/D: Description Quality:** The ad breaks a rule, such as using a superlative expression, an exclamation point, or unnecessary capitalization.
- ✔ **User Name/Password Needed:** The landing page requires login information to view it.

Working with the editors can sometimes be frustrating, and in fact some of their decisions *just don't seem to make sense!* Unfortunately, Yahoo! doesn't make appealing the editorial decision, nonsensical or not, very easy, and ads cannot be moved or resubmitted from the Declined box. You can, however, recreate the ad and then resubmit it, hoping you get a different editor next time! Complaints about the editors are *very* common, and from what I've seen many of these complaints are justified.

All of which leads to this question: How can you talk to someone at Yahoo!? You can find a Support link at the bottom of every page in your account console. It's light gray, so you might miss it — look carefully. This link takes you to a page on which you can access a Support Request Form and enter questions.

You can call, though the phone number's hidden away a little; to save you some time, here's the number: 866-924-6676. Make sure you have your account number (not just the User ID) before calling; you'll find it in the top-right corner of your management console.

There's something we won't cover in this chapter, but that you really should look into before you begin your campaign. I suggest you read about tracking traffic to your site in Chapter 15. At the very least, you'll probably want to turn on *Easy Track* (explained in Chapter 15), a system that sends information to your Web server when someone clicks an ad, so you can see, in your traffic logs, the keyword you bid on, the Match Type, and the actual search query typed by the searcher. You'll also probably want to use the Conversion Counter, which, through the use of a little bit of code on your Web pages, sends information back to Yahoo! so it can keep track of conversion.

Creating More Ads

You've seen how to create ads already, and, of course, you can go back and create more. You may *have* to if they've all been rejected by the editors, of course! But creating more ads is all part of the process of experimentation, finding what works best. Here's how:

1. **Click the Manage Sponsored Search tab or Manage Content Match tab at the top of the page.**

   When you create an ad category, it applies to both Sponsored Search and Content Match campaigns, so creating it in one applies it to the other, too.

2. **Click the Add Listings option on the line below the tabs.**

   You see a page very similar to the one you saw in the original sign-up page for working with keywords (Figure 8-2).

3. **Use the process I discuss in the previous "Entering keywords" section to create your ad and keyword combinations.**

Note that this page has another option: a drop-down list box that lists all your existing ad categories and an additional Unassigned option. You can add an ad to an existing category or place it into the Unassigned category if you wish, and assign it to a particular category later.

Uploading a spreadsheet

Now, you might have jumped a step ahead and thought, "Surely there's got to be a better way. Can't I just upload a spreadsheet containing all my keywords and ads?"

Imagine that you have 500 keywords broken into 50 keyword groups, with different ads for each group. Or perhaps you are working with *thousands* of keywords? Wouldn't it be easier to manage all these in a spreadsheet and just upload the spreadsheet?

Yes it would. Can you do it? Yes, if you ask nicely. As I mention earlier, Gold and Platinum accounts can use the spreadsheet-upload feature — and all accounts, for the first 90 days, are Gold accounts.

Call, ask nicely, and remind Yahoo! that you are a Gold member because you're new, and it'll send you a sample template (the LSOTemplate.xls file) that you can use to create your own upload file. In Figure 8-10, you can see the headings for this spreadsheet. You simply enter all the information for each ad in the appropriate columns and save the file. (Don't put more than 1,500 listings in a single spreadsheet file.)

Figure 8-10:
The ad-
listing
spreadsheet
template.

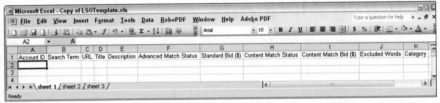

To upload your spreadsheet file, click a Support Center link, which can be found at the bottom of every page in your management console, to access the Support Request Form. And make sure you remind them that you have a Gold account for three months (no, I'm not being anal, someone on the Gold support team actually told me that it would be a good idea to do this, just to be sure the spreadsheet is accepted). To upload your spreadsheet, click the Attachment tab at the top of the form. You'll see controls that let you attach the spreadsheet file to the message.

Note, by the way, that thanks to Yahoo!'s editorial guidelines — and the fact that different editors have different ideas as to what those guidelines actually are — working with spreadsheets is not always easy. "We want to spend much more money with Yahoo!, but they don't make it easy," one client told me. "We spend three times as much on Google as we do on Yahoo!, because Yahoo!'s editors keep slowing down our keyword submissions." This client, by the way, is using hundreds of thousands of keywords, and spending $60,000 a month on Google.

Some third-party bid-management tools that allow you to do this are available. You upload spreadsheets to the bid-management tool, which then submits the data to Yahoo! (See Chapter 16 for information about these tools.)

Copying (and deleting) ads

Of course there are other things you can do with ads; sometimes you'll want to copy them — to use an existing ad as the starting point for a new one — and sometimes you'll want to delete them. Here's how:

1. **In the management console, click the Manage Sponsored Listings tab.**

2. **Click the Manage Listings option on the line under the Manage Sponsored Listings tab.**

3. **Click the check box next to the ad listing you want to copy (or** *listings* **— you can copy multiple listings at the same time).**

4. **Click the Edit Listings button.**

5. **In the box that opens, click the Copy Listings link.**

   You see a box showing all the listing details.

6. **Make any changes you want and add a new keyword for the listing.**

   You can have only one ad for each keyword.

7. **Click the Continue button.**

You can also delete listings, of course; in Step 5, simply click the Delete Listings link.

Managing Your Yahoo! Campaign

Setting up a PPC campaign is just the start . . . PPC campaigns must be *managed.* You need to keep an eye on what's going on, so that you maximize the benefit and minimize the cost. So let's take a look at how to manage your Yahoo! PPC campaign.

The Manage Categories page

As you discover in Chapter 7, you need to watch your bids. You can be leapfrogged by other advertisers or, in some situations, forced to pay more than you should be paying. So start digging into the system and find out how you can keep track of what's going on in your campaign. The Manage Categories page lets you manage keywords and ads *within* a category. You can view all the keywords, and modify bids for each one.

You can view the Manage Categories page for search-engine placement (Sponsored Search results) and for content sites (Content Match) separately. Click the appropriate tab at the top of the page. You see a list of all your categories (Figure 8-11).

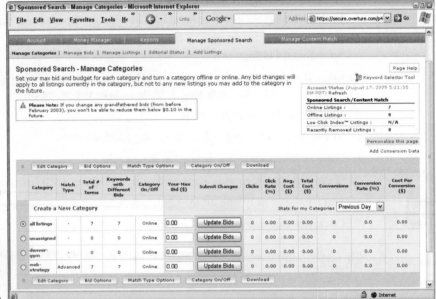

Figure 8-11: Manage your ad (listing) categories here.

All this can seem a little confusing. Here is a summary of the columns in the table:

- ✔ **Category:** The table shows you at least three lines:

  - • **All Listings:** A "super category" showing you all your keywords and their associated ads.

  - • **Unassigned:** Ads that were created and placed into the unassigned category.

  - • **Named Categories:** The categories you created when you first set up the account.

- ✔ **Match Type:** The keyword matching in use: Standard or Advanced. See "Setting Match Type options," later in this chapter, for more information.

- ✔ **Total # of Terms:** The total number of keywords in the category.

- ✔ **Keywords with Different Bids:** The number of ads that are using a bid other than the category Max Bid.

- ✔ **Category On/Off:** Shows whether the category is online (the ads are running) or offline (the ads are not running).

- ✔ **Your Max Bid ($):** The maximum bid price for all ads in the category, unless you individually set ads to different bid prices. When you first begin using your account, using the category created during the Self Serve sign-up process, no Max Bid has been set.

- ✔ **Submit Changes:** Enter a value in the Max Bid column and then click the corresponding Update Bids button to enter a category-wide maximum bid. Be careful; doing this overwrites all the existing individual bids for each listing.

- ✔ **Stats for my Categories:** Notice the drop-down list box below the following column headings. This determines what period the numbers are from: Previous Day, Last Week, Last Month, or Month to Date.

  - • **Clicks:** The number of clicks the ads in the category have received

  - • **Click Rate (%):** The click-through rate — the percentage of ads shown that were clicked upon

  - • **Avg. Cost ($):** The category's average click cost

  - • **Total Cost ($):** The category's total click cost

  - • **Conversions:** The number of conversions on your Web site

  - • **Conversion Rate (%):** The percentage of clicks that turn into a desired action on your site

  - • **Cost Per Conversion ($):** The cost of each conversion

Before I move on, I'd better clarify a few terms here. A *listing* is a single keyword, and its characteristics: the bid and associated ad. Yahoo! also uses the word *term* (as in "Total # of Terms") to mean a keyword listing.

The table also sports a few buttons. You can click an option button to the left of a category name to select the category, and then you can click one of the following buttons to carry out the action:

- ✔ **Edit Category:** Rename or delete the category.

- ✔ **Bid Options:** Turn on Bid to Position or use one maximum bid for all listings in the category. I discuss this a little more in the "Your bidding options" section, later in this chapter.

- ✔ **Match Type Options:** Set all the listings in the category to either Standard or Advanced Match Type. By default, they're set to Standard. See "Setting Match Type options," later in this chapter.

- ✔ **Category On/Off:** Place the entire category, and all its ad listings, online or offline.

- ✔ **Download:** Download the information from the category into a spreadsheet or text file. You'll get a list of all the ads with titles and descriptions and some very basic bid information.

There's one more important thing you can do on this page; you can click a category name to view the ad listings in that particular category in the Manage Bids page, which I show you next.

The Manage Bids page

You saw a page similar to the Manage Bids page (shown in Figure 8-12) when you set up your account, so much of it will already be familiar. The basic aims of this page are to show you how your individual ad/keyword combinations are doing and to allow you to modify the bids (of course you can also change bids in the Manage Categories page).

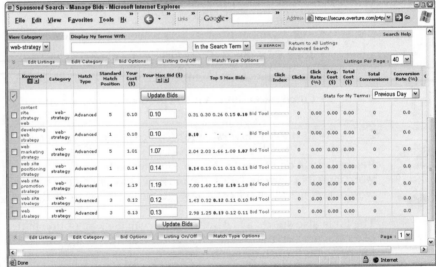

Figure 8-12: The Manage Bids page.

Look at the Top 5 Max Bids column. It shows, yes, the top five bids, but more importantly it shows *your* bid in bold text; if you don't see any bold text, your bid is lower than position #5.

You've already seen some of these columns in the preceding section, so I won't repeat myself. But there are some new ones that you need to know:

✓ **Keywords:** Clicking a keyword opens a box in which you can modify the keyword information. You can move it to another category, change the online/offline status, change the Excluded words (see Chapter 7), change the title, description, and URL, change the bid, change the Match Type, or delete the listing.

✔ **Standard Match Position:** This column shows the position the ad appears in, with the current bid, when using Standard matching (when using Advanced matching, the position may be lower). See "Setting Match Type options," later in this chapter.

✔ **Your Cost ($):** In Chapter 7, I show you the difference between a bid and an actual click price. This column shows the click price, the actual sum you pay if someone clicks your ad.

✔ **Your Max Bid ($):** This shows your current maximum bid. You can type a new number and click the Update Bids button to change your bid.

✔ **Click Index:** This little bar indicates how well your ad is performing compared to the competitors — that is, how often searchers click it. There are five bars, with three bars being average, five bars well above average, and one bar well below average. When there's just one bar, the bar is red, and you risk having the ad removed.

You also have a number of buttons on the Manage Bids page:

✔ **Edit Listings:** Rename or delete the category.

✔ **Edit Category:** Move to another category.

✔ **Bid Options:** Turn on Bid to Position or apply a maximum bid to the listings. See "Your Bidding options," later in this chapter.

✔ **Listing On/Off:** Places the selected listings online or offline.

✔ **Match Type Options:** Set the selected listings to either Standard or Advanced Match Type and add Excluded words. By default, listings are set to Standard match. See "Setting Match Type options," later in this chapter.

Notice also the View Category drop-down list box at the top left of the table. Use this to switch between categories or to view all listings across all categories. You can also use the Display My Terms With text box to search for listings that match certain keywords.

Editing Listings

There are a few ways to edit a listing after it has been created, even after it has begun running in the search results. The Manage Listings page (shown in Figure 8-13) provides a quick way to scan through all the different listings. Remember that you can use the View Category and Display My Terms With components to filter your listings to see just the ones you're interested in.

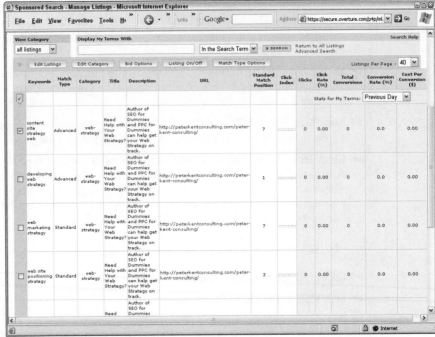

Figure 8-13:
The
Manage
Listings
page.

Most of this table is self-explanatory; it shows the Keywords each listing is matched with, the Match Type you're using, the Title, Description, and URL, and so on. Here's what the buttons can do for you. Select one or more listings you want to edit and then click the appropriate button:

- **Edit Listings:** You can delete a listing or create a new one by copying the selected one, or you can modify the listing's Title, Description, and URL.
- **Edit Category:** Move the listing to another category.
- **Bid Options:** Set a maximum bid, or bid to position (see "Your bidding options," below).
- **Listing On/Off:** Turn the listing on or off.
- **Match Type Options:** Select the Match Type or add Excluded words (see "Setting Match Type options," later in this chapter).

You can also edit listings elsewhere, of course. The Edit Listings button on the Manage Bids page opens the same edit options as it does on the Manage Listing page. Clicking the listing on the Manage Bids page, though, opens a more advanced Keyword Detail page, as you can see in Figure 8-14, in which you can change almost everything related to the listing.

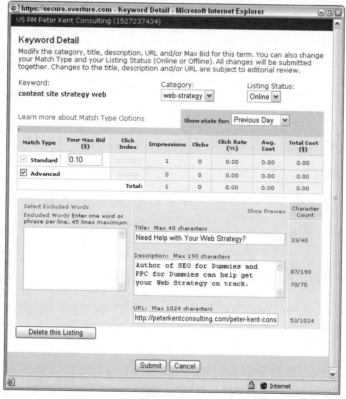

Figure 8-14:
The Keyword Detail page, opened by clicking the listing name on the Manage Bids page.

Modifying Bids

Yahoo! provides a few different ways to modify bids. As you learn in Chapter 7, there are a number of bidding options you could employ, depending on what your competitors are doing.

- ✔ **To change a specific listing's bid,** enter your new bid in the appropriate text box on the Manage Bids page or the Keyword Detail page, which is available by clicking a listing in the Manage Bids page.

- ✔ **To change a group of listings' bids within a category,** select the listings and then click the Bid Options button.

- ✔ **To apply a single bid to all listings in a category,** go to the Manage Category page. This bid can be overridden by later applying a bid to a particular listing.

- ✔ **To bid to position,** click the Bid Options button on the Manage Categories, Manage Bids, or Manage Listings page to apply a simple bidding rule (see Figure 8-15): "Pay as little as possible, up to $x, to keep position y." This can be applied to an entire category, to a group of listings within a category, or to an individual listing.

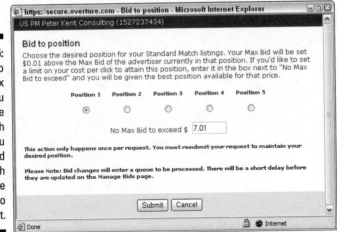

Figure 8-15:
The Bid to
Position box
lets you
define
which
position you
want and
how much
you're
willing to
pay for it.

Setting Match Type options

In Chapter 7, I discuss different keyword matching types. I'm not going to go into detail about these, but I do want to quickly show you how to set the different types.

By default, your listings use Standard match. If you want to use Standard for some and Advanced for others, the first thing you have to do is set Advanced for the entire account: Click the Account tab at the top of the page and then select the Account Set-Up option. Next, click the Option button in the Advanced Match Type area and click the Submit button.

This control turns Advanced Match on and off for the entire account; even if you have a particular listing set to Advanced Match, it won't work if the Account Set-Up Advanced Match option is set to Off.

You can also enter Excluded words in this area: Click the Add Excluded Words link to open a window in which you can type words you want excluded from *all* searches, across your entire account.

After you've turned on Advanced match, you can specify, for a particular listing or category, what matching type to use. Look for:

- ✔ The Match Type column in the Keyword Detail box (displayed when you click a listing in the Manage Bids page).

- ✔ The Match Type Options button in the Manage Categories, Manage Bids, and Manage Listings pages.

The Match Type Options buttons on the Manage Bids and Manage Listings pages (not the Manage Categories page) open a window in which you can both turn Advanced match on and off and enter Excluded words to apply just to the selected listings (see Figure 8-16). Use this carefully, though, and make sure it really did what you intended, as it's a little flakey.

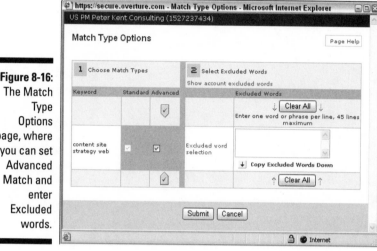

Figure 8-16: The Match Type Options page, where you can set Advanced Match and enter Excluded words.

Removing ads

PPC systems want their advertisers to run ads that encourage searchers to click them; that, after all, is how the PPC company gets paid. If your ads don't get clicked enough, Yahoo! at some point removes them.

You saw earlier the Click Index bar. This indicates, in comparison with other advertisers, how well your ad is doing; if you have one red block on the index bar, you have problems, and the ad may be removed soon. (Note that it takes some time after your ads are released for Yahoo! to determine the click index.)

There's also a Low Click Index Listings line in the Account Status box that appears on most management console pages. This indicates how many listings have the single red bar in the Click Index. A number in here is a warning that you should be thinking about fixing the ads.

Finally, the Account Status box also has a Recently Removed Listings line, indicating how many listings have been removed because of low click rates over the last 90 days. If you click the number, the Removed Listings tab on the Editorial Status page opens, so you can see the listings, modify them, and resubmit them.

How do you fix a removed ad? Read Chapter 6 and try creating the ad again!

Chapter 9

Buying Traffic from Google AdWords

Though Yahoo!'s PPC system (see Chapter 8) is the descendant of the first such system, Google's AdWords system is perhaps the best known, partly due to all the Googlemania seen over the last few years.

Google AdWords is certainly one of the first-tier systems. Not only are AdWords ads placed on the world's most popular search site — Google — but they also appear on a wide variety of other sites, large and small. They are placed onto all the Google search-engine partner sites, and that includes very significant sites, such as AOL.com, Netscape.com, Earthlink.com, and Amazon's A9.com search engine. Of course, these ads also appear on many content sites, such as The New York Times, The Weather Channel, Business.com, and many thousands more, smaller sites. (Though I recommend that you don't use content placement to begin with; I cover this subject in more detail in Chapter 13.)

Most large PPC advertisers use Google along with Yahoo! (and, by the time you read this, possibly MSN). Google AdWords is regarded as an essential part of any PPC campaign; in fact, some companies find that they get better results from Google than from other systems (although other companies, quite possibly, get worse results). Advertisers I've spoken with who are selling to a high-tech audience sometimes claim that they get much better conversions from Google. "Our customers are the sort of people who search on Google," one consulting client told me.

Creating Your Google Account

Start setting up your Google AdWords account by going to AdWords.com. Unlike Yahoo!, which has all sorts of different advertising programs (see Chapter 8), the only program you'll find at the Google AdWords page is the AdWords PPC program.

Before you begin setting up an account, check out the Google Jumpstart service, which is similar to the Yahoo! Fast Track program I discuss in Chapter 8. JumpStart is an easier decision than Fast Track: Not only does Google's staff help you pick keywords, write your ads, and set your bids, it also applies the $299 JumpStart fee to your advertising campaign, so it ends up being free. (Assuming you actually run your campaign; the fee is nonrefundable.)

Note, however, that you should carefully review any bidding done by PPC staff, whether for Google, Yahoo!, or any other system. Based on what you find out in Chapter 7, you may want to revise bids. The PPC firms tend to push the idea that the #1 position is always best, which is not always true.

As with Yahoo!, Google has a special program for large advertisers (though the required budget is much lower for Google). If you *know* you're going to be spending over $4,000 a month on PPC ads, contact Google. Currently, a link at the bottom of the main page says, "Let our specialists design a campaign for you." Click that link and you're taken to a page that contains a contact link near the top of the page for "additional setup and support services."

In this chapter, though, I discuss only the self-service set up. So let's get started setting up your first AdWords account.

1. **Point your browser to http://AdWords.com.**

2. **On the page that appears, click the Click to Begin button.**

   You see the page shown in Figure 9-1.

3. **Select the language your ads will be written in.**

   If you plan to use multiple languages, select them all by holding the Ctrl or Command key on your keyboard while you click the different languages.

4. **Select a Target Customers by Location option.**

   I show you this in more detail in Chapter 12, but for the moment, assume that you're just selecting the basic Countries option.

5. **Click the Continue button to move on to the next step.**

   You see the Target Customers by Country page (Figure 9-2).

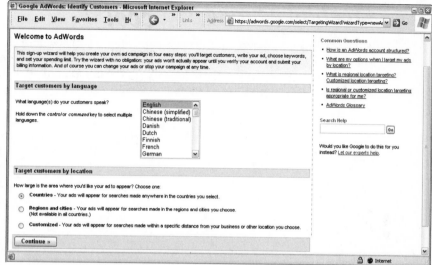

Figure 9-1:
The first
page of the
AdWords
sign-up
wizard.

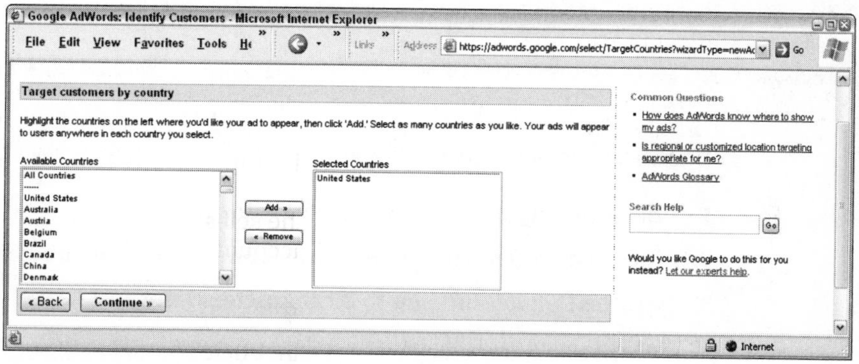

Figure 9-2:
Select the
country or
countries in
which your
ad should
run.

6. **Select the country or countries in which you want to run your ad or select All Countries.**

   You can use the Ctrl or Command key again while clicking to select multiple countries.

7. **Click the Add button to move your selections into the Selected Countries box.**

8. **Click the Continue button to move to the next page, where you create your ad.**

Creating your ad

After creating your account, the next page (Figure 9-3) is where you create your ad. As you type, the sample in the top left changes to show you what the information you are entering will look like in the completed ad. Remember, you'll want to read Chapter 6 before you create your ad.

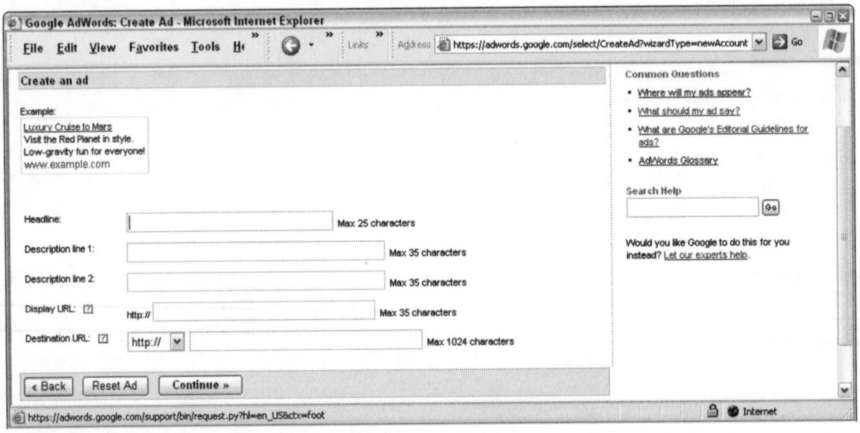

Figure 9-3: Create your ad here.

Follow these steps to create your ad:

1. **Type a Headline, up to 25 characters long.**

2. **Type the two Description lines, each one up to 35 characters long.**

3. **Type the Display URL, up to 35 characters long.**

   This is the actual URL, usually a domain name, that is displayed at the bottom of the ad. As discussed in Chapter 6, Google *does* allow you to mix-case your domain names to make them easier to read, and I advise you to do so.

4. **Type the Destination URL, the URL of the ad's landing page, up to 1,024 characters long.**

5. **Click the Continue button.**

   Google automatically checks to see whether your ad obviously breaks any editorial guidelines (as discussed in Chapter 6). If it does, you see the Request an Exception box that allows you to explain why your ad does not break the rules. You'll be able to continue through the process, and Google will have a live editor check the ad after you complete the process. (If you don't have a problem, of course, when you click Continue you simply move to the next step.)

Note that if you request an exception for your ad, you may slow down approval dramatically. While you can usually get up and running in a few minutes, waiting for approval can change that to many hours. I recommend that you go with a simple ad that doesn't cause a problem so you can get moving and then try the problem ad again later if you wish.

Entering keywords

After you create your ad, you proceed to the page shown in Figure 9-4, where you enter your keywords. You can enter your list directly into the large text box (by now you should have a large list; see Chapter 4).

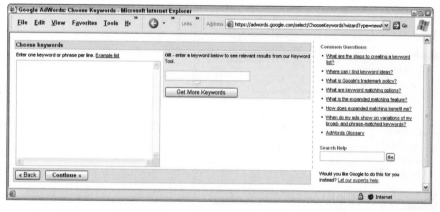

Figure 9-4: Enter your keywords into the large text box.

Notice, though, that Google also provides a keyword-selection tool. Type a keyword into the small text box and click Get More Keywords to see something like what's shown in Figure 9-5. Google shows you two types of keywords: those that contain the phrase you entered, and those that are related to the one you entered — keywords that people searching on your phrase also searched on.

To add keywords from these boxes, click the check boxes next to the phrases (or use the Select All button) and then click the Add Selected Keyword button.

When you have a word in your list, you can modify it to specify the type of matching you want to use for that word (see Chapter 7). Note that, by default, your keywords are Broad matched, which can increase click-throughs from poorly matched keywords. You may want to change keywords to Exact or Phrase match to make sure you get closer matching.

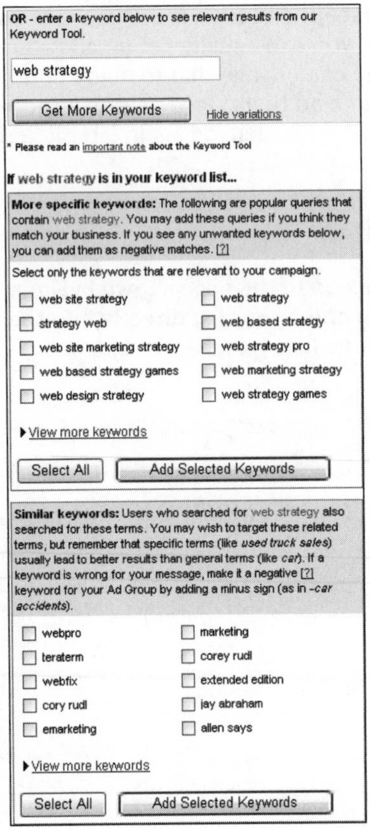

Figure 9-5:
The
keyword
tool
provides a
couple of
different
keyword
lists.

For instance, if you are using the term *rodent racing,*

✔ To **Broad match,** simply enter the term into the large keywords box.

✔ To **Phrase match,** enter the keyword phrase in quotation marks: *"rodent racing"*

✔ To **Exact match,** enter the keyword phrase in square brackets: *[rodent racing]*

✔ To **Negative match,** that is to exclude all terms with the keyword, precede the term with a minus sign: *-extermination* (Thus, if Broad matching, your keywords would not be matched with *rodent extermination.*)

When you've finished your keywords, click the Continue button.

Entering budget information

Now that you have entered your keyword(s), the next screen (Figure 9-6) you encounter is where you enter information about how much you want to spend on your ads.

1. **Select a Pay for This Account Using currency option.**

   This is simply the currency in which you will be billed.

2. **In the Enter your daily budget text box, enter the maximum amount you want to spend every day.**

   After this limit has been reached, your ad will be pulled. It's a good idea to use this number to control your campaign in the first few days to make sure everything's fine and you don't have a runaway ad spend!

3. **In the Enter Your Maximum CPC (Cost Per Click) text box, type the maximum amount you're willing to pay for a click.**

   You'll want to modify the price for particular keywords later (see "Getting Help Placing Bids," later in this chapter).

4. **Click the View Traffic Estimator link to open the traffic estimator (Figure 9-7).**

   This tool shows you the positions in which your ad will be placed for each keyword, based on the sum you have bid and an estimate of the number of clicks per day, the cost per day, and the average cost per click. Remember, your cost per click is not the same as your maximum bid (see Chapter 7).

   The Status column shows whether or not your ad will be displayed for a particular keyword; if it says Inactive, increasing the maximum bid may change it to Active. Note that you'll be able to change bids — and thus positions — for particular keywords later; see "Getting Help Placing Bids," later in this chapter.

5. **When you're finished, click Continue.**

Completing your account sign up

After you enter your budget information. you're ready to finalize your account sign up. In the next screen, (Figure 9-8) you see a confirmation page in which you can review your ad, keywords, and budget. After you have reviewed the confirmation page, click the Continue to Sign Up button.

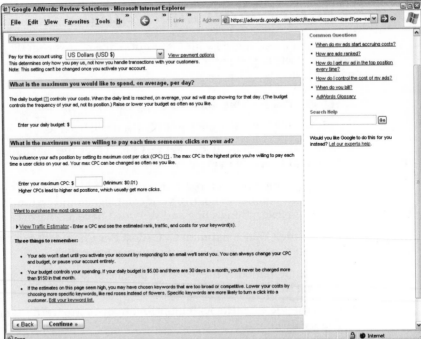

Figure 9-6:
Set your
budget
information
in this
screen.

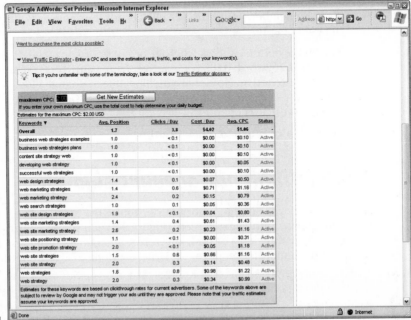

Figure 9-7:
The Traffic
Estimator
gives you an
idea of your
ad positions
and costs.

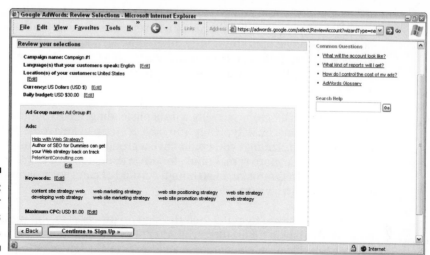

Figure 9-8:
Review your
ad in this
page.

In the next screen, Google will ask if you have a Google account. Google has begun the process of consolidating all its subscriber services into a single account system; with a single Google account you'll be able to check your e-mail, read discussion groups, use Personalized Search, receive Google news and search alerts and via e-mail, use your Froogle Shopping List (you can find information about all these at www.Google.com/accounts/), use your Personalized Homepage (www.Google.com/ig), use Google Talk (talk. Google.com), use the Orkut online community (www.orkut.com) and, of course, manage your AdWord campaigns.

You may not want to have the AdWords account linked to your personal Google account, though; if you are, for instance, setting up AdWords for a client, or setting up an account that will be used by several people, you'll want a separate account. So Google gives you a choice. If you already have a Google account you may, if you wish, use that account for AdWords; click the **Sign in to AdWords with your Google Account** link. Or you can choose to create a new Google account (either because you don't have one, or because you want to keep your existing account separate): click the **Create a new Google Account to be your login to AdWords**.

Whatever your choice, enter the requested login information, then click the Create AdWords Account button, and Google completes the sign-up and sends you an e-mail with further information about how to validate the associated e-mail address.

You have now created an *ad group* in your first *ad campaign*. An *ad campaign* is a project that targets a geographic region and contains one or more ad groups. An *ad group* is a group of keywords to which one or more ads have been assigned. Ad groups are *similar* to Yahoo! Sponsored Search *ad categories*, though not quite the same.

As you see in the preceding chapter, Yahoo! Sponsored Search has *ad listings* within its ad categories; these are single keyword phrases associated with single ads. Google operates a little differently. An *ad group* is a group of key-words with one or more ads associated with them; if you have multiple ads, then Google "rotates" the ads — your reports will show you which ads work best for each keyword.

I think the term *ad group* is really a little misleading; I like to think of it as a *keyword* group because typically you have a group of keywords associated with a single ad. Though you could have a group of keywords associated with multiple ads, it's more rare, I think, for advertisers to have single keywords associated with groups of ads (though certainly I can see situations in which advertisers might want to do this).

Note that you haven't yet finished the sign-up process; as you probably noticed, you haven't paid them yet! After your account has been approved, you get a notification e-mail message. (It may take a few minutes, perhaps much longer if you used the Request an Exception box to appeal an editorial-guidelines decision.) Read the e-mail message, follow the instructions, and log in to your account.

When you first log in to AdWords, you see a notice saying that you haven't yet set up your payment information. Click the Billing Preferences link and enter all the usual stuff — read the terms and conditions (at 1,267 words, they're positively brief compared to Yahoo!'s 18,447 words), enter credit card information and your address, and so on. Note, by the way, that Google charges a $5 activation fee for each account.

Be careful, though. After you complete this process, your campaign will prob-ably start right away. If you're not sure you want this to happen — you may want to look around in the AdWords management console (which we look at next) a while to figure out what's there first — turn off the campaign you cre-ated during the initial setup process. Click the check box next to the cam-paign on the main page you see when you log in; then click the Pause button to pause the campaign.

Removing Content Placement

After you've received your e-mail and verified your account, you can log in to your account; go to `http://AdWords.com/` and do so. You'll see a page similar to that shown in Figure 9-9.

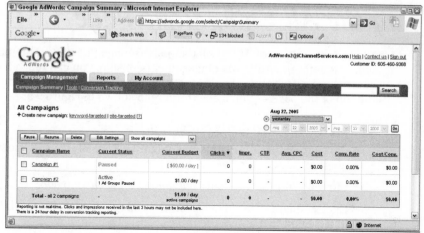

Figure 9-9:
The
AdWords
manage-
ment
console.

As I discuss in Chapter 2, I recommend that you turn off content placement before you begin your campaign. *Content placement* refers to the placement of ads on non-search sites, and it's likely to have a lower return on investment (ROI) than normal search-results placement. So you may want to turn it off to start with and perhaps turn it on and experiment with it later.

This is another way that Google varies from Yahoo!. With Yahoo!, content placement is treated like a totally separate distribution network: You can turn that distribution network on and you can turn it off, and ad listings on each distribution network are managed completely separately. With Google, though, you have one ad management area, not two, and you turn ads on and off selectively within this single area. There is no way to turn off content placement from an "account level" as there is with Yahoo!.

Here's how you go about turning off content placement:

1. **Click the Campaign Management tab at the top of the page.**

2. **Click the name of the campaign you want to modify.**

3. **Click the Edit Campaign Settings link.**

4. **Clear the Content Network check box.**

5. **Click the Save All Changes button.**

Using the All Campaigns Page

Let's take a quick look at the All Campaigns, page, the page that you see when you first enter the AdWords management console; you can reach it if you're somewhere else in the console by clicking the Campaign Management tab at the top of the page — you'll see the screen shown in Figure 9-9:

- ✔ **Campaign Name:** Pretty obvious, eh?
- ✔ **Current Status:** Your campaign might be **Paused** (the ads are not running) or **Active** (they are).
- ✔ **Current Budget:** The daily budget set for the campaign.
- ✔ **Clicks:** The number of clicks on the ads in the campaign in the specified time period (set above the table).
- ✔ **Impr.:** The number of impressions in the specified time period; that is, the number of times the ads have been displayed. (All the subsequent items are related to the time period, too.)
- ✔ **CTR:** The average percentage click-through rate.
- ✔ **Avg. CPC:** The average cost per click.
- ✔ **Cost:** The total cost of the clicks.
- ✔ **Conv. Rate:** The conversion rate for the clicks; I discuss conversion tracking in Chapter 15.
- ✔ **Const/Conv.:** The cost per conversion.

Editing Campaign Settings

Above the All Campaigns table you'll see several buttons. You can use these to Pause or Resume the campaign's ads and to Delete the campaign. You can also use the Edit button to open the Edit Campaign Settings page (shown in Figure 9-10) — click the check box next to a campaign and then click the Edit Settings button.

Here's what you can do in this page:

- ✔ **Change the campaign name.**
- ✔ **Change the daily budget.**

✔ **View a Recommended Budget.**

This is Google's recommendation based on past performance for the keywords in the campaign.

✔ **Turn on the Budget Optimizer for this campaign.**

I discuss the Budget Optimizer in the "Your Bidding Options" section, later in this chapter.

✔ **Specify when the ads should be shown.**

✔ **Automatically optimize ad serving.** With this feature turned on (the default), Google automatically serves ads that have higher click-through rates (CTRs). As I mention earlier, if an ad group has multiple ads within it, those ads "rotate" — with this feature turned on, Google doesn't rotate ads randomly or in sequence; it gives preference to ads that have high CTRs.

✔ **Specify where to show the ads: On the search network and/or on the content network.**

I discuss the content network in Chapter 13.

✔ **Select the language(s) with which the ads should be matched.**

✔ **Select the countries in which the ads should run.**

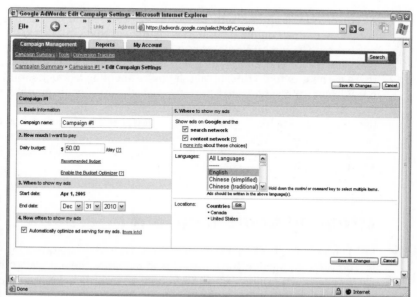

Figure 9-10:
The Edit
Campaign
Settings
page.

Creating More Campaigns, Ad Groups, and Ads

If you wish to create more ads, you have two choices: You can add an ad to an existing ad group (remember, an *ad group* is a collection of one or more keywords associated with one or more ads that Google rotates among the keywords, so you can add another ad to one of these groups), or you can create a new ad group entirely, entering both keywords and ad text.

✔ **To add an ad to an existing group,** open the ad group from the Campaign page, click the Create New Text Ad link. Also note the Create New Image Ad link, which is purely for content ads; Google does not run image ads in search results. See Chapter 13 for more information.

✔ **To create a new ad group,** click the Create New Ad Group link in a campaign page.

You can, of course, also create new campaigns. (*Campaigns* are collections of one or more ad groups.) Click the Create New Campaign: Keyword-Targeted link in the Campaign Summary page. Note that there's also a Create New Campaign: Site-Targeted link, but this is also a content-ad feature, which I go over in Chapter 13.

As I discuss in Chapter 8 with Yahoo! Sponsored Search, you can upload a spreadsheet or a comma-delimited spreadsheet that contains keywords and ads to your Google AdWords account, though Google doesn't necessarily make it easy for you to do. The customer-service rep may actually tell you there *isn't* a way to do this. In fact, if you're spending enough money, they *will* provide such a mechanism. There seems to be no specific guideline — "each request is decided on a case-by-case basis," I was told. As one advertiser told me, "They get much more helpful when you reach a couple of thousand dollars a day!" That's an exaggeration; I'm sure they'll help you with spreadsheet uploads at a much lower spend level, perhaps around $130 a day (Google's $4,000-a-month limit for special assistance).

Using dynamic keyword insertion

You learn in Chapter 7 that including the searched-for keyword into your ad is a powerful thing; that the closer the ad matches, the more effective it is likely to be. Furthermore, Google will bold any words in your ad that match the words in the searcher's query, helping your ad stand out.

Well, Google provides a way for you to automatically insert the keywords used by into your ad. You type *{Keyword:default}* into your ad title or first line (people generally use it in the title, as it's hard to make the description flow properly when you're not sure what phrase will be inserted. For instance, let's say your ad is related to a candle store. You might enter this into your ad title:

```
{Keyword:Votive Candles}
```

When Google displays your ad, in place of this text it will display the keywords that the searcher used. If the searcher uses more than 25 characters in the search phrase, Google won't insert the keywords into the ad; rather, it will use the default phrase instead . . . in this case it would use *Votive Candles*.

You can define how Google capitalizes the inserted keywords, by changing the capitalization of the word *keyword,* like this:

- ✔ {keyword:Votive Candles} — The inserted keywords will be all lower-case; for instance, *buy candles*

- ✔ {Keyword: Votive Candles} — The first letter of the inserted keywords will be uppercase; for instance, *Buy candles*

- ✔ {KeyWord: Votive Candles} — The first letter of each word will be upper-case; for instance, *Buy Candles*

Use this technique carefully, though. It can definitely increase your click-through rate, but that doesn't necessarily mean it's a good idea; your clicks may increase at a greater rate than your sales, leading to lower ROI.

Specifying bids and URLs for keywords

Google provides a little trick that lets you specify, for each keyword in an Ad Group, a particular bid and URL, giving you more control over your campaign, improving tracking, and allowing you to make your landing pages more "relevant" to the keyword the searcher used (see Chapter 5).

Here's how it works. Open the Ad Group you want to modify (click a campaign name in the All Campaigns table, then click an Ad Group name in the Campaign table). Then click the little Edit Keywords link you'll see above the table. You'll see a text box containing all the keywords in the Ad Group. You can now add bids and URLs to each keyword, by appending this text to each line:

```
**bid**url
```

For instance, adding this sets the keyword's bid to 35 cents, and sets the Destination URL to `yoursite.com/shoepage.html`:

```
**0.35**http://yoursite.com/shoepage.html
```

For instance, you could do something like this:

```
content site strategy
          web**1.00**http://yoursite.com/pg1.html
developing web
          strategy**0.55**http://yoursite.com/pg2.html
successful web
          strategies**0.40**http://yoursite.com/pg3.html
web design strategies**1.50**http://yoursite.com/pg4.html
web marketing
          strategies**1.55**http://yoursite.com/pg5.html
web marketing strategy**1.05**http://yoursite.com/pg6.html
```

Managing a Campaign

After you log on to your account, click one of the Campaign titles in the table on the main page, and you'll see a Campaign page (Figure 9-11) listing all the ad groups in your campaign. The table columns require no explanation now that we've seen the All Campaigns table (in the "Using the All Campaigns Page" section, earlier).

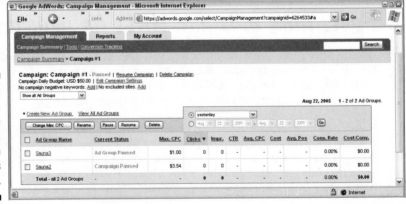

Figure 9-11:
You can
manage
basic
campaign
settings
here.

The Campaign page contains a number of useful buttons. You can, of course, Pause and Resume the ads running in the selected ad group. You can also

Delete an ad group or Rename it. But you can also change the maximum CPC by clicking the check box next to the Ad Group you want to modify, clicking the Change Max CPC button, entering a new maximum CPC into the page that appears, and clicking Save Changes.

By the way, Google has a great little diagnostics tool that you can use to figure out whether your ad is running properly, and if it isn't, why not. On the Campaign Management tab, click the Tools option and then click the Ads Diagnostics Tool link. You'll be able to enter a keyword, google domain, language, and location, and find out if Google thinks your ad should be running under those circumstances . . . and if not, why not.

Managing Your Ad Groups

Click an ad group in the Campaign page, and you'll see the page in which you can manage the keywords and ads in that ad group (see Figure 9-12). This page shows you all the keywords in the ad group. At the top, it shows the first ad in the group, but if the group has multiple ads, you see all of them listed at the bottom of the page, underneath the table, Notice the View All Below link to the right of the sample ad at the top. Clicking this link moves the page down to the bottom to the list of ads. Remember, Google rotates the ads, using them in sequence (and eventually, when it figures out which are most effective, using some more than others).

Figure 9-12:
The Ad Group page.

Keyword	Status [?]	Max CPC Bid	Clicks ▼	Impr.	CTR	Avg. CPC	Cost	Avg. Pos	Conv. Rate	Cost/Conv.
Search Total			0	0	-	-	$0.00	-	0.00%	$0.00
Content Total [?]			0	0	-	-	-	-	0.00%	$0.00
far infrared sauna	Active	$1.00	0	0	-	-	-	-	0.00%	$0.00
far infrared saunas	Active	$1.00	0	0	-	-	-	-	0.00%	$0.00
infrared sauna	Active	$1.00	0	0	-	-	-	-	0.00%	$0.00
infrared sauna heater	Active	$5.00	0	0	-	-	-	-	0.00%	$0.00
infrared sauna kits	Active	$1.00	0	0	-	-	-	-	0.00%	$0.00
infrared saunas	Active	$1.00	0	0	-	-	-	-	0.00%	$0.00
kidneys--effects of infrared sauna	Active	$1.00	0	0	-	-	-	-	0.00%	$0.00
portable far infrared sauna	Active	$1.00	0	0	-	-	-	-	0.00%	$0.00
portable infrared sauna	Active	$1.00	0	0	-	-	-	-	0.00%	$0.00
sauna infrared	Active	$1.00	0	0	-	-	-	-	0.00%	$0.00
saunas	Active	$1.00	0	0	-	-	-	-	0.00%	$0.00
thermal life far infrared saunas	Active	$1.00	0	0	-	-	-	-	0.00%	$0.00

So what's on the table on this page? Notice first, at the top of the keywords list, the Search Total and Content Total lines. Google provides statistics broken down by search-results pages and content pages.

For each keyword in the group, you have a number of familiar statistics: the number of clicks, the click-through rate, and so on. There's also the Status column, which may show Active or Inactive. *Active* means, of course, that the keyword is running (or able to run, assuming the ad group and campaign are active) . . . that an ad from the ad group will appear when the keyword is used in a search.

If the keyword is *Inactive,* you have several choices:

  ✔ **Increase your Maximum CPC (bid).** A link under the Inactive indicator tells you how much you must bid to get the ad running again for this keyword. Click the link to open a page in which you can change the bid.

  ✔ **Edit your keywords.** You can add and remove keywords from the list.

  ✔ **Edit your ads.** You can add or modify ads.

In some cases, you have to bid higher, even if you do change your keywords or ads, simply because your Maximum CPC is too low. We'll look at active and inactive bids in more detail under "Google's minimum bids and the Quality Score," later in this chapter.

The Vagaries of Google Bidding

As I discuss in Chapter 7, Google determines ad position rather differently from most other PPC systems. Compare Google with Yahoo! Sponsored Search:

  ✔ On **Yahoo! Sponsored Search,** you bid for a position. Yahoo! shows you everyone else's bids, and you bid above someone else to take that advertiser's position.

  ✔ On **Google AdWords,** you tell Google how much you're willing to pay, and Google shows you an estimate of what position you'll (probably) be in and how much you'll actually pay. Google never shows you other advertisers' bids or positions.

What's going on here? What's Google hiding? Well, Google can't really show you how it determines your ad's position because it's determined by a number of factors:

1. Your maximum bid

2. Other advertisers' maximum bids

3. The ad's Quality Score

The *Quality Score* is an evaluation of how well your ad performs in conjunction with a particular keyword (an ad may do well for one keyword but badly for another). Google wants the best performing ads possible for two reasons: Google gets paid when you get clicks, and Google is also trying to provide the best possible search results to searchers; ads that get clicked frequently are, presumably, good results for a particular search.

Thus, an ad with a high Quality Score may actually rank higher than an ad with a higher Maximum CPC. That's right, your ad may appear lower than someone paying less than you, or higher than someone paying more than you. We look at the Quality Score in a little more detail next.

Google's minimum bids and the Quality Score

Until 2005, Google had a simple minimum bid: 5 cents. The company has changed the minimum bid methodology now, so different ads and keywords have different minimum bids (with the lowest possible bid being 1 cent). Google now has *quality-based minimum bids.* This means that an ad with a high Quality Score — one on which people are clicking frequently — requires a lower Maximum CPC (maximum bid). When you begin running an ad, you get a default Quality Score, of course, which can rise or drop depending on ad performance.

In addition, Google now has two keyword statuses: *Active* and *Inactive.* If the keyword is *Active,* you have bid enough, or more than enough, for your ad to be displayed. If the keyword is *Inactive,* it means that the associated ad will not run. You have a couple of options:

✔ Increase the Maximum CPC (the maximum bid)

✔ Increase the Quality Score of your ad by improving the ad and re-running it

I discuss at length how to optimize ads to increase click-through in Chapter 6, so I'm not going to go into it here. But you must understand the Quality Score concept to understand how bidding on Google functions. It's not all about bids, and because the bid — the Maximum CPC, as Google calls it — does not directly determine your position, it makes bidding a little tricky.

Of course, when you begin running your ads, you have only one option if a keyword is set to *inactive:* You have to increase Maximum CPC; at the beginning stage, Google uses a default Quality Score because it has no information about how well your ad is running (because it's *not* yet running), so if your ad is inactive it just means Google wants you to bid higher. Later, if your ad drops below the active/inactive line, you can try rewriting the ad or increasing Maximum CPC in order to get it back into the active status.

Before Google introduced its new quality-based minimum bid system, you could bid whatever you wanted on a particular keyword, and Google would assess how well the associated ads did based on the CTR (click-through rate). If the rate dropped too low, Google would stop running ads for that keyword. It wouldn't matter how much you bid, Google would not run the ad for the keyword until you edited the ad.

Google still assesses how well your keyword is performing, but now whether or not an ad runs — whether the keyword is active or not — depends on two factors: your Maximum CPC (maximum cost per click — your bid) and the Quality Score.

This means that if Google makes a keyword inactive, you can still get it running again without editing the associated ad or ads, or without producing a new ad. Now, all you have to do is raise the bid.

As I write this, Google just recently introduced this new system and is quite likely in the middle of adjusting things. Exactly how it works may change somewhat. At the moment, it does appear that there's more to the Quality Score than merely keyword/ad performance. Google states that the Quality Score is based on the "keyword's click-through rate (CTR), relevance of your ad text, historical keyword performance, and other relevancy factors," so the last two factors are significant. *Historical keyword performance* presumably means the performance of this keyword not just for you, but for other advertisers, and *other relevancy factors* could cover a lot of ground. As for *relevance of the ad text,* presumably Google is trying to compare keywords with the ad text to see if they are related in some way, though this is a very hard thing to do in an automated manner.

It appears, for instance, that *other relevancy factors* includes the historical performance of your account. "When we opened a new account," one large advertiser told me, "we found that the minimum required bids were huge, around $5 a click, so we moved the keywords into an existing account we'd had for some years, and the minimum click price instantly dropped below a dollar."

This advertiser is convinced that the new system discourages new advertisers, whether intentionally or not — that new advertisers must pay more per click than established advertisers.

Anyway, regardless of the details of the inner workings of Google's bidding algorithm, the basics are this:

- ✔ Google calculates a Quality Score based on certain characteristics: click-through performance of the keyword/ad combination, performance of the keyword for other advertisers, your account (it's age and performance, perhaps), relevance of the ad text, and so on.

- ✔ Google uses the Quality Score in combination with your bid — the Maximum CPC — to determine whether your ad will run for a particular keyword.

- ✔ If Google decides that your ad *will* run, it uses the Quality Score and bid to determine where the ad will rank.

- ✔ If Google decides that your ad will not run, or if your ad gets a low position, then you have two choices: attempt to increase the Quality Score or increase the bid.

Certainly a large part of the Quality Score is the click-through rate. If the ad simply doesn't get many clicks, then it will have a low score. So consider this:

1. If you bid so low that the ad is positioned low on the page — below the fold — you'll probably get a low click-through rate.

2. Your Quality Score will drop, which will drop your position even further.

3. You'll need a higher bid to maintain the low position.

4. You'll need a much higher bid to push the ad up to a position in which it does get enough clicks to increase the Quality Score.

It's hard to know exactly what's in the minds of the developers of any piece of software, but certainly the Google bidding system does appear to have been built to encourage higher bidding and more competitive bidding and to discourage advertisers from coming in at lower positions.

Google's "discounter"

I mention in Chapter 7 that bidding and click prices are two different things in most PPC systems; that advertisers generally pay 1 cent above the lower bidder, regardless of how high the bid is.

It's harder to see on the Google system because of all this Quality Score stuff, and of course it can't work the same — because in some cases you'll rank above people paying more than you, and sometimes below people paying less than you — but Google does have what it calls its *discounter*, which is part of the ranking algorithm and ensures you pay the "minimum."

Your Maximum CPC (your Maximum Bid) is, on Google as on other systems, the most you are willing to pay. But Google figures out your rank based on the Quality Score and your bid and then charges you one "just 1 cent more than the minimum necessary to keep your position on the page."

When I try to think through this process (based on Quality Score and bid price, find the ad position, which may be above someone paying more or below someone paying less, then charge 1 cent more than, um, er . . .), my head feels like it's going to explode, so I'm not going to go into more detail. However, remember that on the Ad Group page (see Figure 9-12), you'll see both a keyword's Max CPC Bid *and* the Avg. CPC (the average cost per click). As we saw in Chapter 8, Yahoo! shows you both your cost (the actual click cost) and your maximum bid at that very moment. Google can't do that, of course, because it doesn't know where it's going to rank you until the ad actually runs, but it can show you, afterward, what you bid and, on average, what you actually paid.

Improving ad performance

If you find a wide disparity of results in an ad group, you might consider breaking the group into multiple groups, making the ads easier to deal with by having keywords with similar results grouped together. (To grab a list of the keywords in an ad group, click the Edit Keywords link, and you'll see a text box containing the keywords.) Create a new ad (see "Creating More Campaigns, Ad Groups, and Ads" earlier in this chapter), remove keywords from the original group, and place them into the new ad.

You might also consider adding Negative match keywords. If you have a keyword that simply doesn't work well, consider whether people are often using it with other keywords that completely change the meaning and remove these words from consideration by entering them as negative terms. You can quickly set negative keywords by clicking the Campaign Management tab, clicking the Tools option below the tab, and then clicking the Edit Campaign Negative Keywords link.

Getting Help Placing Bids

You've already seen how to place bids on your keywords in various places throughout this chapter. In the following list, I summarize the different ways you can place bids within the tables we've seen, and then I show you a couple of bidding tools.

> ✔ On the Ad Group page, select a keyword and click the Edit CPCs/URLs button.
>
> ✔ In the Campaign page, select an ad group and click the Change Max CPC to set the CPC for all keywords in all ad groups in the campaign.

Simple enough, eh? But there are two more tools you can use, the Budget Optimizer and the Find and Edit Max CPCs tool.

Using the Budget Optimizer

The Budget Optimizer is an automated bidding tool that is designed to get the most clicks for your budget. You tell Google how much you're willing to spend for a particular campaign, and Google tries to get the maximum number of people to your site. (The Budget Optimizer is applied to a campaign, not to an ad group or keyword.)

Note, however, that this is a very crude tool, as you'll see, and should be used with care. Don't blindly accept Google's recommendations! This tool is designed to maximize clicks, not maximize your ROI.

Here's how it works:

1. **On the All Campaigns page, click the check box to the left of the campaign with which you want to use Budget Optimizer.**

2. **Click the Edit Settings button.**

3. **In the Edit Campaign Settings page (which you saw earlier in Figure 9-11), enter a Daily Budget.**

4. **Click the Enable the Budget Optimizer link.**

5. **In the message box that appears, click OK.**

6. **In the Budget Optimizer Setup page, click the Continue button.**

   You'll see the page shown in Figure 9-13.

7. **Select or enter a budget that you want to spend over 30 days.**

   Note that Google provides several choices and estimates how many clicks you're likely to get for each choice, as well as the average cost per click. Note that the more you're willing to spend, the more clicks you will get, but the higher your average click cost will be.

8. **If you enter your own budget number (in the text box above the buttons), you must also enter a Max CPC number (to the right of the budget text box); then click the Refresh Estimates button to see the effect.**

Play with these numbers a little to see what you can turn up. As you can see in Figure 9-13, Google estimates that it can still get significant clicks at a much lower click price.

9. **Click the Save and Activate button.**

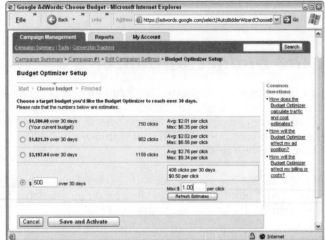

Figure 9-13:
Setting up
the Budget
Optimizer.

That's it; away it goes. Now that you've set up the Optimizer, you can change the budget (or disable the Optimizer if you don't like its advice). The Optimizer runs in 30-day cycles; as soon as one cycle ends, or when you change the budget, the 30-day cycle starts automatically again.

The Optimizer will now set new maximum CPCs for all your keywords; look in an Ad Group page and you'll see, for each keyword, something like *Auto: $0.97.*

Using the Find and Edit Max CPCs tool

This tool enables you to quickly modify maximum CPCs throughout your campaigns in various ways. To get to the Find and Edit Max CPCs tool, click the Campaign Management tab, click the Tools option below the tab, and then click the Find and Edit Max CPCs link; you'll see the page shown in Figure 9-14.

As you can see, this page allows you to modify keywords in a variety of different ways. You can change CPCs for entire campaigns or for specific keywords. You can search for keywords in various different ways — by typing a partial keyword, for instance, or by looking for keywords with a particular CPC or performance history. This is a very flexible tool that allows you complete control for rapidly changing CPCs throughout your account.

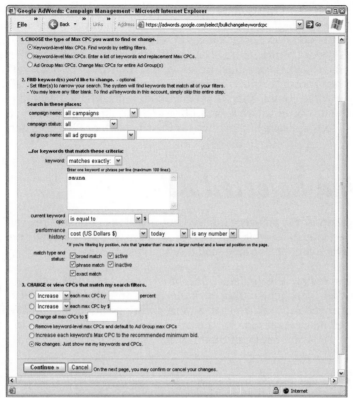

Figure 9-14:
The Find
and Edit
Max CPCs
page.

Changing Matching Options

Earlier, I show you how to change matching options while entering keywords
(by using the " ", [ ], and – symbols; see "Entering keywords" earlier in this
chapter). Google provides a few more tools for modifying matching options:

✔ **Change one matching type to another for a specific ad campaign:** Click
the Campaign Management tab; click the Tools option; click the Change
Keyword Matching Options link.

✔ **Add or remove Negative keywords for a specific ad campaign:** Click
the Campaign Management tab; click the Tools option; click the Edit
Campaign Negative Keywords link.

✔ **Copy Negative keywords between ad campaigns:** Click the Campaign
Management tab; click the Tools option; click the Edit Campaign Negative
Keywords link, select a campaign, and use the Clean Sweep tool.

And now, back to the Quality Score, which we discussed under "The Vagaries of Google Bidding" earlier in the chapter. The Quality Score also comes into play in the decision Google makes in relation to Broad and Phrase matching. For a keyword phrase to be Broad or Phrase matched with another search term, the Quality Score must be above a certain level. (What level? Only the algorithm knows . . . this is all behind the scenes.) The idea is that if you have a keyword/ad combination that isn't doing well with the Exact phrase, why would it do better with a *similar* phrase? So you may have a term that is active for the Exact phrase but inactive for Broad-match or Phrase-match terms.

Reviewing Rejected Ads

Google approves ads very quickly, but that doesn't mean they can't be rejected later. If an ad is rejected for some reason after initially being approved, you receive an e-mail notification.

You can review rejected ads (*disapproved ads,* as Google calls them); click the Campaign Management tab, click the Tools option, and then click the Disapproved Ads link. You see a table showing your ads that have been rejected and the reasons for their rejection; you'll also be able to edit any rejected ads and resubmit them.

Chapter 10

Harnessing MSN Keywords

· ·

In This Chapter

▶ Creating your AdCenter Account

▶ Working with keywords and ad parameters

▶ Managing your MSN Keywords campaigns

▶ Using the Price Estimation tool

· ·

*B*ig changes are on the way in the PPC business. Microsoft is entering the fray with its new *MSN Keywords* program, part of the *MSN AdCenter* advertising business (http://adcenter.msn.com). Here's the situation at this very moment:

  ✔ MSN has some of the most popular Web sites in the world, with huge amounts of traffic and searches every day. In fact somewhere around 16 percent of the English-speaking world's Web searches are carried out through MSN, making MSN the third-largest search system (after Google and Yahoo!).

  ✔ MSN currently runs mostly Yahoo! Search Marketing ads. MSN is part of Yahoo!'s "partner" network, so if you place an ad into Yahoo! Search Marketing (see Chapter 8), the ad will also be displayed on MSN Web sites' search results.

  ✔ MSN is already running test programs for its new MSN Keywords program in Singapore and France.

  ✔ MSN is also running a test program in the United States, but only for high-volume advertisers.

  ✔ The test program mixes both MSN Keywords ads — ads sold directly by MSN to advertisers — with Yahoo! Search Marketing ads. The ads will not appear on the same pages, but different searches will pull ads from one or the other system.

That's the situation late in 2005. By the time you read this, the situation may be very different. Microsoft's plan is to fully implement MSN Keywords by the spring or summer of 2006; almost certainly by June of 2006, when its contract with Yahoo! Search Marketing expires. (At one point, Microsoft implied that the program would be fully operational by March of 2006 at the latest.)

You can expect that the launch of MSN Keywords will lead to another spurt of innovation in the PPC field. Why? Because MSN is upping the ante and introducing some interesting new features that are not available to Yahoo! and Google PPC customers unless they use more advanced systems (see Chapter 16). For instance, MSN Keywords provides

✔ **Dayparting:** Define what times of day your ads should run.

✔ **Demographic targeting:** Display ads dependent on the searcher's demographic characteristics, such as age or lifestyle.

✔ **Ad parameters:** You can associate special blocks of text with each keyword, allowing you to create one base ad and then insert a piece of text into the ad depending on the particular keyword.

I've no doubt that Yahoo! and Google programmers are talking right now about how to stay at the front of the PPC game, so we should be seeing some interesting developments in 2006.

It will also be interesting to see if Yahoo! sues MSN over patent infringements, as it did Google (Yahoo! and Google settled, with Google agreeing to license several patents).

Creating Your MSN AdCenter Account

The first step to using MSN Keywords is to set up an MSN AdCenter account. AdCenter is Microsoft's advertising umbrella; MSN Keywords is just one of the various advertising products that Microsoft sells.

Begin by visiting MSN AdCenter (`http://adcenter.msn.com`) and clicking the Sign Up and Create Account link. The first couple of steps are basic account-admin steps; name, address, billing information, and so on. After you've created an account, log in and get started.

In the MSN Keywords system, the categorization works like this:

✔ A **campaign** is a group of one or more advertising **orders,** with a particular budget and an overall starting and ending date.

✔ An **order** is a group of ads and associated keywords; in Google, it's called an *Ad Group.* Individual orders can have their own starting and ending dates.

Here's how to set up a campaign. When you first log in, you're in Step 1 of the setup wizard, as you can see in Figure 10-1.

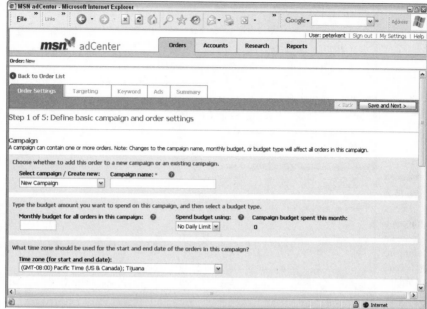

Figure 10-1:
The MSN
Keywords
setup
wizard.

1. **Enter a campaign name.**

2. **Enter a Monthly budget for all orders in this campaign.**

   This is the total monthly amount you're willing to spend for all the ads you're going to create.

3. **Select a budget type from the Spend Budget Using drop-down list box.**

   If you select Daily Limit, MSN divides your monthly budget into a daily budget and attempts to spend that amount each day. If you select No Daily Limit, MSN tries to spend all the money as quickly as possible.

4. **Select your local time zone so you can enter start and stop times in local time.**

5. **Scroll down the page to see the components shown in Figure 10-2.**

6. **Enter an order name.**

   Remember, an "order" is a group of ads and keywords.

   Note that the Start Date is set to the current day, and the End Date is set to a year from today.

7. **If you want to change either date, click the appropriate ellipsis button (...).**

8. **Select the language you're going to use for the ad and keywords.**

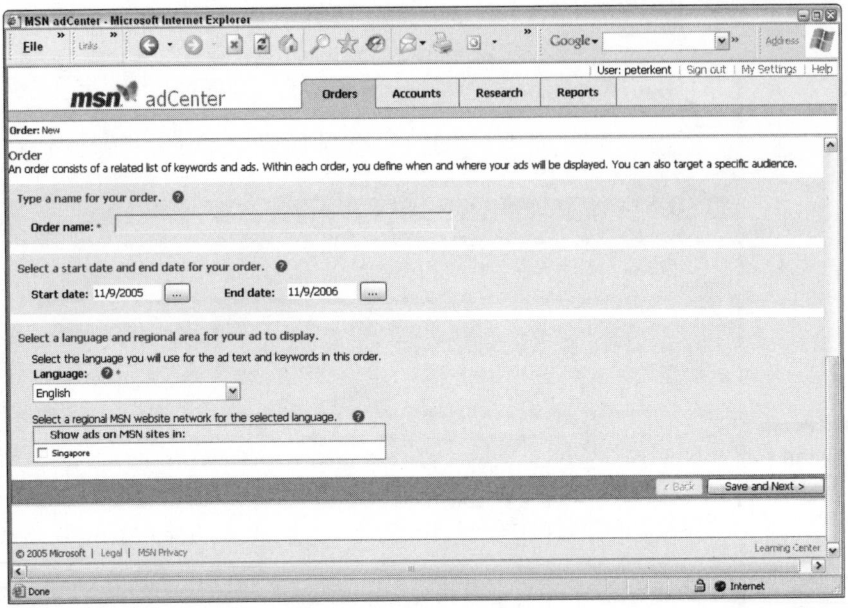

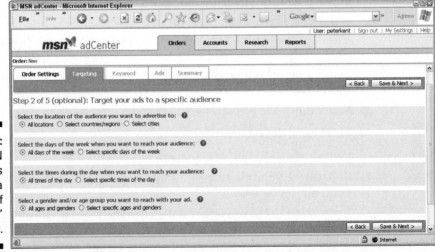

Figure 10-2:
Here's
where you
begin
setting up
the first ad
"order."

9. **Check the check boxes for the countries in which you want MSN to run the ads on its search engines.**

10. **Click the Save & Next button, and you'll see a page in which you can set up ad targeting (Figure 10-3).**

Figure 10-3:
MSN
Keywords
has a
variety of
"targeting"
options.

You can target by location, days of the week, times, and gender or age group. I talk about targeting location in Chapter 12, so I won't go into detail here; however, note that if you make no choices here, MSN runs your ad in all countries. So at the very least, you may want to click the Select Countries/Regions option button and select the country in which you want the ad to run.

11. **If you want to change one of the other three targeting types — days of the week, times during the day, or gender and /or age group — select the appropriate Select Specific option button, then click the Save & Next button.**

    In Figure 10-4, you can see the controls used for setting the days of the week on which you want to run your ads. You can specify particular days on which the ads run, specify different bids for different days, or a combination of both.

12. **Click a day in the Available Days of the Week box — or hold the Ctrl or Command key and click two or more days — and then click the > button to move those times into the Selected Days of the Week box.**

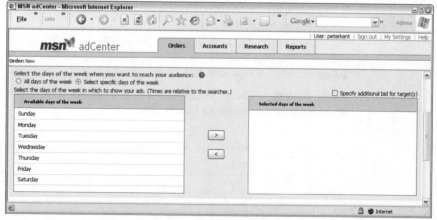

Figure 10-4:
You can run the ads on particular days.

13. **If you want to have different bids for different days, click the Specify Additional Bid for Target(s) check box.**

    A Bid Amount box opens (see Figure 10-5).

14. **Type the bids into the Bid Amount boxes.**

    If, for some reason, searches on particular days are more valuable, you can bid more for them.

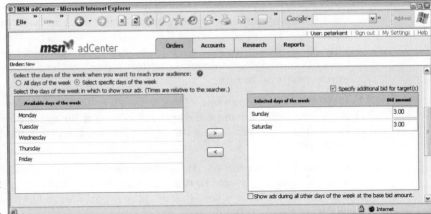

Figure 10-5:
You can
specify
different
bids for
different
days.

15. **You can also choose to run ads on the non-selected days at the base bid amount by clicking the Show Ads During All Other Days of the Week at the Base Bid Amount check box.**

16. **If you click the Select Specific Times of the Day option button, you'll see the controls shown in Figure 10-6.**

    These controls work in the same way as the Specific Days of the Week controls: You can specify the times you want the ad to run, and specify different bids for different time periods.

17. **If you click the Select Specific Ages and Genders option button, you'll see the controls shown in Figure 10-7.**

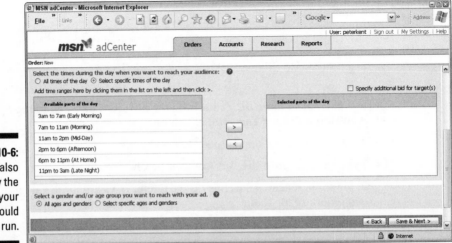

Figure 10-6:
You can also
specify the
times your
ads should
run.

To be more precise, you're not really selecting ages or genders — MSN can't really block the ages or gender you don't want to target because it doesn't know the age and gender of all searchers. But it does know the age and gender of *some* searchers, so you can bid more for the particular gender and age groups you are most interested in, increasing the likelihood that your ad will be displayed to those people.

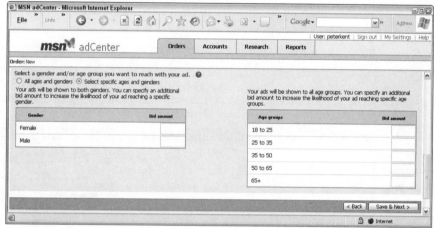

Figure 10-7: Enter specific bids for each gender and age range.

18. **When you've made all your targeting choices, click the Save & Next button to continue to the next step: adding keywords.**

Adding your keywords

After making your targeting choices, you enter your keywords (see Figure 10-8). You can enter your keywords in a number of different ways:

- **Type them one by one.** Each time you begin typing a keyword, another line opens below the current one so you'll be able to type the next keyword.

- **Import an Excel or CSV file.** You can create a list of keywords in another program and quickly import it into the system.

- **Use the Keyword Research Tool.** This provides a simple way to find keywords and immediately add them to your list.

- **Import a list from the Clipboard.** You can select a list from the Keyword Research Tool, under the Research tab, copy it, and then come back to this area and "import" the list.

TIP

Note, however, that this technique does not work when using the Keyword Research Tool under the Orders tab. This feature does *not* allow you to import a list of keywords from the Windows Clipboard; you can't select keywords in another application and paste them in using this option.

It's nice that MSN offers a way to import keyword files. As I point out in the two preceding chapters, neither Google nor Yahoo! makes this very easy. What MSN lacks, though, at present at least, is the ability to copy a list from another program and quickly paste it into the system.

Figure 10-8:
Type your keywords into this table.

Typing the keywords

Entering keywords by hand is simple. Type the keyword, press Tab, and then type the bid you want to make for the keyword. Press Tab again and you'll be on the next line, on which you can enter another keyword. Make sure you click the Save & Next button at the bottom of the page when you are finished.

Importing keywords from a file

Unlike Google and Yahoo!, MSN makes importing large keyword lists pretty easy. You can upload an Excel file or a Comma Separated Values text file (CSV). Here's how:

1. **Click the Import/Export menu at the top of the keyword list.**

2. **Click the Import from a File option, and the box shown in Figure 10-9 opens.**

3. **To download a sample, click the Excel or CSV link, and save to your computer.**

4. **Open the file to see a sample.**

   You can see both types of import files in Figure 10-10.

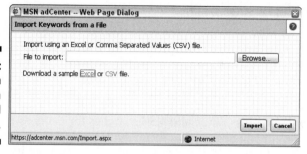

5. Create a new file with your data in the same format.

As you can see in the example files, you can add a bid for the different match types; see *Working with different match types* for a description of these match types, later in this chapter.

6. Click the Browse button in the Import Keywords from a File dialog box to find your import file.

7. Click the Import button.

Your keyword file will be imported, and the words added to the keyword list.

8. Click the Save & Next button at the bottom of the page to save your changes.

Note, by the way, that you can also export keywords from MSN. Select the Import/Export menu at the top of the keyword list and then select Export.

Using the Keyword Research Tool

If you haven't yet done your keyword research — see Chapter 4 — you can use MSN's Keyword Research Tool. Click the Show Keyword Research Tool check box in the top left of the Keyword page (see Figure 10-8), and a frame opens on the right side of the browser. You can create more room, if you wish, by dragging the frame border to the left.

Type a keyword and press Enter, and MSN searches for matches. The list of matches includes the number of times each term has been searched for during the current month and the previous month. If you want to use any of these terms, click the appropriate check box, and the term is added to the Keyword Collection box, as you can see in Figure 10-11.

Click the Add to Order button at the bottom, and the selected keywords are added to the list in the left pane, where you can enter a bid for the terms. To close the research tool, click the little X in the top-right corner of the frame.

Remember, whenever you make a change to the order that you want to save, click the Save & Next button at the bottom of the page before doing anything else.

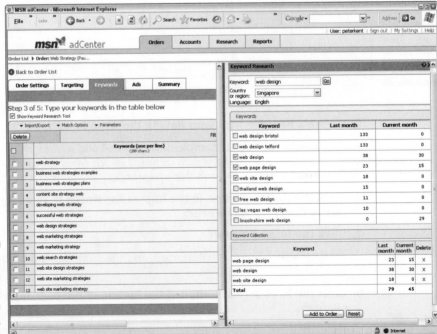

Figure 10-11:
MSN's
Keyword
Research
Tool.

Importing from the Keyword Research Tool

There's another way to get to the Keyword Research Tool: You can click the Research tab at the top of the page, and the Keyword Research Tool is displayed. The advantage to working here is that you have more room — you have the entire width of the browser rather than just a small portion of its width.

You can quickly get keywords from the tool into an ad order by clicking the Copy button in the Keyword Collection box, returning to the order (click the Orders tab, then the Order ID in the Select an Order table), clicking the Keywords tab, clicking Import/Export at the top of the table, and selecting the Import from Clipboard option. As mentioned before, this is a special Clipboard, not the normal Windows Clipboard — you can't use this feature to import from other programs.

Working with different match types

MSN has four different matching options, which are actually the same as the ones used by Google: Broad, Phrase, Exact, and Negative (see Chapter 7). By default, your keywords are *Broad matched.* That is, a keyword is matched with phrases that include your keywords, but that may have the words in a different order, and may include other words. If you are bidding on *video games,* and someone searches for *buy video games, games video,* or even *stop kids playing video games,* your ad will be matched.

The bid you enter into MSN's Keyword table (Figure 10-8) is the bid for matching the keyword with a Broad-matched term, but you can also bid on other forms; click Match Options at the top of the table and select Phrase Match or Exact Match from the drop-down menu. New columns appear in your table, in which you can enter bids for particular keywords, for Phrase matches (your keywords must appear exactly as you typed, though other words can appear around them), and for Exact matches (the ad is matched with your exact phrase only). Thus, MSN allows you to bid differently for different matching options. Rather than bidding *only* for one type of matching, you can bid more for more exact matches, and less, perhaps much less, for much broader matches.

In addition, MSN allows you to add Negative keywords to particular keywords. Click Match Options at the top of the table and select Negative Match, and a Negative Match column is added to the table. Now you can enter negative terms for each keyword. Imagine you have the keyword phrase *video games,* but you don't sell PS2 video games. Entering **ps2** into the Negative Match field for that keyword phrase ensures that your ad is never matched with a search term that includes *ps2.*

As mentioned earlier, make sure you save any changes you make before moving to another screen, or you'll lose them.

Working with parameters

MSN has a very unusual system called *parameters,* something you won't find with Google or Yahoo!. These are text fragments that are automatically placed into your ad, triggered by particular keywords. As you find out earlier in this book (Chapter 6), the closer the ad matches the keywords typed, the better. Parameters provide a way to help you get your ads to match keywords very closely. You can now create large numbers of ads that are mostly the same, yet customized for particular keyword phrases.

You can associate up to three blocks of text — three *parameters* — with each keyword phrase. In addition, there's a fourth, fixed parameter, the keyword. That is, you can tell MSN to insert the keyword that the searcher typed into a particular location in the ad.

Working with parameters is a two-step process. First, you define the parameters under the Keywords tab. Later, when creating your ad under the Ads tab, you specify where in the ad you want the parameters placed by using little {parameter} tags.

Here's an example of how you might use this system. If you have a video-game store that sells a variety of games — Gameboy, Xbox, GameCube, Playstation 2, and so on — and you have a different number of titles for each system and a different discount on each, your ad could include this line:

```
{param1} {keyword} titles! {param2} Off!
```

In the Keywords page, you enter the appropriate parameters for each keyword, as illustrated in Table 10-1.

Table 10-1	Example Keyword Parameters	
Keyword	*Param1*	*Param2*
psp	5,000	10%
psp video game	5,000	10%
Xbox	3,000	12%
xbox games	3,000	12%

Now, if your ad is matched with the term *psp video game,* the ad will say this:

```
5,000 psp video game titles! 10% Off!
```

How do you get these parameters into the Keyword table? There are a couple of ways. Look back at Figure 10-10, and you'll notice that the Import file format includes fields for Param1, Param2, Param3; in other words you can add these parameters to your import file along with the keywords and bids.

Or you can add them to the table manually, while entering your keywords. Click Parameters at the top of the table, and select the parameter you want to include from the drop-down menu: Insert Parameter {param1}, for instance. Each time you select one of these parameters, MSN adds a field to the table, in which you can type the parameter you want to use for each keyword. Note, by the way, that when you do this, you'll only be able to add parameters for new keywords, not existing ones.

Creating the ad

After you've finished with the keywords, click the Save & Next button to move on to the Ads tab (see Figure 10-12). Enter your Ad Title (25 characters), Ad Description (70 characters), Display URL (35 characters), and Destination URL (1,022 characters).

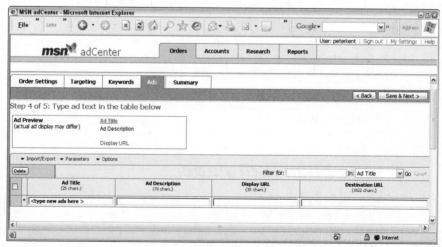

Figure 10-12: Creating the ad.

Remember, you can use parameters in the ads if you wish. Where you want to place parameter 1 into the ad, for instance, simply type **{param1}**. If you want to drop the keyword into the ad, type **{keyword}**.

Note that you can create multiple ads for the order. As with Google, for instance, the system rotates ads among the keywords.

Importing your ads

You can also import ads in much the same way you can import keywords, as I show you earlier in this chapter (use the Export/Import menu at the top of the ad table). Again, you can download a sample Excel or CSV file. For instance, here are the contents of the sample CSV file:

```
title,description,display url,url
Tennis instructions ,Improve your tennis
        skills,http://www.tennis.com,http://www.
        tennis.com
Tennis classes ,Improve your tennis
        skills,http://www.tennis.com,http://www.
        tennis.com
Tennis Gear,Improve your tennis
        skills,http://www.tennis.com,http://www.
        tennis.com
Tennis racquets,Improve your tennis
        skills,http://www.tennis.com,http://www.
        tennis.com
```

If you are creating a lot of ads, you'll want to use import files. It's much easier to create all this information in an Excel spreadsheet file and import it than it is to enter it directly into the MSN pages.

When you finish creating your ads, click Save & Next to proceed to the Summary page.

The Summary page

The next step, after creating your ads, is the Summary page, shown in Figure 10-13. You see the list of all the keywords and, at the bottom of the page, the ads that are part of the advertising "order." Check the keywords, and in particular read the ad text, and make sure everything's okay; if not, you can click a check box next to the keyword or ad and then click the Edit Keywords or Edit Ad button. You'll be able to delete a keyword or change a bid, or you can modify the ad.

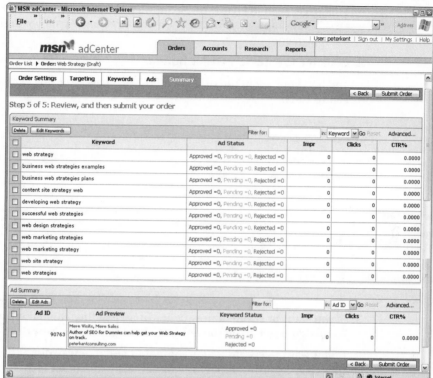

Figure 10-13:
The
Summary
page.

When you've reviewed everything, click the Submit Order button, and your order is submitted to MSN for approval.

Managing Your Campaigns

Unlike Google and Yahoo!, in which you set up your account by using a wizard and manage the account in a totally separate area, the process we just saw for creating your MSN ads happens on the same screens you use to manage the campaign.

Creating new campaigns and orders

You can create new campaigns and orders at any time. Here's how:

1. **Click the Orders tab at the top of the page to get to the Select an Order page.**

This page, seen in Figure 10-14, shows a list of all the *orders* you've created. The campaign to which each order belongs is shown in the Campaign column.

2. Click the Create New Order button.

You find yourself in the original Step 1 of 5 page you saw earlier (refer to Figure 10-1).

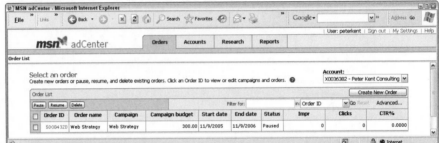

Figure 10-14:
The Orders
tab.

3. If you want to create a new order in an existing campaign, select the campaign name from the Select Campaign/Create New drop-down list.

4. If you want to create a new campaign and a new order at the same time, select New Campaign from the drop-down list box.

5. Continue the process I showed you earlier, in the "Creating Your MSN AdCenter Account" section, beginning from Step 2.

Viewing campaign and order results

In order to see how a campaign and its orders are going, click the Orders tab at the top of the page (see Figure 10-14). This table shows you, for each order, the number of impressions (Impr), the number of clicks, and the click-through rate (CTR%).

Click a particular order to get to the order Summary page (Figure 10-13). This table shows the same three statistics.

Now, remember that the description here is based on early days for MSN Keywords. The system will undoubtedly develop and evolve, so what you see may be a little different, and I'm sure some things will have to change soon because, at present, the system isn't as easy to use as it should be. Bidding, for instance, isn't so easy at present; you currently select a particular keyword and click Edit Keywords to change bids.

Using the Price Estimation tool

Note that, similar to Google and dissimilar to Yahoo!, MSN doesn't make it easy to see the effect of a bid on your ad position. MSN does, however, provide a simple price-estimation tool to show you the *likely* effect of a bid. Here's how you use it:

1. **Click the Research tab and then click the Price Estimation tab on the bar that appears.**

2. **In the tool, select the Language and the Country or Region.**

   MSN shows you information for a particular area, not for the entire network.

3. **Type your keywords and bid amounts into the table and click Estimate.**

   MSN searches for the data and returns both an Estimated Position and Estimated Monthly Cost (see Figure 10-15).

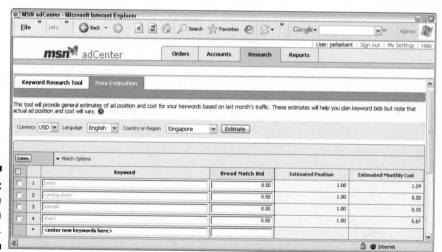

Figure 10-15: The Price Estimation page.

Chapter 11

Using the Second- and Third-Tier PPC Systems

*I*n the preceding chapters, I discuss the three giants in the PPC business: Google, Yahoo!, and MSN. But there's more to PPC than these three companies — much more.

Working with the big three is definitely easier than working with the second- and third-tier systems for a number of reasons. First, if you're trying to generate large amounts of traffic, you almost *have* to work with the top tier. These three systems are responsible for over 90 percent of all search results. And of all the "content" pages carrying PPC ads, the vast majority carry Google and Yahoo! ads (primarily Google).

In addition, the tools provided by the big systems tend to be much better than the smaller systems, which makes sense — after all, the bigger systems have far more money to spend than the smaller systems. Google, for instance, generated $2.6 *billion* in PPC revenues in the first six months of 2005, so it should be able to pay a few programmers to spiff up its tools and a few writers to produce documentation.

Where do these smaller systems place their ads? They build partner networks of small search systems, often incorporated into content sites. For instance, ePilot has over 300 partner sites, including Fitness.com, index.com, SearchBug.com, PageSeeker, and so on. You may never have heard of any of these systems. They are not search-destination sites, not the sort of places most people go when they want to carry out a search. But they get enough combined traffic to generate billions of searches — ePilot, for instance, claims to have 3 billion searches each month across its network, and Searchfeed expects to hit 2 billion searches a month by the end of 2005. A smaller second-tier system, Mirago, claims half a billion searches a month, and even at the bottom end of Tier II, a system such as Clicksor claims 350 million searches a month.

Three Reasons to Use Tier II Systems

There are essentially three reasons to use the second-tier systems:

- ✔ You need more clicks.
- ✔ You need lower-priced clicks.
- ✔ You need more clicks at lower prices.

Many companies use the first-tier *and* smaller systems because they can't get enough traffic out of the big guys. The advertisers are doing well, bringing visitors to their sites, making sales. . . . but heck, if 1,000 visitors are a good thing, wouldn't 2,000 be twice as good? The smaller PPC systems provide another source of visitors, another place to advertise. In the same way that Dell advertises on national TV *and* in local magazines, advertising in smaller PPC systems is simply another way to advertise.

Some companies have tried the big guys and can't make it work. The clicks are just way too expensive. But the smaller systems can provide clicks at a much lower cost than the big guys, allowing some companies to make money from PPC even if they can't use Google, Yahoo!, or MSN.

Finally, for some, it's a combination. They've found a way to buy low-cost clicks on the big guys, and they'd like to buy more. But doing so means using more-expensive keywords. The only option for expansion is to check the smaller systems.

How much cheaper are clicks on the second-tier systems? Table 11-1 shows some examples, comparing Yahoo! Search Marketing with one well-known second-tier system, ePilot (www.ePilot.com). The prices show how much you'll pay for a click if you place your ad into the #1 position (at the time of writing, of course; prices change); that is, they're not the top bids, they're the actual prices paid.

Table 11-1	Comparing Click Prices between First- and Second-Tier Systems		
Keyword	*Yahoo!*	*ePilot*	*% of Yahoo!*
accident attorney	$4.26	$0.08	1.9
accident attorney new york	$10.01	$0.01	0.1

Keyword	Yahoo!	ePilot	% of Yahoo!
shoes	$0.86	$0.14	16.3
coach handbag	$1.95	$0.01	0.51
mortgage broker	$3.90	$0.43	11.0
mortgage brocker	$0.10	$0.01	10.0
mortgage broker los angeles	$4.76	$0.01	0.21
paintball	$0.41	$0.06	14.6
paintball denver	$0.10	$0.01	10.0
paintball dallas	$0.91	$0.01	11.0
pizza chicago	$0.24	$0.01	0.42
pizza equipment	$0.71	$0.01	1.4
buy laptop phoenix	$0.10	$0.01	10.0
mp3	$0.40	$0.07	17.5

Look at some of those percentages! In some cases, ePilot's prices are below —
sometimes well below — 1 percent of the Yahoo! price. Consider also that
these are the top prices; as you saw in Chapter 7, prices often drop dramatically after the first two or three positions.

However, there's a drawback to picking low positions on the second-tier
system. If you go for the rock-bottom prices, you may find that you get very,
very few clicks because lower positions may not be distributed to the PPC
system's partner sites, which is, after all, where most of the traffic comes
from. On ePilot, for instance, the minimum bid price is 1 cent, but you must
bid at least 7 cents in order to get full distribution.

Will Tier 11 Systems Work for You?

You'll find similar price differentials as those in Table 11-1 with most of the
second-tier PPC systems, not just with ePilot (though ePilot claims to have
lower prices than most of its second-tier competitors). As you can see, these
systems can provide very low click costs. If your numbers (see Chapter 3)
simply didn't work with the big systems, you'll find it much more likely that
they will work with these smaller systems.

There's a catch, of course. If the big systems provide over 90 percent of
all search results, that leaves just 10 percent for dozens of other systems.
Prices may be much lower, but it's often much harder to get clicks out of

these systems. That's not always the case, though. You may find the smaller systems actually provide *more* clicks. Why? Because the clicks on the major systems may be so expensive that you can't afford to buy them, so you bid low, generating relatively few bids. Conversely, on the smaller systems, bids are so cheap you can bid up, and generate more traffic.

Some merchants have tremendous success with the smaller systems. Others say they simply can't make them work. I believe it's a matter of experimentation, that if you work with a few systems, you may well find some that perform very well.

Another thing to consider, though, is that conversion rates are often much lower for these smaller systems. In some cases, conversion rates may be as low as 10 percent of the conversion rates from the larger systems. Why is this? I don't know for sure, but I'm guessing that a lot of the traffic generated by smaller systems is "incidental," people searching on sites they just happen to be on at a particular moment. These searches are less-qualified prospects, and so convert at lower rates. If someone is serious about searching, she goes to a major search engine to carry out her search — these searchers are highly qualified prospects. However, when you consider the much lower click prices of the smaller systems, your return on investment (ROI) may still be much higher.

Here are a couple of bidding strategies used on the smaller PPC systems:

- ✔ **Bid High:** Bids are cheap, so you bid high to get as much traffic as possible. Even with lower conversion rates, the low bid price may make it profitable.

- ✔ **Bid Low and let traffic dribble in:** You may find that even though clicks are cheap, conversion rates are so low that you're still losing money. So you might bid as low as you can go and simply let the traffic dribble in at very low prices, allowing you to make a profit despite low conversions.

The bottom line is this: Working with second-tier systems absolutely *can* work, but there's no guarantee.

Finding Tier II Systems

These are the systems that I think of as *Tier II* systems. Many are quite well known in the business, and in some cases serve literally billions of search results each month; the smaller ones still tend to provide hundreds of millions of monthly search results.

- 7Search.com
- AJInteractive (AskJeeves, iWon, Excite, and MaxOnline, `http://SponsoredListings.Ask.com/`)
- Blowsearch (`http://blowsearch.com`)
- Brainfox (`http://brainfox.com`)
- Business.com
- Clicksor (`www.Clicksor.com`)
- Enhance Interactive (`www.Enhance.com`, formerly Ah-Ha.com)
- ePilot (`http://ePilot.com`)
- Findology (`www.Findology.com`)
- GenieKnows.com
- goClick.com
- Kanoodle (`www.Kanoodle.com`)
- LookSmart (`www.LookSmart.com`)
- Lycos InSite AdBuyer (Lycos, HotBot, AngelFire, and so on, `http://insite.lycos.com/adbuyer/overview.asp`)
- Mamma (`www.mamma.com`)
- Mirago (`www.Mirago.com`)
- Miva (`www.Miva.com`, formerly FindWhat.com and eSpotting)
- myGeek (`www.MyGeek.com`)
- PageSeeker (`www.PageSeeker.com`)
- Search123 (`www.Search123.com`)
- Search*feed*.com
- Snap (`www.Snap.com`)
- Turbo10 (`www.Turbo10.com`)

Which systems do you go for first? Hard to say. There are no hard and fast rules on these systems; what works for you might not work for me, so to a great degree it's a matter of experimentation. AJInteractive is a pretty big network; it feeds ads to AskJeeves (the third-largest search system in the English-speaking world) and Excite. Some of the better known and more commonly used networks are Miva, goClick, ePilot, Enhance, Search*feed*, LookSmart, myGeek, and Enhance.

By the way, this list doesn't include content-placement systems, which I discuss in Chapter 13. While both Google and Yahoo! distribute their ads on content sites, not just search sites, a number of smaller systems do the same.

Tier II Features

Different systems have different features, of course, and overall you'll find that the Tier II systems are much simpler, with much more basic features, than the first-tier systems. But because the Tier II systems have to work harder for their money, they have in some cases developed features that you may not find on the major PPC systems. For instance, ePilot allows you to place small *Keyword Sponsor Boxes* (as you can see in Figure 11-1) to the right of the search results (though these are a fixed $50 per month and are not PPC ads).

Miva provides a Pay Per Call feature, allowing even businesses without a Web presence to buy PPC ads; I show you this type of system in Chapter 14. And Tier II systems are also more likely to make an import feature available, allowing you to import files containing ads and keywords. (Google makes this available only to large advertisers, and Yahoo! makes it available for a limited time, though it hides it away for some reason — MSN does make it easily available, though.)

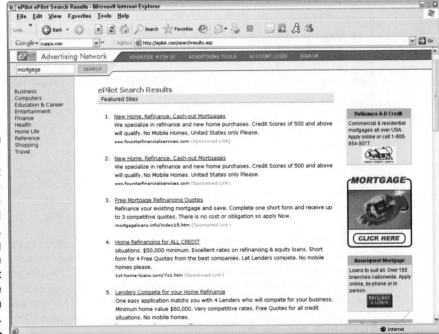

Figure 11-1: ePilot allows you to place little ad boxes, including logos, on the right side of the search results.

Working with Tier III Systems

There are also many, many systems that I think of as *Tier III systems* — much smaller systems, less well known, with very limited ad distribution. A good place to find these systems is at PayPerClickSearchEngines.com; this site has an index of over 650 PPC systems.

The big question is, should you use them? They have a number of problems:

- ✔ These systems typically generate extremely low levels of traffic.

- ✔ Many have very low conversion rates.

- ✔ They still take time and energy — and sometimes initial sign-up fees and deposits — to get running. Combine that with limited traffic and low conversion rates, and you have a high investment for a very low payback!

- ✔ Some of these systems border on fraudulent, making money not by selling PPC ads but by charging nonrefundable sign-up fees. You'll pay your fee and probably never see any traffic.

That's not to say you should never use these systems. In fact, you may want to look for highly targeted third-tier systems that match your business. For instance, are you selling products wholesale? Maybe you should try advertising on WholesaleGopher.com (Figure 11-2). Is your site related in some way to science? Perhaps you should place ads on SciSeek.com.

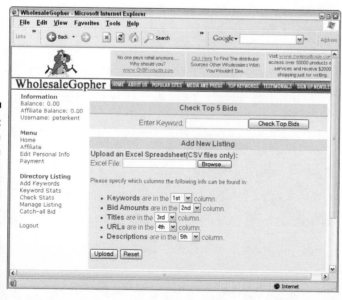

Figure 11-2: Wholesale Gopher.com provides a simple file upload system to help you load ads and keywords.

However, while it may be worthwhile working with the specialty systems, remember that the more general third-tier systems are likely to be a lot of work for very little payback.

Chapter 12

Using Geo-Targeting

The Internet provides a way to reach people across the nation and across the world. But increasingly, it's being used to reach people across town. *Local search* is the generic term given to the ability to search for information related to a particular location — a state or city, for instance, or even a particular zip code. The major search engines use various methods for helping with local searches; they have partnerships with Yellow Pages companies, they search Web pages for geographic information, and so on.

From the PPC advertiser's perspective, though, the questions become, "How do I target my ads geographically? How do I display my ads just to people in particular geographic locations?" For example, here are some situations in which geo-targeting would be very useful:

✔ A company selling furniture may ship only within one country; it doesn't want to display its ads to people in other countries.

✔ A hotel in Palm Springs may want to advertise to people in Southern California who are looking for weekend breaks but not to people elsewhere in the country who are not likely to go to Palm Springs for a couple of days.

✔ A nightclub in Phoenix doesn't want its ad appearing for people outside the Phoenix area.

✔ A dentist in Surprise, Arizona, just northwest of Phoenix, doesn't want his ad appearing for people in Phoenix itself, or in Scottsdale, in Chandler, in Mesa . . . because he knows people in those areas aren't likely to drive 20 or 30 miles to visit a dentist.

There are many reasons to geo-target, and virtually all PPC advertisers do geo-target at least at the most basic level: specifying in which country the ad should run.

Why Is Geo-Targeting So Important?

In Chapter 3, I discuss *W2S* (Web to Store) and Off-Channel shoppers. In that discussion, I point out these concepts:

- Most Internet users are "off-channel" or W2S shoppers.

- They spend more money offline, after online research, than they spend online.

- Almost half spend extra dollars on products they didn't research online after they're in the brick-and-mortar store.

- According to one survey, during the last three months of 2004 the average W2S buyer spent $250 online (29 percent), $400 offline on researched products (47 percent), and $200 offline on additional purchases (24 percent). That's 29 percent online and 71 percent offline!

Furthermore, another recent study found that 25 percent of all searches made by people researching products were made by people looking for local merchants.

Although most people think of e-commerce as a purely online thing, *online* marketing predominantly generates *offline* sales. In other words, many people search for information online and then make their purchases at a local store. Thus, many businesses are trying to target people in their own areas to get them to walk into their brick-and-mortar stores. Geo-targeting helps you find those people.

But geo-targeting helps you do something else. In Chapter 6, I explain that one challenge of PPC advertising is discouraging the wrong people from clicking your ads. Geo-targeting allows you to reduce (though not eliminate, as you find out in this chapter) the number of people who see your ad who are not in your area. By carefully targeting the right people in the right areas, you can reduce wasted clicks and increase your advertising ROI (return on investment).

How Does Local Search Work?

Local search is based on several different methodologies, including *geolocation,* the science of trying to figure out where the heck a computer actually *is,* geographically speaking. When a computer contacts a Web site, it says something like, "Hi, I'm computer 67.176.77.58 [the computer's IP number, at least for the moment]; can you search for information about *rodent racing* and send me the results?" How do you figure out whether that computer is in Colorado and wants information about prairie-dog racing, or is in Florida and is interested in the famous African Gambian pouch rat races?

Local search generally works in a few basic ways (different services use different combinations of these methods):

- **Search terms:** If someone types *dentist new york,* the search engine can be pretty sure that she's looking for a dentist in New York, not a dentist in Oklahoma City. Simple, eh?

- **Partner sites:** A PPC service can also guess at a location based on the Web site someone is using. If someone is searching at `www.google.fr`, there's a good bet that person is in France; if someone searches at `www.yahoo.co.uk`, that person is probably in the United Kingdom. In other cases, partner sites could be even more specific, related to a particular region or even a specific city.

- **IP numbers:** IP (Internet Protocol) numbers identify computers on the Internet. Every computer connected to the Internet at any moment has a unique IP number.

The first two methods are pretty easy to understand; identifying computers by IP numbers may require a little more explanation.

With information being sent to and fro — from thousands of computers to millions of Web sites and back — there has to be a way for the information to be "addressed" so that the various servers on the Internet know where to deliver the information. Thus, every computer connected to the Internet has an *IP number,* or *IP address.* In some cases, computers "own" a particular IP number; turn the computer off and turn it on next week, and it will still have the same number (this is known as a *static IP number).*

Often, however, computers share IP numbers; log out of a dial-up account now and dial back in five minutes, and your computer will be assigned a different IP number (known as a *dynamic IP number).* That IP number is "shared" among many computers, but at any moment only one computer can use the number.

Take a look at this IP number:

```
67.176.77.58
```

This number uniquely identifies a particular computer in Colorado. If a Web server sends a page to that address, there's only one place the page can go because, at that particular moment, only one computer on the entire Internet uses that number to identify itself. It's like a telephone number. Every telephone in the entire world has a unique number (when you include the country code). Pick up the phone and dial the full number, and there's only one telephone that you can possibly be connected to.

An IP number is a *hierarchical* system. A block of numbers is assigned to a particular organization or company. That organization or company then assigns blocks of numbers to other organizations or companies, which can then assign their numbers to different organizations, companies, or divisions within a company, and so on.

Consider again, `67.176.77.58`. This number is "owned" by Comcast Cable Communications, a large, American cable-TV company. In fact, Comcast "owns" a large block of numbers:

```
67.160.0.0–67.191.255.255
```

Within that large block lies another block that is used by Comcast Cable Communications in Colorado:

```
67.176.0.0–67.176.127.255
```

Clearly `67.176.77.58` lies within this block.

Want to see geo-location at work? There are a number of sites you can go to that will tell you where you are, or at least where the site thinks you are. I just visited IP2Location (`www.ip2location.com`; see Figure 12-1), and it was able to tell me my city correctly, (though not my zip code, latitude, or longitude).

Now, geo-targeting with IP numbers is not perfect; it's definitely an imprecise science, for a few reasons. First, you can't always assume that a number that is assigned to a company in a particular area is being used in that area. It's possible for two computers using two IP numbers just one digit apart — 67.176.77.58 and 67.176.77.59, for instance — to be thousands of miles apart. An IP number assigned to an organization in one area can be used by many different computers in many different locations. For example, a computer in San Francisco that has been assigned a block of IP numbers may use those numbers for computers in various branch offices in San Diego, in Oklahoma City, in Seattle, and so on.

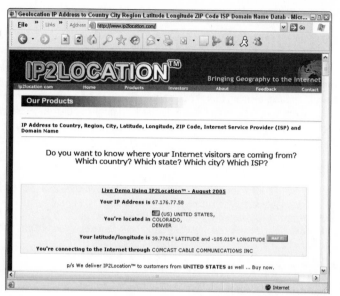

Figure 12-1:
IP2Location
is one of a
number of
services
that can
figure out
where an IP
number is
located. It's
usually
more or less
correct,
though your
mileage will
vary.

Second, dynamic IP numbers are "here today, there tomorrow." When you dial into an ISP's network and are assigned an IP number, you could be in California, while the computer that just assigned the IP number to your computer for the current session could be in Virginia. But when you log off and someone logs on and takes your number, the new computer might be in Wyoming or Florida. There are other cases in which IP locating doesn't work, too. To see this in action for yourself, search for *anonymous browsing* at any major search engine and then visit one of the anonymous Web-browsing sites. Use one of these systems to visit an IP location site, such as www.ip2location.com, and see where it thinks you're coming from; quite likely, somewhere on the other side of the country or the world.

So it's not always easy for search engines to figure out where you are or what ad is most appropriate. For instance, while writing this chapter, I did various searches looking for examples of geo-targeted PPC ads. I was searching for *mortgages california* and *pizza new york*. Google did, in fact, show me businesses in California and New York, but in addition, it kept showing me businesses in Colorado. Why? Because it had figured out (using my computer's IP number) that I was actually in Colorado while doing the searches. I wasn't looking for Coloradan businesses, but Google showed them to me. On the other hand, as explained above, in many cases the PPC system cannot use your IP number to figure out where you are and has to work purely on the search terms you enter.

Still, geolocation is getting better all the time because the basic geographic information about where blocks of IP numbers have been assigned is being combined with other clues about where particular IP numbers within those blocks actually lie.

Finding more location clues

While the authorities that assign blocks of IP numbers provide very basic geographic information, this can then be combined with other clues, such as hostnames, to find where someone is searching from. For example, it's possible, using tools such as *traceroute,* to trace the path from one computer to another. When you do this, you get not only the IP numbers but the hostnames of the servers between the start point and the destination computer, as with this traceroute from a computer in Australia to 67.176.77.58:

```
1   FastEthernet6-0.civ-service1.Canberra.telstra.net (203.50.1.65)
2   GigabitEthernet3-0.civ-core2.Canberra.telstra.net (203.50.10.129)
3   GigabitEthernet2-2.dkn-core1.Canberra.telstra.net (203.50.6.126)
4   Pos4-1.ken-core4.Sydney.telstra.net (203.50.6.69)
5   10GigabitEthernet3-0.pad-core4.Sydney.telstra.net (203.50.6.86)
6   10GigabitEthernet2-2.syd-core01.Sydney.net.reach.com (203.50.13.38)
7   i-6-1.wil-core02.net.reach.com (202.84.249.201)
8   sl-gw28-ana-10-0.sprintlink.net (144.223.58.221)
9   sl-bb21-ana-11-0.sprintlink.net (144.232.1.29)
10  sl-bb22-ana-15-0.sprintlink.net (144.232.1.174)
11  sprint-gw.la2ca.ip.att.net (192.205.32.185)
12  tbr1-p014001.la2ca.ip.att.net (12.123.29.2)
13  12.122.10.25 (12.122.10.25)
14  12.122.9.138 (12.122.9.138)
15  12.122.12.134 (12.122.12.134)
16  gar1-p360.dvmco.ip.att.net (12.123.36.73)
17  12.125.159.90 (12.125.159.90)
18  68.86.103.141 (68.86.103.141)
19  68.86.103.2 (68.86.103.2)
20  * * *
21  c-67-176-77-58.hsd1.co.comcast.net (67.176.77.58)
```

A *hostname* is a name assigned to a computer. The Internet actually used IP numbers for addressing, but to make things easier for us mere mortals — and in particular the server administrators who have to manage servers — names can also be applied to computers. Notice something about the hostnames above? Some of them have geographic information embedded in them: Canberra, Sydney, co (Colorado), la2ca (Los Angeles, California, perhaps?), and so on. Another clue: Some major ISPs assign blocks of IP numbers geographically, so after you crack the code, you can begin to figure out where people using that ISP actually live. By using clues such as these, geolocation engineers at various companies specializing in this science can get pretty accurate about locating IP numbers. Not perfect, but close much of the time.

Creating Your Ads

When creating geo-targeted ads, it's a good idea to ad local terms to the ad. If you're a dentist in New York, say so. (Google places a line containing geographic information below the ad, as you see in the next section, but not all

PPC systems do that, and even Google recommends that you still use geographical terms in the ad.)

In your keyword list, you can include regional terms if you wish, but you can also include more general terms because the PPC system is, in effect, targeting regionally for you. For instance, if you're a dentist in New York, including *dentist* in your keyword list is the equivalent of including *dentist new york* because the PPC system will match you for *dentist new york* automatically.

By the way, you might remember from Chapter 9 that Google's click prices are to some degree dependent on how well an ad performs; the more click-throughs, the lower the price to get a particular position. Well, one advantage of geo-targeting with Google is that an ad is likely to perform better, thus reducing the click price. If you're targeting the term *dentist,* you'll probably get a higher click-through rate (and a lower price) if you carefully geo-target the term.

Consider, by the way, that some products and services are going to work better with geo-targeting than others. You may find that advertising your local bookstore doesn't work well, for instance, because — and this is a supposition on my part, I could be wrong — most people searching for books online are going to buy online. Many fewer are searching for local bookstores because either they already have their favorite local store, or they are looking for a local chain store, but they are less likely to search for an independent local store.

Remember, there are different types of targeting. Someone identified through IP tracking as searching in Denver for *buy books* is less likely to be looking for a local store than someone who searches on, for instance, *denver bookstore.*

Businesses that typically do well with local search are those that provide a product or service that *has* to be bought locally (doctors and dentists, pet grooming services, and hair salons, for example), businesses selling products that are almost always bought locally (hardware stores and appliance stores, for instance), and businesses selling products that are often researched online and bought offline (such as electronics and furniture).

Using Google Local Targeting

Google has a service called *local targeting* by which you can specify the areas in which you want your ads to run. For instance, I just found these ads by doing several searches on Google:

Denver Attorney
Local lawyer directory. Area lawyer
listings in all specialities. Free!
www.LegalListings.net
Colorado

NYC Food Delivery
Order food online from
hundreds of NYC restaurants!
www.Delivery.com
New York, NY

Dallas Cowboys Tickets
Tickets To all Dallas Cowboys Games
buy online view schedules & seating
www.tadfw.com
Texas

Facial Cosmetic Surgeon
Board Certified Years of Experience
Request a Free Consultation Today
www.DrBurres.com
Los Angeles, CA

You can quickly tell that all these ads are locally targeted by the location names underneath each one. On Google — though not on most local-search PPC ads — an extra line is added to locally targeted ads showing a location name. This helps the ad in several ways:

✔ **It attracts the eye of people quickly scanning the page.** You may have heard of the "cocktail-party effect," in which you can be at a noisy party, but when someone across the room speaks your name, you instantly hear it above the hubbub. Well, this is the same concept: As searchers scan down the page, familiar words — such as their city or state — "pop out" at them.

✔ **It encourages people in the area to click.** If a user is looking for video games, and an ad from a local store pops up, the user may well click.

✔ **It discourages people who are not in the area from clicking.** A searcher looking for a shoe store in Alabama is not likely to click an ad for a store in Arkansas.

In Chapter 9, you find out how to set up an account with Google AdWords. I return to that subject here, but this time look at how to use geo-targeting for your ads. When you begin setting up an account, or creating a new keyword-targeted campaign (click the Create a New Campaign: Keyword-Targeted link), you see the Target Customers by Location choices:

✔ **Country Targeting:** You can specify the countries in which you want your ads displayed; in fact you *must* choose at the least a country, even if you don't do any further geo-targeting.

✔ **Regional and City Targeting:** Specify the regions in which you want your ads to run. This isn't available in every country — fewer than a couple of dozen at present — and the type of targeting varies between countries. In fact, most choices are broader regions, not cities. In the United States, you can target by states and by metropolitan areas; in the United Kingdom, you can target by country — England, Wales, Scotland, Northern Ireland, the Isle of Man, and the Channel Islands. In Canada, you can target by province.

✔ **Customized Location Targeting:** This form of targeting allows you to specify an address or geographic location and a radius, and Google attempts to target searchers within that circle.

Local targeting while setting up your account

In Chapter 9, you see how to set up a Google account, but I skipped over how to use local targeting. In this section, I revisit that topic and show you how you can specify, while creating your account, where your ads should run.

In the first setup screen, you have some location options (see Figure 12-2).

As you can see, you have three choices available to you at the bottom of the page: Countries (the default), Regions and Cities, and Customized. I discuss each option in turn in the following sections.

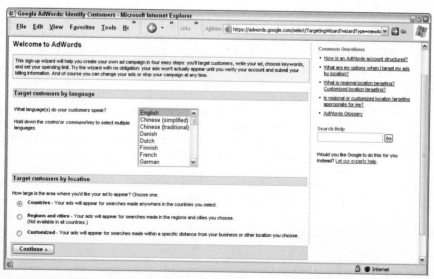

Figure 12-2:
Your first local-targeting options when setting up a Google account.

Targeting countries

Targeting countries is very quick and easy, and in fact every advertiser has to do this to some degree. Targeting by country is also very accurate. You'll get a very low rate of false locations because locating a country based on an IP number is fairly easy.

When you select the Countries option and click Continue, you see the page shown in Figure 12-3. You can click a country in which you want your ads to appear and then click the Add button to add them to the Selected Countries list.

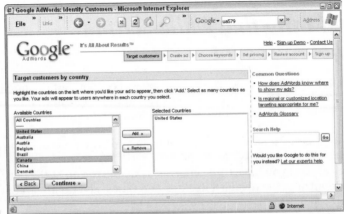

Figure 12-3: Selecting different countries.

If you want your ads to appear in two or more countries, either add each country one by one or select multiple countries at once and then click the Add button. You can select multiple countries by holding the Ctrl or Command button down while you click them.

Remember that if you select a country, the ad will be displayed to people anywhere within that country. What if, however, you want to display ads to people in one country and part of another? If you're in Seattle, Washington, and you want your ads to appear throughout northern Washington *and* southern British Columbia, in Canada, what do you do?

You use the Customized method, which I explain in the upcoming section, "Targeting by address or longitude/latitude."

Targeting regions and cities

It's important to note that with Google, if you use anything but the most basic geo-targeting — targeting by country — your ad will not be included on some significant partner sites, including AOL.com. Some advertisers create campaigns that are targeted by regions and cities, or that use customized geo-targeting, *and* create broader, country-targeted campaigns to ensure they appear on AOL.

To target particular regions and cities, select the Regions and Cities option button on the first setup page and then click Continue. You see the page shown in Figure 12-4. Unfortunately, at present, you can select regions and cities only within a single country. In order to target cities in multiple countries, you have to create separate campaigns for each country (you can, of course, add campaigns later; see Chapter 9).

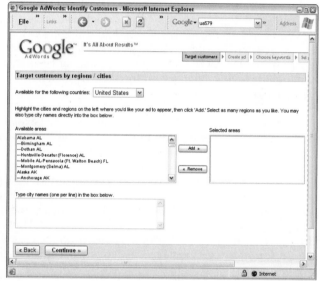

Figure 12-4: Selecting different regions and cities.

Select the country from the drop-down list box near the top, and the contents of the Available Areas box change. Click a region in which you want to advertise and then click Add.

Again, if you want to select multiple cities or regions, you can press the Ctrl or Command key and click on each one before clicking the Add button.

You can also type city names into the text box near the bottom of the page. However, note that Google doesn't accept all city names; it accepts Denver, Colorado, but not Lakewood, Colorado. Also, note that it's a good idea to include a state or province name; in some cases Google does not accept the city without this additional information.

Unfortunately Google does *not* display a confirmation showing your choices. If it accepts your choices, or the cities you typed into the text box at the bottom, after you click Continue, you simply end up in the Create an Ad page.

If it doesn't like something you did, such as typing a city name it doesn't recognize, Google displays the Target Customers by Regions/Cities page again, with an error message at the top of the page.

Targeting by address or longitude/latitude

Google provides three more ways to specify a geographical location. You can provide a street address, which is an easy way to geo-target for many businesses — simply enter your business address. You can also provide a latitude or longitude specifying a location. Finally, you can provide a variety of coordinates to map out an irregular shape.

In effect, what you are doing here is providing Google with a very specific area in which you want to run your ads. Each time someone searches for keywords that match your ad, Google uses the searcher's IP number to figure out, as closely as possible, where that person is, then converts that location to latitude and longitude coordinates, and then sees if the coordinates lie within the area you specified. If it does, your ad is displayed.

Remember, of course, that this isn't incredibly accurate. As I explain earlier, in some cases Google may be off by hundreds, if not thousands, of miles. But even when Google's guess is close, as it usually is, it still may be off enough to place someone you want to get to outside your region, and someone who you don't care about inside. In some cases, Google can have a good guess at what city the searcher is in; in other cases it may figure out the zip code. But the actual searcher's location could be just over the border in the next city, or outside the city limits, or perhaps in an adjacent zip code. Thus, really tight targeting generally doesn't work. Don't bother trying to create a one-mile-radius circle, for instance. Google *will* accept such a small region, but it won't work well for you.

When you select Customized on the first setup page and then click Continue, you see the page shown in Figure 12-5. Your first choice, of course, is to decide whether to specify an address or coordinates. In the illustration, I clicked Use a Physical Address, and Google added the address fields to the page. I then just enter my business address.

You must also select a distance in the Define the Distance text box. The address specifies the center of a circle, while the distance defines the radius of a circle around that point. If you enter, for instance, **50**, Google does its best to display the ad to people within 50 miles of your location in any direction — throughout a circle 100 miles wide.

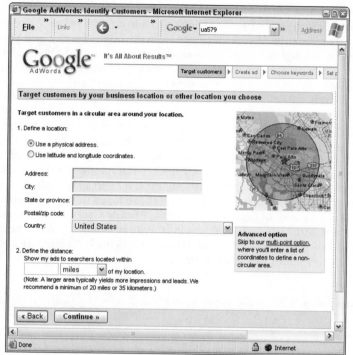

Figure 12-5:
Defining a
circle
around an
address.

How wide should you make this circle?

- ✔ **The smaller the circle, the less accurate the geo-targeting.** Quite frankly, it's *very* hard for anyone to define a location based on IP number down to, say, a five-mile radius. Even a 10- or 20-mile radius is tough. Google recommends a radius of at least 20 miles.

- ✔ **The smaller the circle, the fewer the clicks.**

- ✔ **If you use too small of a radius, you'll miss some people who are actually within the area you are trying to target.** Because of the innate inaccuracy of IP locating, Google will not show the ad to people who it *thinks* are outside the radius but are actually within it.

You can experiment with this radius size later, so go ahead and make it as large as seems reasonable. You can still use terms in your ad to discourage people on the outer edges of the radius from clicking if they really aren't close to you.

Specifying the center and radius of a circle isn't the only way to create a geo-targeting location. Perhaps you can't provide an address at the center of the circle. For instance, if your business is on the edge of a city, and you want to advertise throughout that city, you want your business to be on the edge, not in the center, of the circle. In this case, you can define a point on the map by using latitude and longitude coordinates. Click the Use Latitude and Longitude Coordinates option button, and you'll see the page shown in Figure 12-6.

Of course, the question you're thinking right now is, 'Where the heck do I get coordinates from?' It's really not that difficult. You simply need a map that provides latitude and longitude. Now, most city maps, the typical "A to Z" type maps, *don't* provide this information. But hiking-type maps *do* provide this information, as do atlases (though you'll need to find an atlas with enough detail, of course). You can find these maps in many bookstores and hiking stores and, of course, your public library. Generally *topographic* maps and maps with *GPS grids* have the information you need. You'll need a map that can provide all three coordinate numbers for both latitude and longitude: degrees, minutes, and seconds.

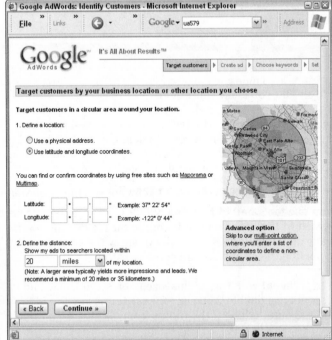

Figure 12-6:
Defining a circle around coordinates.

You can also find maps with this information online. The most popular mapping systems — Google Maps, Yahoo! Maps, and MapQuest — do *not* provide this information, but sites such as Multimap.com can help you find exact coordinates. (Google also recommends Maporama.com, but this service currently provides degrees and minutes but not seconds.) If you're using Multimap.com's system, simply center your area in the map, as Multimap.com always shows you the coordinates of the center of the map. Wherever you go to get your coordinates, you should end up with coordinates that look something like this:

```
Lat: 39:43:58N (39.7326) Lon: 104:58:56W (-104.9822)
```

For instance, the Latitude number above is 39:43:58N, which means 39 degrees, 43 minutes, and 58 seconds north of the equator. The Longitude is 104:58:56W, which means 104 degrees, 58 minutes, and 56 seconds west of the prime meridian, which runs through Greenwich, England. (The other numbers, in parentheses, are *decimal degrees,* simply another way to measure coordinates; you can ignore these. Google requires the more traditional DMS — degrees, minutes, and seconds — coordinates.)

By the way, a degree of latitude is around 69 miles; a minute of latitude is, therefore, about 1.15 miles, and a second of latitude is 101 feet. As for longitude, it depends on where you are because the distance between lines of longitude shrinks as you move toward the poles. At 38 degrees north (which runs through Northern California, a little north of San Francisco), a degree of longitude is 54.6 miles, one minute is about 0.91 miles, and one second is 80 feet.

Creating strange shapes

If you want to get really fancy, you can create different shapes, both regular and irregular, instead of a circle to indicate your search area. For example, if your business sits close to Navy Pier in Chicago, a city that stretches north and south on the west banks of Lake Michigan, you may well want your area to encompass a rectangular region running north and south, but extending west a shorter distance. You can, if you wish, provide coordinates for the corners of your rectangle.

To create a shape other than a circle, click the Multi-point Option link on the page shown in Figure 12-5 (it's in the Advanced Option box), and you'll see the page shown in Figure 12-7. It's really quite simple to specify the region you want covered. Using a paper or online map, find the coordinates of the corners of the shape you want to create and then enter them into the large text box in this format:

```
39* 43' 58",-104* 58' 56"
```

Press Enter after each pair of coordinates; each corner point should appear on its own line.

Keep these tips in mind as you enter your coordinates:

- ✔ **Enter the latitude first, then the longitude.**

- ✔ **Don't separate numbers with colons; rather, use the * (asterisk), ', and " to denote degrees, minutes, and seconds, respectively.**

- ✔ **Separate the latitude and longitude coordinates with a comma.**

- ✔ **Do not use cardinal directions (N, S, W, and E).** Rather, use the minus sign (–) to denote latitudes south of the equator or longitudes west of the Greenwich meridian. In the example above, -104* means 104 degrees west of Greenwich.

- ✔ **Enter points in order.** Google runs a line from the first point to the second, the second to the third, and so on, in order to create the shape, so the last point you enter will be joined to the first.

When you click Continue in any of these geo-targeting pages, Google checks for errors in what you have entered and then, if all is okay, drops you into the Create an Ad page, so you can continue with the normal account sign-up process; see Chapter 9 for the details.

Figure 12-7:
Creating a noncircular region.

Using geo-targeting in the Google management console

You can, of course, add and modify local-targeted campaigns while working within the Google account-management console. Local targeting is applied to an entire campaign, not to an ad group or a particular keyword, so you'll create and edit local-targeted campaigns from the Campaign page.

✔ **To edit an existing campaign,** adding or modifying local targeting, select the check box next to the campaign name and click the Edit Settings button. On the Edit Campaign Settings page, click the Edit button in the Location box. A wizard leads you through the process.

✔ **To create a new local-targeted campaign,** click the Keyword-Targeted or Site-Targeted link.

You can local-target either kind of campaign. I talk about keyword-targeted campaigns in Chapter 9, and you find out about site-targeted campaigns in Chapter 13.

Using Yahoo! Local Advertising

Yahoo! provides a couple of ways to target ads locally:

✔ **Local Sponsored Search:** This is simply localized PPC, which you find out about in this section.

✔ **Local Listing:** This is a way to enter your business into the Yahoo! Local Search (for free or for $9.95 per month with enhanced features). I don't cover this because it's not a PPC advertising service. But it's worth checking out if you have a local business (see `http://search marketing.yahoo.com/local/`).

There's an important difference between the Yahoo! and Google systems. Yahoo! provides an intermediate step between the ad and the advertiser's Web site, a "locator page." You can see this in action in Figures 12-8 and 12-9. In Figure 12-8, you see some search results. Notice that the first two PPC ads have the words *Local Info* after their URLs. This indicates, of course, that these are Local Advertising (geo-targeted) ads.

If you click the second ad, you see the *locator page,* shown in Figure 12-9. The locator page is placed inside a horizontal frame in the Web browser, and below, in another frame, is the actual Web site (assuming the advertiser *has* a Web site; this system is design to allow businesses without Web sites to advertise through Yahoo!'s PPC system).

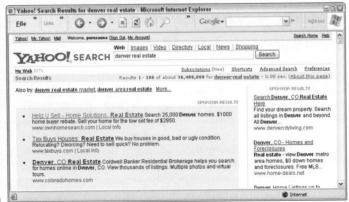

Figure 12-8:
Yahoo!'s
Local
Advertising
ads contain
the words
Local Info
after the
URL.

The locator page includes an address, phone number, e-mail address (if applicable), description, and map. Under the Business Info tab, the advertiser may have entered more information, such as the business's hours and the types of payments accepted. The searcher can print the page (you'll notice the little Print This Page link and icon in the upper right) and close the locator frame if he wishes and remain on the advertiser's Web site by clicking the little Close link.

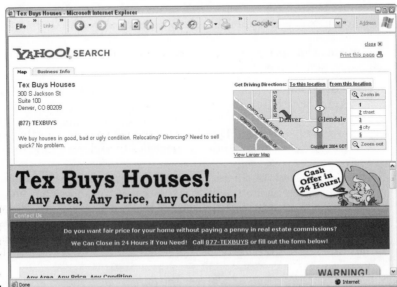

Figure 12-9:
A PPC ad's
locator
page.

Note also, by the way, that Yahoo! provides geo-targeting at a level lower than merely country targeting only within the United States, at least at the time of writing. In other words, no city or regional targeting in countries other than the United States.

Setting up Local Advertising

Unlike Google, Yahoo! treats Local Advertising as a separate product. You can't set up local targeting during your initial sign-up process if you choose the regular Sponsored Search program; you must select the Local Advertising option. (Here's the direct link: http://SearchMarketing.Yahoo.com/local/ls.php.) Yahoo! regards the two things as totally separate, so you can't, for instance, change a Sponsored Search ad to a Local Advertising ad later.

As with Sponsored Search, Yahoo! has a Fast Track service that, for $99, helps you set up your account. The Fast Track service will

✔ Set up the software for you.

✔ Turn on your account more quickly — three business days instead of five.

✔ Determine an area for your geo-targeting.

✔ Write your ads and business description.

✔ Recommend a budget for your campaign.

✔ Provide a proposal document showing an estimate of clicks and prices, keywords, bid amounts, and the recommended ads.

To begin setting up your account with the Self Serve option, click the SIGN UP button at the bottom of the Self Serve column. The first step is to provide a username and password, and you'll then enter the setup wizard.

In Figure 12-10, you can see the first step in the process, in which you begin by entering business information:

1. **Enter your business address.**

   Note that the address is required, although you can click the Do Not Display My Business Address check box to exclude it from the locator page.

2. **Click the Confirm Map link.**

   Yahoo! opens a secondary window with, if you're lucky, a map showing the address you entered (see Figure 12-11). However, sometimes this map does not appear; you may have to try refreshing the browser window (in Internet Explorer, press F5 or right-click and select Refresh).

3. **Check your position on the map carefully.**

   Does the red arrow really point to your location? Zoom in closely to make sure it's on the exact spot. Note that even if Yahoo! Maps can find your position accurately doesn't mean that this system will find you. In recent tests, this system was shown to be pretty inaccurate, though maybe Yahoo! will have gotten the bugs out by the time you read this.

4. **If the arrow is not in the correct position, click on the correct position.**

   You may have to zoom out first if Yahoo! is way off target, as it sometimes is. Then zoom all the way in, to the closest position, and if necessary click again on the position to get it "spot on." You may have to zoom in and out a few times to get this right. (Zoom too far in, and your position may not be visible.) You can also move the map by clicking near an edge; Yahoo! redraws the map with the position on which you clicked in the center of the map.

5. **When you have the right position, switch to the zoom level with which you want your map displayed in your locator page.**

   You can use the top position or the position one zoom level down.

6. **Click the Save button to close the window.**

7. **Back in the main window (Figure 12-10), select a Business Type from the drop-down list box.**

8. **Type your business name into the Business Name text box, up to 50 characters.**

   When you do that, Yahoo! changes the Title field, turning it into a drop-down list box containing both the business name you just entered and another entry — the city name appended to the business name.

9. **From the Title drop-down list box, select the title you want to use for your PPC ad.**

10. **Enter the URL of the ad's landing page.**

11. **Type the ad Description, up to 190 characters.**

12. **From the Target Listings to Customers drop-down list box, select the radius of the circle around your business location in which you want to advertise your business.**

    You can select a radius as small as 0.5 miles, though it won't do you much good. As explained earlier in this chapter, because of the inaccuracy of IP targeting, small regions are not going to perform well.

    Remember, the smaller the circle, the fewer clicks you'll get, and the more local clicks you'll miss. The larger the circle, the more clicks you'll get overall, and the more non-local clicks you'll get.

13. **When you've entered all the information, click the Preview Locator Page button.**

    Yahoo! opens a new window, showing you what your locator page will look like (see Figure 12-12). Close the window when you have finished with it.

You can add another business location, if you wish, which will be displayed under the Additional Locations tab in the final ad.

14. **Click the Add Another Listing button at the bottom of the Location Information page and repeat Steps 1 to 13 for the new location.**

    Don't click this button just to explore! If you get into another listing page, Yahoo! won't let you out until you really do add another listing.

15. **When you are ready to continue to the next step, click the Continue button.**

    You find yourself at the Select Your Keywords page that I show you in Chapter 8, back in the regular Sponsored Search account setup.

Setting up Sponsored Search

See Chapter 8 for more information on setting up Sponsored Search; it's much the same process as the rest of the Local Advertising setup process. There are a few differences, of course; when setting up Local Advertising you have to "represent and warrant" that the keywords you are going to use "accurately describe the goods or services offered at each of my store locations or service areas," for instance. And, of course, you've already set up your ads, so that step is omitted.

Working with MSN Location Targeting

MSN also allows geo-targeting; you can target particular countries, regions, or cities. In Figure 12-13 you can see the components used to select the location in which you want the ads to run; in this case, you can select the cities.

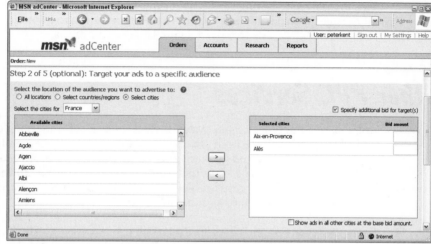

Figure 12-13: MSN allows you to target by country, region, and, in this case, city.

At present you can only select cities within one country; if you want multiple countries, you have to create separate ad campaigns. As you can see, you select a country from the Select the Cities For drop-down list box, then click on the cities in which you want the ads to run; press the Ctrl or Command key to select multiple cities, or press the Shift key and the first and last cities in a range that you want to select. Then click the > button to add the selected cities to the Selected Cities box.

MSN actually allows several types of targeting.

✔ You can specify where you want to run your ads (what countries, regions, or cities).

✔ You can specify where you want to run your ads, and specify different bids for different areas — click the Specify Additional Bid for Target(s) check box to do this.

✔ You can run ads in all areas, but specify bids for specific locations and then use the base bid for all other locations — to do this click the Specify Additional Bid for Target(s) check box and then click the Show Ads in All Other Cities at the Base Bid Amount check box.

Don't Forget the Yellow Pages

We'll be looking at the Yellow Pages, among other forms of PPC, in Chapter 14. But for now, you should know that the Yellow Pages present a geo-targeting opportunity in a way that normal search engines cannot. Why? Because what do you do when you use a Yellow Pages search system? You tell the search system where you to search! You typically provide a zip code, or a city and state.

This makes geo-targeting *very* easy for the Yellow Page companies. SuperPages.com, for instance, can use this information to allow advertisers to target their PPC ads to a particular city, zip code, or state.

Other PPC Services

Don't expect the types of geo-targeting features you get from Google, Yahoo!, and MSN to be available from other PPC services. Most of the smaller PPC systems either provide no geo-targeting or provide rather basic geo-targeting tools. The smaller PPC systems have fewer resources to apply to this whole (complicated and expensive) geo-targeting thing, and so you may find that their services are not quite as sophisticated.

Kanoodle (www.kanoodle.com), for instance, has a service called LocalTarget that does geo-targeting using the second method I mentioned earlier in the chapter: It places ads on Web sites it knows to be local. Kanoodle built a network of local sites and uses it to allow customers to target specific sites. Quigo (see Chapter 13) does something similar; you can use the system to place ads on newspaper sites in particular regions, for instance.

More common is the most basic geo-targeting: country and regional targeting. myGeek, for instance, allows you to select different regions: North America (the United States and Canada), Central and South America (does that include Mexico?), Western Europe, Eastern Europe, Australia, Asia, Africa, Pacific Rim, and the Middle East.

Also, note that some systems may partner with Yellow Pages sites, such as SuperPages, and use Yellow Pages ads as local ads; I discuss Yellow Pages systems in Chapter 14.

Chapter 13

Working with Content or Contextual Placement

I mention *content* or *contextual* placement of ads a number of times in this book, mostly telling you not to use it! Certainly, advertisers in the PPC field widely believe that such ad placement is not as productive as placing ads in search results and is also often open to click fraud (as I explain in Chapter 17).

But that's not to say you *shouldn't* use content placement; it just means you should use it with care. Even if, overall, it is less productive than search-result placement, that doesn't mean it is not still profitable in some cases. You may want to postpone using content placement until you are comfortable working with search-result placement, but you may want to use it at some point nonetheless.

What Is Content Placement?

PPC as a business began with search-engine placement; ads are placed on search-results pages after someone searches, based on the keywords the person entered into the search engine.

But you can also place ads on Web pages that are *content* pages, pages that are not search-results pages. In this context, in fact, the term *content page* pretty much means "any page that doesn't contain search results."

How does a PPC system decide what ads go onto what page? There are a couple of different ways:

- ✔ Contextual placement
- ✔ Selective placement

Because no search keywords are involved, the ads are placed onto the page depending on the *context* of the page — which is why these ads are often called *contextual.* That is, the ad is chosen depending on what the PPC system finds on the page. In other words, the PC system reads the page, figures out what the page is about predominantly, and then places ads on the page that match this subject. In Figure 13-1, you can see an example of contextually placed ads; these are placed by Google AdWords' distribution service, Google AdSense.

Ads can be placed onto a page in another way: An advertiser can choose the type of sites, or even the specific sites, that should carry the ads. For instance, an advertiser might say, "Place this ad on sports pages on a newspaper's Web site," or even, "Place this ad on sports pages in newspapers in Colorado." In Figure 13-2, you can see an example of this; these are ads placed onto the Denver Post Sports Page, delivered through the Quigo advertising system, and placed by choice, not by keyword context (Quigo calls this its *PageMatch* service). Notice that none of these ads are related to sports — they are ads for mortgages, DSL service, and a "people finder" service. One ad has made an attempt at relevance — "Sports Fans! Stanford Funding is your source . . ." — but it's not really relevant, is it? Another mortgage company, in an ad not shown here, did something similar: "Hey, Denver fans!!!!! We are Colorado's Wholesale Lender!" The advertisers know that their ads will run on the sports page, but still, the ads are not related to sports in any way. (Note, by the way, that Quigo also allows advertisers to use automatic, keyword-based ad placement, using its *Contextual Placement* service.)

Figure 13-1:
Ads placed
by Google,
dependent
on the
context of
the words in
the page.

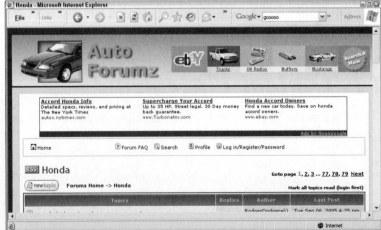

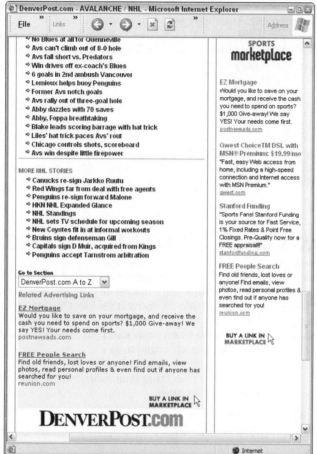

Figure 13-2:
Ads placed by Quigo, onto the Denver Post Web site.

You can think of different levels of relevance, then, with content placement:

- ✔ **An ad is placed automatically by the PPC service, based on keywords in the page.** An attempt is made to make the ads relevant to the page, with varying degrees of success.

- ✔ **An ad is placed on a page, with some degree of relevance.** An ad for climbing gear might be placed onto a site related to rock climbing. Google provides a service called *site targeting* that allows you to do this, for example.

- ✔ **A totally irrelevant ad is placed, by choice, on a page.** For instance, a mortgage lender places an ad on the local newspaper's Web site, trying to reach residents of the city without regard to what subject area the page falls under. (Such ads have *extremely* low conversion rates, by the way.)

Actually I have noticed yet another form of content-ad placement recently, *post-search* placement. The only company I know of doing this is AlmondNet (www.almondnet.com), and although this is a relatively little-known company, it has at least one large partner; at the time of writing, Wiley Publishing, the publisher of the very tome you hold in your hands, is running AlmondNet ads on the Dummies.com site.

It works like this. When someone searches on an AlmondNet partner site, a cookie is placed on the searcher's computer, with information about what he searched for. Later, when viewing a content page that carries AlmondNet ads, the searcher will see adds related to his earlier search; the ads, in fact, may have nothing whatsoever to do with the content of the page, but are related to what AlmondNet knows the person was interested in earlier.

The Problems with Content Placement

Again, I want to stress that I'm definitely *not* saying that you should never use content-placement ads. They can work very well in some situations. But such placement has a number of problems. Industry-wide, the advice you'll hear is this: "Content placement doesn't work as well as search-result placement." So the first reason to beware is that vast combined experience says there's a problem. But here are a few specific problems:

- Searchers are in a state of mind that is more receptive to advertising than people reading content sites.
- Content ads are often not well-matched.
- Click fraud is more prevalent for content ads.
- Your ad may appear where you don't want it to.

Searchers are more receptive

One major problem is that the viewer of the ad on a content page is in a different state of mind, a less receptive state of mind. When someone uses a search engine, you can be *very* sure of one thing: That person is searching for something (and your product or service may fit the bill perfectly). On the other hand, when someone reads an article on a Web site, he may have no desire to go further than the information he is currently reading. When someone uses a search engine, there's a very good chance he's looking for product information (research shows that product research is a very common use of search engines). When someone reads an article on a Web site, he or she may have no interest in purchasing anything. The searcher is a great prospect; the reader is merely a tangential prospect.

But, you might be thinking, isn't using content-placement ads very similar to placing ads in newspapers and magazines? And if that works, why shouldn't this? To that I respond that placing ads in newspapers and magazines often *doesn't* work. The psychology of advertising is a fascinating subject, but one thing you can be pretty sure of is that, to paraphrase 19th-century merchant John Wanamaker, *half the money spent on advertising is wasted.* (That may be an underestimate.)

Generating results from print advertising is very expensive, often too expensive for any company that has to show a direct result between ads and sales, and indeed this is a real problem in the print world. How do you ensure that people reading an article read the ads? (Though, in many cases, print materials are purchased *for* the ads; many people buy the Sunday newspapers to peruse the classifieds, for instance.) In any case, what's important is the comparison between content placement and search-result placement, not with other forms of advertising. Search-results PPC is an unusually effective form of advertising because it reaches people when they are seeking something.

It's hard to match ads with content

Another problem with content placement is that ads are often badly matched to content sites. Remember the three placement techniques I discussed earlier? Forget intentionally placing irrelevant ads onto content pages; this is so ineffective that it's not even worth discussing. But consider the other two methods: automatic, keyword-based choices and "manual choices."

Automatic ad placement in content pages doesn't work as well as automatic placement in search-results pages. When ads are placed on search-results pages, the choice is based on exactly what the searcher types into the search box, generally one to four words. It's relatively easy to match those keywords with the keywords advertisers have associated with their ads. It's *much* harder to examine, for example, an article in a Web page and say "this page is about subject *x*" and then find matching ads. Consequently, PPC systems often don't do as good of a job matching ads to pages.

Here's an example. I read a message in TravelForumz.com from someone who would be spending four hours in Madrid between flights and wanted to know what he could do during that time. Google placed several ads related to Madrid, but none were relevant; one was about finding an apartment in Madrid, and three were about planning trips to Madrid (he already has a trip planned). So I jumped over to do a search on *Madrid sightseeing* at Google. This time, out of six ads, five were relevant. So you can see that it's much more difficult to figure out what a page is really about than it is to figure out what a searcher wants.

As for the final method of matching — manually choosing sites on which to place relevant ads — the degree of success depends on how much effort you put into making your choices and the degree of control the PPC system gives you. Can you, for instance, choose to place ads on "Outdoor Recreation" sites, or do you get finer targeting choices, such as "Rock Climbing" sites and "Kayaking" sites. The greater the degree of "granularity" in your choices, the better your chances of success.

Beware click fraud!

Another huge problem for content-placement ads is the prevalence of click fraud. This is a problem in particular for Google AdWords (though probably also, soon, for Yahoo!'s PPC system, too). I cover click fraud in detail in Chapter 17, but for the moment let me just explain the two basic reasons why people engage in click fraud:

- **To drive up a competitor's ad costs:** That's most easily done through search-engine result pages.

- **To make money:** The crook places PPC ads on his site, such as ads from AdSense or the Yahoo! Publisher Network (see Chapter 18). This wicked person then clicks those ads — the advertiser gets charged by Google or Yahoo!, and the fraudster takes his cut.

So content-placement is a big target for fraud, in particular for high-click-price keywords. As you find out in Chapter 17, click fraud is *very* common. Fraudulent clicks are, of course, nonproductive clicks, forcing your costs up and your return on investment (ROI) down.

It's difficult to control where your ad appears

The final problem with content placement: Content ads are often placed on sites that you might prefer they not be placed on. For instance, ads are often placed on sites that distribute spyware. One second-tier PPC system (Miva) carefully checks its content partners to see whether they distribute spyware and drops them if they do. In mid-2005, in the 10-Q corporate report, Miva stated that dropping the spyware sites had already cost the company 5 percent of its revenues and that the percentage "would be higher" once it finishes dumping the spyware site.

But other PPC systems have not been so careful about the spyware problem, including, perhaps, the major systems. If you're interested, do a little search at some of the sites mentioned in Chapter 20 for *ppc spyware*.

In some cases, your ads may appear on sites that you don't want to be associated with for other reasons. For instance, a number of companies and organizations were very upset to find their ads running on a virulently racist white-supremacy Web site. Kraft didn't like it; nor did Wal-Mart, Amazon.com, Jennie-O, or Bass Pro Shops — or the NAACP!

Some PPC systems provide tools that you can use to block particular sites and allow you to choose where your ads may be placed. But on any large network, it's next to impossible to make sure your ads appear only where you would be happy to find them.

Using Content Placement Despite the Problems

Okay, having said all that, there still is a reason to work with a PPC service's content network: If you can make money on search results, maybe you can make money on the content network.

Most of these problems reduce click-through and, perhaps, conversions from the click-throughs — less-receptive viewers and poor ad matching lead to fewer clicks, and click fraud leads to more clicks but fewer conversions. So your click costs can be higher and conversions lower, with the end result that your ROI is lower. But that doesn't necessarily mean that the ROI is too low to be profitable.

It's just a numbers game. There's an ROI line below which you can't go, and where that line sits depends on many factors. For some businesses, the ROI line will definitely be crossed by using the content network — it just won't work. For other businesses, it may still be viable.

Working with Google's Content Network

In Chapter 9, I leave the discussion of Google's *content network* up in the air, and I pick up that discussion here. The ads you create on Google AdWords can run on the *search network,* the *content network,* or both networks. Where do content-network ads run? Google AdWords run on major content sites, such as About.com and Lycos, The New York Times and the Miami Herald, Business.com and iVillage, The Weather Channel and HowStuffWorks, Food.com and HGTV.com, and many others.

They can also be placed in e-mail newsletters and even in e-mail messages themselves. If you have a Google e-mail account (Gmail: www.gmail.com), you'll find ads placed into the e-mail messages you have received (see Figure 13-3).

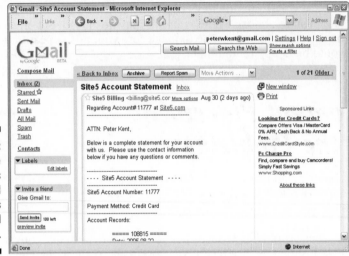

Figure 13-3: Google AdWords ads placed into e-mails in the Gmail system.

Furthermore, Google has what it calls its *AdSense* program (see Chapter 18). This allows just about any Web publisher to sign up to run Google AdWords ads. Certainly there are standards, but many, many sites have signed up and run AdWords. So AdWords are running on thousands of different sites.

In fact, Google has long-term plans to put ads just about everywhere. Google is, contrary to popular understanding, an advertising company, not a search company. (It's now possible to buy print-magazine ads through Google.)

Configuring the content network

In Chapter 9, I have you turn off the content network. If you're interested in using Google's content network, now is the time to turn it on. Remember that you can determine which ads are placed onto the content network on a campaign basis. So on the All Campaigns screen, click the check box next to a campaign and then click the Edit Settings button. Or, within a Campaign page, click the Edit Campaign Settings link near the top of the page. Either way, the Edit Campaign Settings page appears. Follow these instructions to get your campaigns going on content sites:

1. **If you want the campaign's ads to run on the content network, make sure the content network check box is checked in the Where to Show My Ads box.**

2. **Click the Save All Changes button to save your changes.**

   Google also lets you block certain sites from running your ads (remember the white-supremacy site?).

3. **If you want to keep your ads off of certain sites, click the Tools link under the Campaign Management tab and then click the Site Exclusion link.**

   You see the page shown in Figure 13-4.

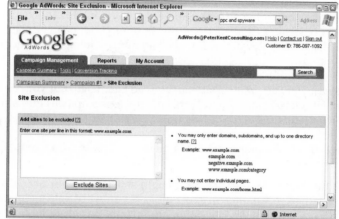

Figure 13-4:
Blocks sites from running your ads here.

4. **Simply type the domain of the sites you want to block into the text box.**

   You can type domain names in the form `www.domain.com`, `domain.com`, or `sub.domain.com`. You can also block a particular directory within a site: `domain.com/directory`.

Using site targeting

Google also provides a tool called *site targeting,* which allows you to target your ad campaign much more specifically than merely turning on the content network. You can place rock-climbing ads on rock-climbing sites, on indoor-climbing sites, on mountain-sports sites, on outdoor-activity sites, and so on.

There's more, though. Site-targeted ads run by themselves; rather than sharing an ad position with other ads, site-targeted text ads expand to take up an entire ad position (I discuss this in the "Google's different content network ad formats" section, later in this chapter). And you can run image ads, even animated image ads, in site-targeted campaigns. Finally, remember the discussion about brand advertising in Chapter 3? You may recall that I'm no great fan of the concept of brand advertising. However, you'll also recall that I *do* believe that very tightly targeted ads, placed on specific sites related to your business, *can* sometimes be of value. Google's site targeting allows you to specify particular sites, even a single site, on which you want to place an ad.

Note that Google's site-targeting is in addition to the normal keyword-based content advertising; it doesn't replace it. It's simply one more way to target ads. You can use it in addition to, or instead of, the keyword-based content network. So if you don't use site targeting, your ads can still be placed onto content sites by using the *content network* setting we just looked at.

Also note that this is *not* a PPC system; it's actually a CPM (cost per thousand impressions; remember, *M* is the Roman numeral for 1,000) system. That is, you bid a particular CPM sum, not the amount you'll pay per click. To make this totally clear, you will pay for 1,000 ad impressions, even if nobody ever clicks your ad.

By the way, you can create a site-targeted ad campaign, but you cannot change a non-site-targeted campaign (a *keyword-targeted* campaign) into a site-targeted campaign. Here, then is how to set up a new site-targeted campaign.

1. **In the All Campaigns window, click the Create New Campaign: Site-targeted link.**

2. **In the first page that appears, begin setting up your account as explained in Chapter 9. Proceed as if you were setting up a normal PPC ad, naming the campaign and group, targeting by language and location, and so on.**

3. **Follow the various steps until you get to the Target Ad page (see Figure 13-5).**

4. **If you know of a site on which you want to place ads — one that already displays Google AdWords — you can enter the domain name into the large text box.**

5. **If you know of a site similar to the type of site on which you want to place ads — even though the site you have in mind *doesn't* carry AdWords — you can enter that domain name.**

   Google examines the site you enter and tries to find matching sites in its network.

6. **You can also enter keywords in the same text box to help Google pick sites that are appropriate.**

7. **Click the Continue button.**

   Google examines your entries and then displays the page shown in Figure 13-6.

   If some of the domain names you entered are of sites that are not available, Google displays the View Unavailable Sites link.

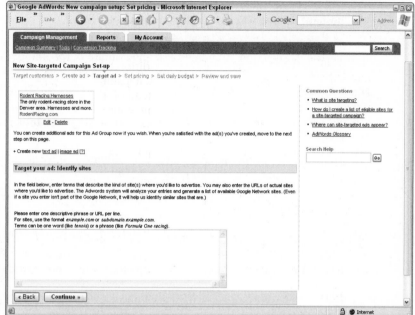

Figure 13-5:
Enter
domain
names and
keywords
here.

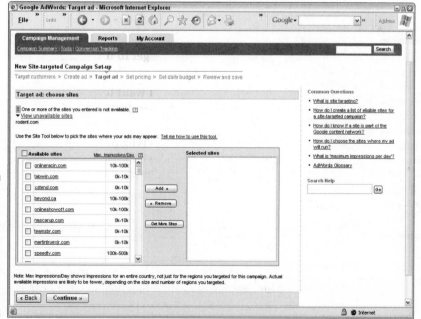

Figure 13-6:
Google
displays
appropriate
sites; select
the ones
you want to
work with.

8. **If it appears, click the View Unavailable Sites link and the unavailable domain names will be displayed under the link.**

   The Available Sites list shows sites that Google believes are appropriate. The list shows domain names and an estimate of the amount of traffic on the site — the number of page impressions every day. This is *not* how often your ad will appear, just the number of pages carrying AdWords displayed every day.

9. **To review a site, click the link, and a secondary window opens to that site.**

10. **To add a site to the Selected sites list, select a site by clicking the check box and then clicking the Add button.**

    You can also select all the entries by clicking the check box next to the Available Sites label.

11. **You can ask Google to find more matching sites by clicking the Get More Sites button.**

    It might not do so until you've placed at least one site into the Selected Sites list.

12. **When you've selected all the sites you want to use, click the Continue button, and you'll see the page shown in Figure 13-7.**

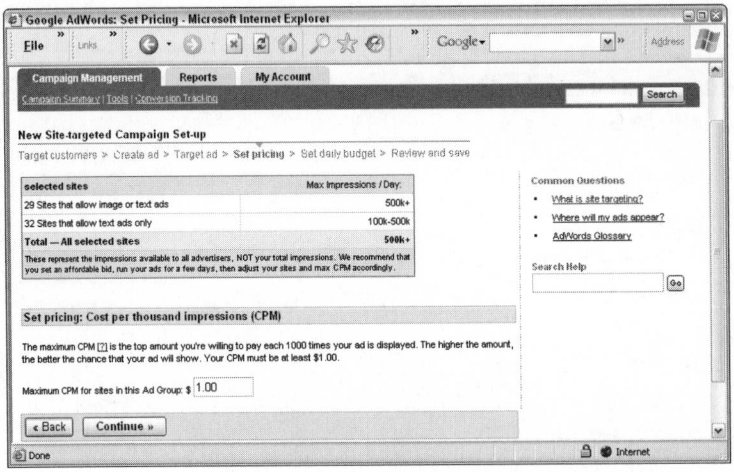

Figure 13-7:
Google shows you the number of sites it will work with and how many page impressions a day are likely.

The page in Figure 13-7 shows you the number of sites you've selected, breaking them down into sites that accept image ads and those that don't. (I discuss image ads in the next section.)

13. **Enter the Maximum CPM — cost per thousand ad impressions — that you are willing to pay to have your ads run on these sites.**

This sum must be at least $1; that is, every time your ad is displayed, you could pay at least a tenth of a cent. (As with Maximum CPC charges, the AdWords discounter ensures you pay the minimum required to maintain a position, not necessarily the maximum CPM you enter here; see Chapter 9 for information.)

Note that your ad competes not only with other site-targeted ads, but also with ads running on the normal PPC content-network model. Google calculates an "effective CPM" (eCPM) number based on cost-per-click charges under the PPC model. Thus, if the average ad is clicked upon 1 percent of the time and pays 20 cents per click, the effective CPM rate would be $2 (1 percent of 1,000 is 10, 10 times 20 cents is $2).

14. **Click the Continue button and you see the Set Your Daily Budget page.**

15. **Enter your maximum daily budget and click Continue.**

    You see the Review Your Selections page.

16. **You can now click Create Another Ad Group or Save Campaign.**

By the way, before ads appear on the content network, they have to be reviewed by Google, so there may be some delay.

Google's different content network ad formats

Google allows a number of different ad formats in site-targeted ads. The first thing to consider is that the normal text ads are displayed as *expanded text ads* when run in a site-targeting campaign, and *sometimes* when run with automatic keyword-based placement. Expanded-text ads are larger than normal, as you can see in Figure 13-8. Compare the two ads in this figure with the four normally displayed in a box of this size, as shown at the top of Figure 13-9.

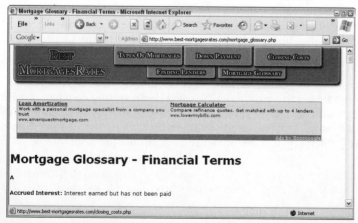

Figure 13-8: Expanded text ads take up more room than normal.

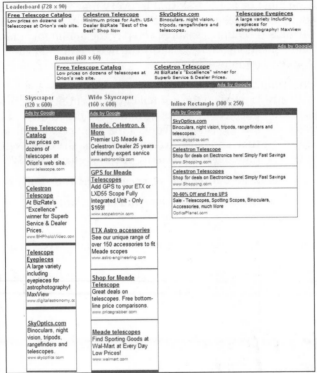

Figure 13-9:
Five of
Google's
dozen or so
ad boxes.

Google also allows you to create five different types of image ads for placement on content sites. In Figure 13-9, you can see a number of ad boxes containing text ads; there are actually around a dozen of these text-ad boxes, but the five I've shown here are the ones that can also contain images . . . as you can see in Figure 13-10.

How do you create these image ads? In the management console, in an Ad Group page, you can find a + Create New Image Ad link. Clicking this link, not surprisingly, opens a page in which you can create an image ad (see Figure 13-11), uploading your image and entering the Display and Destination URLs.

As for site-targeting, for some reason (perhaps a design bug that may be fixed by the time you read this), when you begin setting up a site-targeting ad campaign, you *have* to begin by creating a text ad. However, after you've created that first ad, you can create another, by clicking the + Create New Image Ad link (which you can see in Figure 13-5, shown previously).

Figure 13-10:
The same ad boxes shown in Figure 13-9 . . . this time carrying image ads.

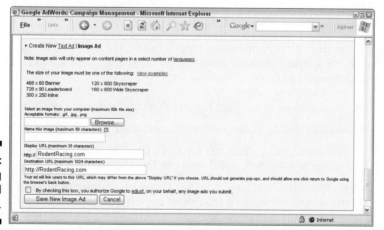

Figure 13-11:
Uploading an image ad is simple.

It's a simple matter of uploading an image by using the Select an Image text box and the Browse button. These images can be .gif, .jpg, or .png formats in any of the following sizes:

✔ Banner (468 x 60 pixels)

✔ Leaderboard (728 x 90 pixels)

✔ Inline Rectangle (300 x 250 pixels)

✔ Skyscraper (120 x 600 pixels)

✔ Wide Skyscraper (160 x 600 pixels)

Note, however, that you may want to use slightly shorter formats to allow for the resizing that Google usually carries out in order to provide space for a couple of text links (see the bottom of the images in Figure 13-10). These sizes would be:

✔ Banner: 468x49 pixels

✔ Leaderboard: 728x79 pixels

✔ Inline Rectangle: 300x239 pixels

✔ Skyscraper: 120x578 pixels

✔ Wide Skyscraper: 160x578 pixels

You also need to type a name into the Name This Image box. This is merely a descriptive name used for managing your ads. Of course, as with text ads, you also need to include the Display URL, which appears at the bottom of the image ad, and the Destination URL.

You can use up to 50 images in your account, each up to 50K each. You can even upload animated images (animated gifs), though there are some restrictions:

✔ "Strobing" or other flashing and distracting ads are prohibited.

✔ Ads containing games with prizes or other compensation aren't allowed.

✔ The animation cannot run for more than 30 seconds at a speed of 15–20 frames per second, but the ad can loop up to three times.

✔ No "trick to click" ads, ads that simulate a mouse pointer moving onto the ad and clicking, or that simulate, for instance, messages boxes in order to encourage clicks.

✔ No animations that expand beyond the ad box (though, considering you can only upload rectangular images of a specified size, I'm not sure how this could be achieved).

Google reviews all the ads and looks for ads that "contribute to a positive user experience," so Google's editors can reject ads for many reasons. There are various other guidelines for images, both animated and static, so read carefully the guidelines carefully (which you can find in the Help area; see the Help link in the top right corner of every page).

Using Yahoo!'s Content Match

There's less to say about Yahoo!'s Content Match system; it's a simpler system with fewer options. In Chapter 8, I point out that you can turn Yahoo!'s content-placement system — *Content Match* — on and off in the Account Set-Up page (click the Account tab and then the Account Set-Up option).

You can then manage your ads under the Manage Content Match tab, in the same way you learned in Chapter 8 Yahoo! manages search-placement (*Sponsored Search*) and content-placement (*Content Match*) campaigns separately, at least as far as management goes, but in the same way. Ads are all created in the same place, though — click the Manage Sponsored Search tab, then the Add Listings option.

Yahoo! currently *doesn't* provide the same sorts of tools that Google has to allow you to specify where your ads are placed; either you choose to let Yahoo! run your ads on the content network, or you don't.

Using Other Content Placement Systems

Google and Yahoo! are not the only players in content placement. I show you some of the other content-placement systems in Chapter 2, and there are more, of course. Each system is a little different, but after you understand the major players, working with the secondary content-placement firms is generally pretty straightforward.

For instance, there's Quigo (`www.adsonar.com`), which has partnerships with many well-known sites, such as Cars.com, GolfDigest.com, Discovery.com, HomeStore.com, theKnot.com, and many newspaper sites. In fact, Quigo may be the largest of the independents in this area.

Quigo provides three types of placement, which you can see in Figure 13-12:

✔ **Run of Site:** Your ad will be placed anywhere on a particular site.

✔ **PageMatch:** You specify the area of a site, or a particular page, on which you want the ads placed, such as *Good Morning America Home Page (ABC)*, *VenturaCountyStar.com Weather Main Page*, or *"eBay Search" Main Page on SuperPages.com*.

✔ **Contextual Placement:** You select a category — BMW, Honda, Cold Remedies, Optometry, Manchester United, and so on — from a very large list, and Quigo uses keyword analysis of all the pages in its network to find applicable pages for placement.

Quigo has a nice little tool that can help you narrow down contextual placement; enter a URL, of your site or someone else's, and Quigo will suggest categories that it feels match.

If you choose the category based *contextual placement,* you still get to bid on position in particular sites, as you can see in Figure 13-13. Quigo has relationships with various sites that sell their ads independently. Thus you can bid separately for position in the specified category, within, say, the Houston Chronicle, or the Boulder Daily Camera. Quigo also has another "site," the *AdSonar Network,* which essentially means "all sites." If you choose not to bid on a particular site, your ad *may* still end up on the site, through the bid you make on the AdSonar Network. But bidding for a category on a particular site gives you priority on that site, so you are likely to rank higher than ads bid through the AdSonar network.

Figure 13-12:
Quigo's system for choosing the placement of your content ads.

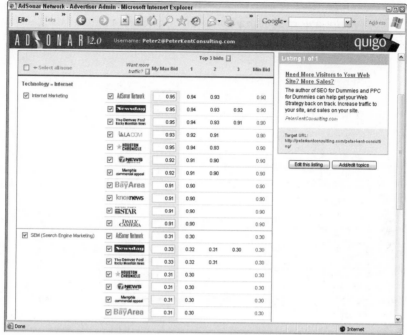

Figure 13-13:
Quigo lets
you bid on
categories,
within
particular
sites.

By the way, Quigo is similar to Google in the fact that placement of ads is
not based purely on bid price, it's also based on click-through. And you can
assign multiple ads to the same pages; when Quigo begins running your ads,
it will rotate through them equally, but as it watches your campaign it begins
dropping the ads that don't perform well.

A company called adMarketPlace (www.adMarketPlace.net) has a network
of sites on which advertisers can place PPC ads. (This is the company that
operates eBay's Keywords PPC program.) adMarketPlace allows you to place
image ads in five different, standard IAB (Interactive Advertising Bureau)
sizes, into various site categories — Travel, Health & Medicine, Religion, Small
Business, and so on. You can use your own images or lay your text over the
top of one of the available templates. This system uses a combination of categorization and keywords to target your ads to the right sites.

Vibrant Media (www.VibrantMedia.com) has three systems: *IntelliTXT*
(which underlines words, as I show you in Chapter 2); *IntelliTXT plus an
Image* (pretty much the same, but the pop-up ad can include a small image);
and *SmartAD,* a more typical content-placement system that puts image ads
onto relevant pages.

Kontera (www.Kontera.com) has a similar underlined-word system called *DynamiContext*. Kontera also provides traditional text ads placed within the page (Figure 13-14).

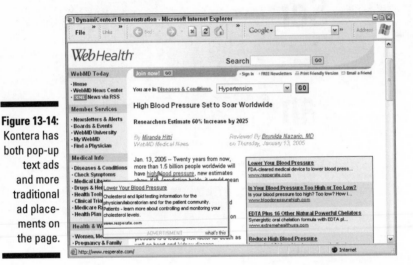

Figure 13-14: Kontera has both pop-up text ads and more traditional ad placements on the page.

Plenty more are out there. In fact, some sites sell PPC directly, rather than through a network. (You find out about building your own PPC system in Chapter 18.) One good place to look for content placement is www.payper clicksearchengines.com, which lists hundreds of PPC sites.

Chapter 14

Other PPC Services — Shopping Directories, Yellow Pages, and More

. . . .

In This Chapter

▶ Working with vertical targeting

▶ Using shopping directories

▶ Working with Pay Per Action ads

▶ Working with the Yellow Pages

▶ Using paid inclusion and trusted feeds

▶ Using Pay Per Call

. . . .

Pay Per Click is worth billions of dollars a year, and it's growing fast. Google alone currently makes around $5 billion a year from PPC ads, and its ad revenues doubled from $2.5 billion in about a year. Everyone wants a piece of the action, and those who already have a piece are looking for more.

With this much money sloshing around in the PPC bucket, and with enormous interest in this new form of advertising, it's natural that the PPC companies should be looking for different ways to sell clicks. In this chapter, I show you a few different forms of PPC advertising you may run into, or with which you may want to experiment.

Using Vertical Targeting

One trend in the business is for finer forms of targeting. You find out about *geo-targeting* in Chapter 12, and in Chapter 10 you see how MSN is introducing the ability to target, to some degree, by age and gender. There are other ways to target, too, in particular what is sometimes called *vertical* targeting — targeting more directly by subject.

For instance, imagine that you're selling cruises. You can, of course, target through the use of keywords in the major PPC systems — you can bid on keywords such as *cruise, mediterranean cruise, caribbean cruise,* and so on. But another way to target would be by advertising directly through the Yahoo! Travel site (`http://travel.yahoo.com`). Now, one way to advertise in Yahoo! Travel is simply to buy Sponsored Search ads (see Chapter 8); if you do a simple travel search on this site, Yahoo! searches its regular directory and displays normal Sponsored Search ads. But in addition, you can place ads onto the pages in the travel-research and planning areas, including Yahoo! Travel Deals and Yahoo! Travel Guides. For instance, notice the list of cruises on the right side of the page shown in Figure 14-1. These may not look like ads, but they are; they are submitted through Yahoo! Travel Submit (`http://searchmarketing.yahoo.com/trvlsb`).

These are still PPC ads, but they're *not* bid-for-placement ads. Rather, Yahoo! charges a fixed fee, depending on the category, as shown in Table 14-1.

Figure 14-1:
A Yahoo!
Travel page
showing
PPC ads in
the middle
of the page.

Table 14-1	Yahoo! Travel's Price Categories
Category	*Price Per Click*
Air	$ 0.32
Car Rental	$ 0.42
Cruises	$ 0.57
Destination > Attractions/Activities	$ 0.20
Destination > Events	$ 0.20
Lodging	$ 0.47
Rail, Ground Transport, and Ferry	$ 0.42
Vacation Packages	$ 0.57
Vacation Rentals	$ 0.57

Keep your eyes open for more of this form of vertical targeting; I'm sure it will develop further. As an example, Business.com sells PPC ads, starting at 40 cents per click, that are distributed on the Business.com, BusinessWeek, Forbes, Inc., CNet, and Internet.com Web sites.

Using the Shopping Directories

Another class of PPC advertising is known as *shopping directories* or *price comparison* services. Again, Yahoo! has one of these — Yahoo! Shopping — but a number of others are available, such as PriceGrabber, Shopping.com, and Shopzilla/BizRate.

There are two basic types of PPC shopping directories — fixed click price and bid for position. (There's one more type, the free-listing systems, of which I know of two: Froogle.com — owned by Google, of course — and PriceSCAN.)

Typically, these systems don't carry what might be thought of as *ads;* rather, they carry *product listings.* You upload, in a text file or spreadsheet, product information, such as product name, model number, brand, description, a link to an image, and so on, for all your products. The product information is displayed when someone searches or browses a category, and if someone clicks, you are charged the click fee.

Note one interesting twist to the bid-for-position model. Shopping directories typically have a sort function that allows searchers to sort search results by price and, sometimes, by other characteristics. So if you are bidding for position, the bid determines only your original position, which may be lost when the searcher re-sorts.

Here are a couple of important things to consider with these shopping directories: First, click prices are often much lower than the normal PPC systems' — clicks on the Yahoo! Shopping DVD category are 16 cents, for instance (as a comparison, I found the top bid for *buy dvd* on Yahoo! is currently $1.17). On the other hand, these systems are price-comparison systems and so can be very competitive. If you don't have very competitive pricing, you probably won't be able to make these systems work for you.

Here are a few shopping directory systems:

- ✔ **Yahoo! Shopping** (`http://shopping.yahoo.com`): Use Product Submit to place products into this system (`http://search marketing.yahoo.com/shopsb`). Fixed click rates vary from 12 cents to 80 cents per click. (And if you have a Yahoo! Merchant Solutions e-commerce system, you get a 20-percent discount off these rates.)

- ✔ **PriceGrabber** (`www.PriceGrabber.com`): This system syndicates its content widely, so signing up with PriceGrabber gets you into DogPile, Metacrawler, PricingCentral.com, and the Spanish-language version, PrecioMania.

- ✔ **Shopping.com** (`www.Shopping.com`): A popular directory (Figure 14-2) with a minimum click price dependent on category and bidding for position above that click price.

- ✔ **Shopzilla** (`www.Shopzilla.com`): This is the new name for BizRate, a company that's been around for a while. It's a bid-for-position system with a base price of 10 cents. This company distributes its ads to Lycos and Time Warner, among others.

- ✔ **NexTag** (`www.NexTag.com`): This is one of the world's largest shopping directories, and the only one I'm aware of that allows advertisers to list not only products but also services. Unlike most of these directories, which require that you upload a data file containing product information, NexTag also allows you to enter product information directly through a Web form.

- ✔ **PriceWatch** (`www.PriceWatch.com`): A very popular site with geeks, this system is a directory of mainly computer equipment, software, and electronics, with a few other categories added recently, such as books, jewelry, and watches. The people running this show are hard to communicate with, so you may have to try a few times in order to get their attention; they want companies selling boxed retail products for more than a year.

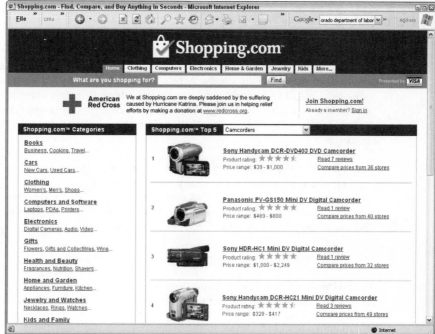

Figure 14-2:
Shopping.
com, a well-
known PPC
shopping
directory.

✔ **PriceSaving.com** (www.PriceSaving.com): Recently renamed from iBuyer.net.

✔ **InStore** (www.InStore.com): This is AOL's shopping directory. You need some clout to get in here, though some listings are fed from other systems, such as Shopzilla and SmartBargains.

✔ **MSN Shopping** (http://shopping.msn.com): This is a very exclusive shopping directory system, with only a couple hundred stores.

✔ **mySimon** (www.mySimon.com): This is owned by CNET and thus feeds results to several sites, such as Computer Shopper and CNET reviews.

✔ **Kelkoo** (www.Kelkoo.com): Owned by Yahoo!, this system runs shopping directories in ten different European countries, from Belgium to the United Kingdom.

Note that not all of these shopping directories have simple sign-up procedures like the typical PPC system. If you want to advertise on some of the preceding systems, you have to talk with the company's staff and go through an approval process first.

PPA or CPA Services

Is this the next wave in advertising, or just a niche form? PPA means *Pay Per Action,* sometimes known as CPA (*Cost Per Action*). The main player in this game is Snap.com. Snap.com combines advertising and tracking (which I talk about in Chapter 15) and then charges not for an intermediate step — a click on the ad — but for the final action: the "desired business results, including sales, downloads, leads, subscriptions, or other actions important to the advertiser."

Such a model dramatically reduces the likelihood of click fraud (see Chapter 17), so it will be attractive to many advertisers. Of course, some of the stated actions are open to fraud, too; downloads, leads, and unpaid subscriptions can all be manipulated (though with more effort than just clicking). Also, Snap.com is a small system, little known to the public.

Snap.com offers three different forms of advertising:

- ✔ **Cost-Per-Click (CPC):** Snap.com uses the original term for PPC, Cost Per Click; you pay when someone clicks your ad. The minimum bid amount is currently 5 cents.

- ✔ **Fixed-Cost-Per-Action (FCPA):** You pay a fixed sum when someone completes a particular action, such as making a purchase, registering for service, providing customer-lead information, and so on. The minimum bid amount is $1.

- ✔ **Variable-Cost-Per-Action (VCPA):** You pay a percentage of the purchase price when someone buys from you after reaching your site through Snap.com. The minimum bid amount is 5 percent.

Here's a question that may have come to you. If you only pay for an actual action that takes place, what if your Web site is badly designed and "converts" very poorly? That is, your site does a really bad job of getting people to actually carry out the action. Why would a company want to carry your ads?

It probably wouldn't. Which is why, when you sign up for a Snap.com account, you're asked for an "Estimated Conversion Rate," which will be used by the system to prioritize your ad. Snap.com then tracks your conversions and uses them to determine how well your site should rank in the search results.

Hey, Snap.com's not stupid. It doesn't want lousy Web sites that don't convert because if your site doesn't convert (when using the CPA model), then it doesn't get paid. So it's not going to continue sending you traffic if you can't convert it into sales.

Working with the Yellow Pages

The Yellow Pages (YP) companies are getting in on the PPC act. The Yellow Pages business is a tremendously profitable one — the YP companies are awash in cash. But they're worried. They can see what's going on, with billions of dollars being spent on Internet advertising, in particular with PPC. And they are beginning to hear murmurs from their traditional advertisers, comments like this one from a good friend who owns a gym:

> "I'm not renewing my Yellow Page ads . . . the business I'm getting these days is coming from people searching online, not through the Yellow Pages, so why bother?"

Hmmm, trouble afoot for the YP companies! As a reaction to these forces, the Yellow Page companies have invested hundreds of millions of dollars building their own search sites, such as Verizon's SuperPages.com, Bell South's RealPages.com, and DexMedia's DexOnline.com.

YP companies are doing a variety of things in the search arena. Not only are they running their own search sites, they are also signing distribution agreements with major search engines to contribute information to those engines' search results. In addition, they are selling PPC ads directly on their own sites (see Figure 14-3) and distributing PPC ads to the major PPC systems, including Google and Yahoo!.

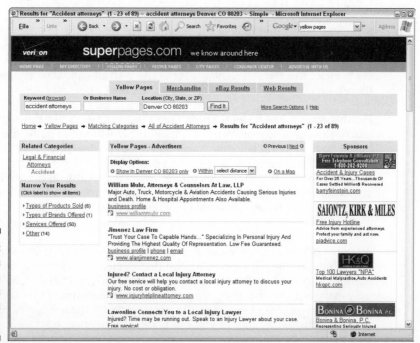

Figure 14-3: PPC ads running on Verizon's SuperPages .com site.

The easiest system to place ads into is probably SuperPages; it has a simple sign-up process that actually pulls existing business information from the directory — assuming you're in there — then lets you choose whether you want national, state, metro, or city coverage.

Using Paid Inclusion and Trusted Feeds

There are a couple more PPC systems that you may not have heard of: *paid inclusion* and *trusted feeds.* First, a couple of definitions:

- ✔ **Paid inclusion:** You pay a search engine a fee to index pages on your Web site. You then pay when someone clicks a link to your site on the search engine's search-results page.

    Currently, only one major search engine uses Paid Inclusion: Yahoo!. While earlier paid-inclusion systems did *not* charge a click fee, Yahoo! does.

- ✔ **Trusted feeds:** You upload a data file containing information about the pages on your Web site. When someone clicks a link in the search results, you're charged a fee. The only major system using trusted feeds is, again, Yahoo!

Note that these two systems are different from the PPC ads we look at elsewhere in this book. In fact, the information seen by the searcher doesn't even look like an ad; it looks like normal *organic,* or nonpaid, search results.

Search at Yahoo! and look at the results page. Ignore the PPC ads at the top and the side; instead, look at the normal, nonpaid search results. Some of these results *could be* paid-inclusion results or trusted-feed results. If you click one of these results, the owner of the Web site *might* be charged a fee; there's no way to know whether that's the case or not.

For this reason, the Federal Trade Commission doesn't like these things much, and consumer-advocate complaints have targeted paid inclusion based on the federal law that "prohibits unfair or deceptive acts or practices in or affecting commerce [such as] a representation, omission, or practice that is likely to mislead the consumer acting reasonably in the circumstances, to the consumer's detriment." Furthermore, Google's founders have stated that they do not approve of mixing paid and nonpaid results like this and say that Google will *not* use such techniques.

A couple of years ago, a few search engines used paid inclusion and trusted feeds, but currently, thanks to a great degree to industry consolidation (that is, Yahoo! gobbled up AltaVista, Inktomi, and FAST/AllTheWeb), Yahoo! is the only major system that uses either of these mechanisms. There *are* some small search engines using them, but working with these engines is unlikely to be worthwhile. In fact, as you see in the next section, paid inclusion might be worth avoiding anyway.

What is paid inclusion . . . and should you use it?

Paid inclusion — which Yahoo! refers to as *Search Submit Express* (`http://searchmarketing.yahoo.com/srchsb`) — really doesn't buy you much. You pay Yahoo! to index pages on your Web site so they will appear in Yahoo!'s search index.

The deal from Yahoo! is this: "We might come by your Web site and index your pages, but if you pay us, we'll *definitely* come by within a day or two and we'll come back every two days."

The problem is that paid inclusion is expensive: $49 for the first page, $29 each for the next nine, and $10 for every page after that. That's an annual fee; on top of that, you'll pay either 15 cents or 30 cents each time someone clicks the link in Yahoo!'s search results (depending on the category). It *might* be worth doing for some important pages, but in general, I think paid inclusion is a bad deal. If you play your cards right, you can get your site indexed by Yahoo! for free anyway, so why pay? (How do you get your site indexed by Yahoo!, you ask? Read *Search Engine Optimization For Dummies* [Wiley] to find out.) There are a number of other serious questions about paid inclusion that I don't have space for here, but do discuss them in detail in the wonderful tome (written by yours truly) just mentioned.

As you can tell, I'm no fan of paid inclusion. Trusted feeds, though . . . that's another matter.

Why are trusted feeds so trusted?

First, let me say that I'm setting aside my ethics hat and putting on my marketing hat. I still have questions about whether a search engine should mix paid and nonpaid results together in a way that is not clear to the searcher. But the fact is, this can be an effective marketing tool for Web site owners.

What's the difference between paid inclusion and trusted feed?

- ✔ With **paid inclusion,** you simply provide the URL of the page you want indexed, and the search engine goes to the site and indexes the page.
- ✔ With **trusted feeds,** you provide a data file, such as an Excel spreadsheet, containing information about the pages on your site; each entry in the data file refers to a particular page.

Providing the data in an Excel spreadsheet allows you to submit data to the search engines so they don't have to crawl to your Web site to pick it up. It also allows you to submit the relevant data, ignoring irrelevant page content — which raises the question, "Isn't this just a legal form of cloaking?" (*Cloaking* is a technique for showing a search engine a different page than the one a site visitor would actually see, and it's frowned upon by the search engines . . . unless you pay them, evidently!)

Now, the search engines have argued that paid inclusion and trusted feeds are not advertising because there's no guarantee your ad will run. (True, but that's also the case with more traditional PPC.) Your Web pages still have to compete with nonpaid, organic pages in the search engine's normal algorithm.

That's true for paid inclusion (another reason not to bother . . . what's the advantage?). With trusted feeds, it's not entirely true — and here's why trusted feeds *can* be a good marketing tool. With a trusted feed, the search engine doesn't analyze your page, it analyzes the information you provide *about* the page. And it's much easier to manipulate a few keywords to get a high ranking in the search results than it is to optimize a Web page to get a high ranking. In fact, Yahoo!'s staff (remember, Yahoo! is the only significant player with a trusted-feed program these days) will even tell you it'll help you optimize your data feed for the best results.

What does this all cost? Well, it's free to get started. Yahoo! assumes you'll be submitting a data file with information about at least 1,000 pages, and its "guidelines" suggest you should be willing to spend at least $5,000 a month on clicks, though this is more of a filter intended to remove small merchants than an actual contractual obligation. Then, each time someone clicks one of your links, you pay a fee that varies depending on category; in the jewelry category, for instance, it was (last time I looked) 28 cents per click.

By the way, if you're interested in trying the trusted feed (which Yahoo! calls *Search Submit Pro;* `http://searchmarketing.yahoo.com/srchsb`), call and talk to the Yahoo! folks nicely, and they'll probably give you a week's worth of free clicks.

Using Pay Per Call

Finally, let's take a quick look at another form of PPC: Pay Per *Call*. With Pay Per Call, rather than paying for every click to your site, you pay for a phone call. Your ad is designed to get people to pick up the phone and call you, not to visit your site, so you could run Pay Per Call ads even if you don't have a Web site. In fact, most businesses really can't use Pay Per Click. Either they simply don't have a Web site or they do have a site but it's just a primitive information-only site that would require a large investment in time and energy to make it something worth landing on. Ninety-eight percent of all businesses have never purchased Pay Per Click ads; Pay Per Call is an attempt to tap into this vast market. Remember also that a large proportion of Web searches are carried out by people searching for products locally, so if you serve a particular geographic market, Pay Per Call might make sense.

What's more valuable: a click or a call? I would have to say that a phone call is more valuable than a click. A single click has little value, which is why conversion rates are typically in the low single digits. A click is something quick and simple, something that can be done with little effort and that is easily reversed. A call, though, now that's something more. Calling a store takes a much greater commitment than a mere click. Calls are very valuable things and have *much* higher conversion rates. And incidentally, it's much easier to track conversion rates with Pay Per Call; all you need is a pencil and a piece of paper, not all the complicated stuff I show you in Chapter 15.

Not surprisingly, Pay Per Call ads begin at a much higher price; for instance, Ingenio's starting bid is $2 (you'll find out about Ingenio in a moment).

Here's an example: I searched on AOL for the term *real estate denver;* you can see the results in Figure 14-4. Notice the first result, *Brass Key Property Brokers.* A phone number is listed with a little icon. Click the link, and an information page opens (Figure 14-5); note that the advertiser is *not* charged at this point. You'll notice that there's no link to a Web site in this ad, but there is a very prominent phone number. Pick up the phone and call this number, and the call is logged and the business charged for the call. This phone number is not the business's normal phone number; it's a number set up for the purpose of the Pay Per Call campaign (the number forwards the call to any number the advertiser defines).

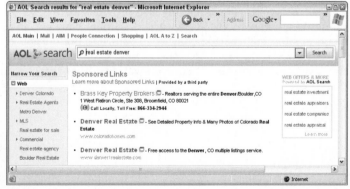

Figure 14-4:
A Pay Per
Call ad,
running on
AOL.

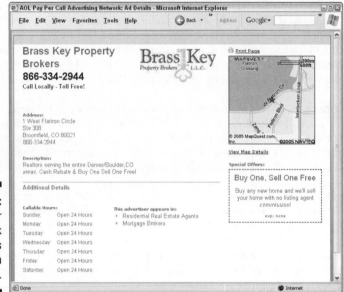

Brass Key Property Brokers
866-334-2944
Call Locally - Toll Free!

Address:
1 West Flatiron Circle
Ste 308
Broomfield, CO 80021
866-334-2944

Description:
Realtors serving the entire Denver/Boulder,CO areas. Cash Rebate & Buy One Sell One Free!

Additional Details

Callable Hours:

Sunday:	Open 24 Hours
Monday:	Open 24 Hours
Tuesday:	Open 24 Hours
Wednesday:	Open 24 Hours
Thursday:	Open 24 Hours
Friday:	Open 24 Hours
Saturday:	Open 24 Hours

This advertiser appears in:
› Residential Real Estate Agents
› Mortgage Brokers

Print Page

View Map Details

Special Offers:

Buy One, Sell One Free

Buy any new home and we'll sell your home with no listing agent commission!

exp: none

Figure 14-5: The Pay Per Call ad's link leads to this information page.

By the way, Pay Per Call services typically have a number of controls that save you money. You're charged only if the call is completed, for instance; if someone calls but hangs up before the call is answered, it's not counted. In fact, if the call *is* answered but lasts only a few seconds (10 seconds on some systems, up to 30 seconds on others), the advertiser isn't charged. And some systems don't charge for multiple calls from the same number within a particular period; if someone calls five times in one day, you're only charged once.

So, where can you buy Pay Per Call ads? One major distributor of Pay Per Call ads is Ingenio (www.ingenio.com); the AOL ad I just showed you is distributed to AOL by Ingenio. The company also provides Miva (www.Miva.com), a second-tier PPC company (see Chapter 11), with its Pay Per Call service, as well as other sites, such as go2.com, Snap.com, and BizJournals.com. There's also Jingle Networks (www.JingleNetworks.com), a service that distributes Pay Per Call ads to Free411.com and various other search systems.

Part III
Managing Your Campaign

The 5th Wave   By Rich Tennant

"Come on Walt—time to freshen the company
Web page."

In this part . . .

Here's a prescription for PPC failure: Set your campaign up, let it run, and then come back in a few weeks and see what happened.

Unfortunately, PPC campaigns need managing. If you don't keep a close eye on the ads, bad things can happen! You can pay so much for the ads that you lose money because it costs more to get a new customer than you make from that new customer; that's a *very* common problem. Or perhaps your ad positions slip down to where they're bringing in very little traffic, even if it is profitable.

Or how about this slightly more complicated situation: All your ads are profitable, but some are much more profitable than others. If you're not watching and experimenting, you won't realize that you could dump some of the less-profitable ads, drop the money into the more-profitable ones, and increase your profits for the same ad expenditure.

And let's not forget *click fraud.* The PPC equivalent of shoplifting, click fraud could easily cost you 20 percent of your ad expenditures, and in some cases has cost as much as 80 percent of a company's PPC ad dollars . . . not something to treat lightly. Click fraud can be the difference between a successful PPC campaign and a total loser, even at low levels of fraud.

So, dear reader, flip the page and read on. You've finished the first two parts of the book, but as far as your PPC campaigns go, you have only just begun.

Chapter 15

Using Click Tracking and Conversion Tracking Tools

Someone (it might have been me) once said, "Business is numbers." In order to effectively run just about any business, or any component of a business, you have to understand the numbers. *The numbers* can be summarized thusly:

✔ You need to know what "goes in."

✔ You need to know what "comes out."

At the most basic level, if what goes in is less than what comes out, you're doing well; if you spend less on the business than what the business makes, you're making, in very general terms, a profit. If more goes in than comes out, you're losing money.

These are very basic concepts, but they are often forgotten in the PPC world. It's certainly not the fault of the PPC firms: All sorts of great tools for tracking the numbers are available to you. Yet I often talk with companies engaged in PPC campaigns that really don't know the answers to these very basic questions:

✔ Are you making money from your PPC campaigns?

✔ What's your ROI (return on investment)?

✔ Which keywords work best for you?

✔ Which PPC services work best for you?

Too many PPC advertisers don't "know the numbers," which leads to a number of ill effects. They may be losing money but aren't aware of it. Or perhaps they are doing well but don't realize the opportunity they're losing if only they would invest more. Perhaps they are doing well in some ways, poorly in others, and don't realize that, with a few tweaks, they could turn a mediocre, or perhaps even failing, advertising campaign into a successful one.

This chapter is about the numbers, or rather, about how to track them. Chapter 3 *explains* the numbers; this chapter explains how to find out what they are.

Tracking the Sales Funnel from A to Z

In order to get a good picture of what's working and what isn't, you want to track from the very beginning of the process to the end and see what's in between. Here are typical steps in the sales process:

1. Someone searches on your keywords.

2. Your ad is displayed.

3. Someone clicks the ad.

4. The clicker arrives on your site.

5. The visitor moves around on your site.

6. The visitor begins a sales process — perhaps placing something into a shopping-cart system.

7. The visitor completes the sales process.

8. The visitor returns and buys again.

Note that this is a *funnel*. If you've ever worked in sales, you probably know the term *sales funnel;* the idea is that throughout the sales process, people drop out, so that each step in the process has a smaller number of people in it than the prior step and a larger number than the subsequent step.

And so it is with the funnel outlined above. Thousands of people search on keywords that match your ads. Your ad is displayed for some of these searchers (but, depending on competitors, not all). Some of the searchers click your ad. Most, but not all, of the clickers arrive at your site (for various reasons, it's never 100 percent). Some of these people leave immediately, while others move around the site. Some of those visitors who stay then begin to make a purchase, but many who start to buy don't finish, leaving a smaller number of buyers. Finally, a smaller number still comes back to buy again. For each person reaching Step 8 in the above funnel, thousands will have started at Step 1, the vast majority dropping out step-by-step.

Why do you care? You need to know more than just whether or not you're making money. The question is, *how do you reduce the number of people dropping out at each step?* This is one of the most basic concepts of e-commerce, one that most in the business don't understand. Take a second look at these steps and the questions you should ask at each step in Table 15-1. (I omit the first step because PPC systems typically tell you the number of times ads are displayed, not the number of times it could potentially have been displayed; that is, the number of times search terms were used that matched your keywords yet your ad wasn't displayed.)

Table 15-1	Understanding the Sales Funnel
Action	*Questions to Ask*
Ad is displayed.	
Searcher clicks.	Why aren't more clicking? Badly written ad? Offer not strong enough?
Clicker arrives on your site.	Why don't more arrive? Server problems? Pages not loading quickly enough?
Visitor moves around on site.	Why aren't more getting involved in the site? Poor site design? Poor marketing message?
Visitor begins sales process.	Why aren't more starting to buy? Uncompetitive pricing? Poor marketing message?
Visitor completes sales process.	Why are people dropping out of sales process? Too complicated? Shipping charges too high?
Visitor returns and buys again.	Why don't people return?

As you can see, knowing what is happening at each point is very important. It can mean the difference between success and failure.

Using the Reports

Virtually all PPC systems have reports of various kinds. The core reports, of course, show you the basics: the first few steps in the funnel (starting at Step 2 in our funnel, the number of ad *impressions*). I suggest you spend an hour or two just digging around, figuring out your options — in both Google and

Yahoo!, click the Reports tab you'll see at the top of most pages to find the reports. The major systems have reports that cut and dice the information just about any way you can imagine (see Figure 15-1): reports that show statistics for each keyword, for each ad group, for different URLs, and so on.

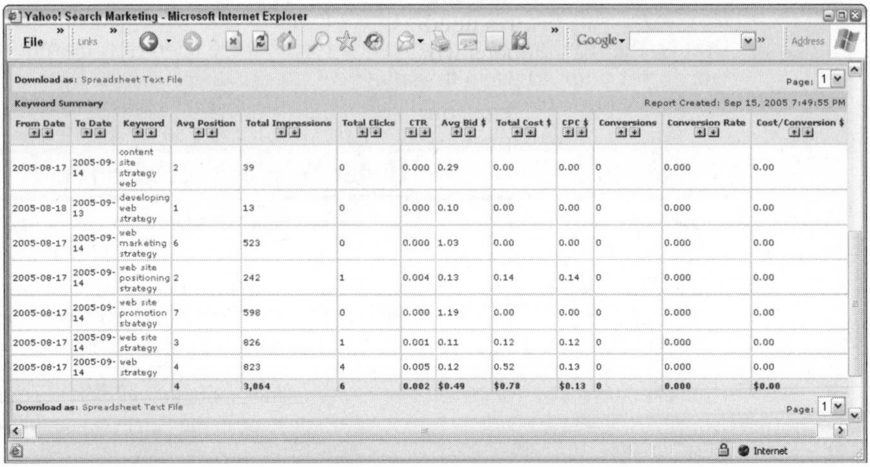

Figure 15-1:
A Yahoo!
Keyword
report.

From Date	To Date	Keyword	Avg Position	Total Impressions	Total Clicks	CTR	Avg Bid $	Total Cost $	CPC $	Conversions	Conversion Rate	Cost/Conversion $
2005-08-17	2005-09-14	content site strategy web	2	39	0	0.000	0.29	0.00	0.00	0	0.000	0.00
2005-08-18	2005-09-13	developing web strategy	1	13	0	0.000	0.10	0.00	0.00	0	0.000	0.00
2005-08-17	2005-09-14	web marketing strategy	6	523	0	0.000	1.03	0.00	0.00	0	0.000	0.00
2005-08-17	2005-09-14	web site positioning strategy	2	242	1	0.004	0.13	0.14	0.14	0	0.000	0.00
2005-08-17	2005-09-14	web site promotion strategy	7	598	0	0.000	1.19	0.00	0.00	0	0.000	0.00
2005-08-17	2005-09-14	web site strategy	3	826	1	0.001	0.11	0.12	0.12	0	0.000	0.00
2005-08-17	2005-09-14	web strategy	4	823	4	0.005	0.12	0.52	0.13	0	0.000	0.00
			4	3,064	6	0.002	$0.49	$0.78	$0.13	0	0.000	$0.00

Of course, the core information in these reports is constant. For each ad, or keyword, or category, or whatever, the reports show

- ✓ **Impressions:** How often the ads were displayed
- ✓ **Total Clicks:** How often the ads were clicked
- ✓ **CTR (click-through rate):** The percentage of ad impressions that were clicked
- ✓ **Total Cost:** The total spent for the clicks
- ✓ **Cost Per Click:** The average cost of each click

If you use some of the tracking techniques I show you in the next section, you may have some more information on your reports:

- ✓ **Total Conversions:** The total number of conversions from the clicks — the number of sales or leads, for instance
- ✓ **Conversion Rate:** The percentage of clicks that led to a conversion
- ✓ **Cost Per Conversion:** The price of those conversions

Working with Basic Tracking Techniques

The basic reports provide the information that the PPC system knows about: the processes they can measure directly, such as how often your ads appear and how often they are clicked. But in order to calculate conversion rates and costs, the reports need more information; they need, in effect, for you to tell them what happens when people arrive on your site.

The major PPC systems, and many second-tier systems, provide tracking tools. I don't have space to show you all of these tools, but they all function in similar ways, though you should note that some tools are better than others. Yahoo!, for instance, has some very basic tools available for free but charges for more advanced tools. (Note that the basic tools won't help you see every step in the funnel but still provide important information.)

Regardless of which tracking tool you use, there are two basic tracking techniques:

✔ Placing JavaScript tracking codes into your pages

✔ Placing special tags at the end of URLs

As an example, let's head to the next section and take a look at how Yahoo! manages this.

Using JavaScript tracking codes

Yahoo! has something called *Conversion Counter.* (Click the Account tab and then click the Account Set-Up option to find the page where you can set up this system — you'll find the code you need at the bottom of the page.) Yahoo! provides a simple piece of JavaScript code that you place onto your "conversion" page. If, for instance, you're selling products, you could put the code on the sales-confirmation page; if you're trying to gather leads, you could put the code on a confirmation page displayed after someone submits contact information; if you're trying to get people to call you, you could put the code on a page that displays a phone number.

This piece of code is placed onto the page — what Yahoo! terms the *transaction completion* page — between the <HEAD> and </HEAD> tags. When someone clicks a PPC ad, Yahoo! sets a cookie on the searcher's computer (a *cookie* is a little text file saved by the user's browser on the computer's hard drive). Later, when, for instance, the visitor purchases an item and completes the transaction, the page on which this script is placed loads. The script is run by the buyer's browser and sends information to the Yahoo! servers. Yahoo! knows the visitor came from the PPC ads because it can read the cookie that was set earlier. The server will know that someone who clicked a Yahoo! PPC ad arrived at your site and completed a transaction.

Note that *no* tracking is perfect. Some information will be lost. For instance, if a buyer has JavaScript turned off in his browser, then this script won't run, and the information will be lost. Or if the user's browser blocks cookies, it won't work either.

Using URL tags

Another tracking technique is to provide information to your Web server's traffic logs by adding special codes to the PPC ad's Destination URL. When you click a link in a browser, the URL in the link is passed to the Web server — that's how the server knows which page to send. So it's possible to add codes to the URLs to provide more information to the server.

Yahoo! has a system called *Easy Track* that passes information about the search term the searcher used, the keyword it was associated with to display your ad, and the match type (see Chapter 7). Not all servers can handle this information, so you need to talk to your server administrator or whoever manages your server traffic reports. But as far as Yahoo! goes, it's very easy to set up. Simply go to the Account Set-Up page, click the On option button in the Easy Track box, and click Submit. That's it, you've turned on the feature, and the PPC ad URLs will contain the extra information.

More advanced tracking

The big PPC companies have more advanced tracking tools that you can use if you're a larger advertiser or if you pay. Yahoo!, for instance, has *Marketing Console,* which starts at $149 a month. Marketing Console can actually incorporate information, such as how much each transaction is worth, into the PPC stats; in other words, you can track not merely what percentage of clicks turn into transactions, but what sort of transactions and how much each transaction is worth, allowing the tool to include an *ROAS* number: return on advertising spend. (Marketing Console also has a built-in bid-management tool, a subject I discuss in Chapter 16.)

What's the difference between ROAS and ROI? ROI takes into consideration the gross profit on your transactions. ROAS is simply a measure of the actual revenues generated by each dollar of advertising spend.

Marketing Console actually has three different JavaScript "tags" you can place into your pages (see Figure 15-2) so that the system can track much more than just conversions:

- ✔ **Universal Tag:** This is placed onto *every* page on your site, so Yahoo! knows when someone arrives on your site, regardless of which page he lands on. (This tag must be present on a page for the next two tags to function.)

- ✔ **Shopper Tag:** This is placed into Web pages that are part of your "shopping-cart" system, so you know how many visitors go to the next step and become shoppers. (If you can program your e-commerce system to drop a transaction ID into the tag, Yahoo! can even identify which click led to which transaction.)

- ✔ **Conversion Tag:** This is placed on a page that is displayed after a conversion has occurred, such as a sales-confirmation page. You can enter an average transaction value into the tag so Yahoo! can keep track of average ROAS, or even program your e-commerce system to drop the *actual* transaction value — and transaction ID — into the tags so Yahoo! can match a click with a particular transaction and the actual value of this transaction.

These tags allow Marketing Console to track more steps in the funnel. The system knows how often an ad is displayed, how often people click, how many clickers arrive on the site, how many begin a sales process, and how many complete the sales process.

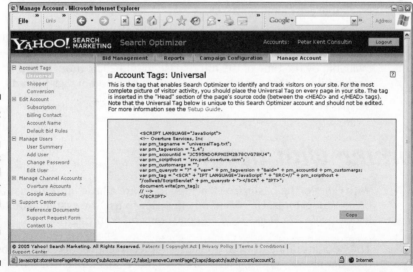

Figure 15-2:
Yahoo!
Marketing
Console's
Universal
tag, used for
tracking
traffic
through
your site.

But Marketing Console can even help with the last step in the funnel: getting buyers to return and buy again. Because Marketing Console sets a cookie on the visitor's computer (assuming cookies are turned on in the browser, which is usually the case), Yahoo! can track two more important statistics:

✔ How long it takes for the person to buy; if he goes away and comes back a month later, Yahoo! can track that

✔ If and when the person returns to buy again

By the way, Yahoo!'s Marketing Console can even incorporate data from Google PPC campaigns. You can have Google e-mail reports to a dedicated Yahoo! Marketing Console e-mail account, allowing Marketing Console to import the data into the system.

And Marketing Console can help with other campaigns. It automates the process of creating specially tagged URLs for *any* of your PPC or other advertising campaigns to allow Marketing Console to track the results of those, too. You select a *tactic:* Advertisement, Affiliate, Comparison (shopping directories, as explained in Chapter 14), Contextual, Paid Placement (PPC), and so on. Then Yahoo! displays a list of matching companies. Pick Paid Placement and you'll see 7Search, Business.com, e-Pilot, GoClick, Kanoodle, and so on. Yahoo! then provides a tracking code you can place into your Destination URLs, such as this one created for a Kanoodle campaign:

```
ovmkt=JC595NDORPNIJM1VSU5U8CTKLO
```

These codes identify where the visitor is arriving from, so Yahoo! can track what those visitors do on the site; you can even enter basic cost information so Yahoo! can calculate ROAS.

At the time of writing, MSN was still in beta testing and had no built-in tracking mechanisms available. I think you can assume that something will be available by the time of the full release in mid-2006, though, and it will be very similar to that used by Yahoo!; a combination of tags placed into the page and codes dropped into the Destination URL.

Working with Google

With Google, the basic, free tracking tools are a little more robust than the basic Yahoo! tools. Unfortunately in order to use the system, you have to put little *Google Site Stats - send feedback* tags on your pages.

The Google administration console's tables won't report conversion initially (see Chapter 9); rather, there's a Learn More link in place of the conversion data. Click this, and Google leads you into a wizard that helps you create the tags you need for your page. As with Yahoo!, Google allows you to track several different types of events:

- **Purchase/Sale:** Placed on a sales-confirmation page to track sales and ROI

- **Lead:** Placed on a confirmation page from a lead-information submission form

- **Sign-up:** Placed on a confirmation page from a sign-up-submission form (such as a newsletter sign-up)

- **Views of a key page:** Placed on any single, important page you want to track

- **Other:** Views of all other pages you want to track combined

Google also allows you to track your campaigns running through other companies' ad systems (Figure 15-3), using tracking URLs in the same way Yahoo! Marketing Console does.

Figure 15-3:
Google's Cross Channel Tracking system lets you track other, non-Google advertising campaigns.

Using Advanced Third-Party Systems

Some great third-party tools are available for tracking PPC campaigns. In fact, the major Web-traffic stats firms have incorporated lots of PPC features into their products over the last few years. There are two basic types of programs: ones you install on your own Web server, and "hosted" services that you pay for monthly and that run on the software company's servers.

These are very cool systems. Not only do they provide a wealth of information about conversions and ROI, they also show you your Web site with statistics laid on top of the pages (see Figure 15-4). So, for instance, you can see how many people click each link on a page. You can "follow" people through your site, seeing what they do, and you can even see how people coming from different sources — different PPC campaigns, for instance, act differently.

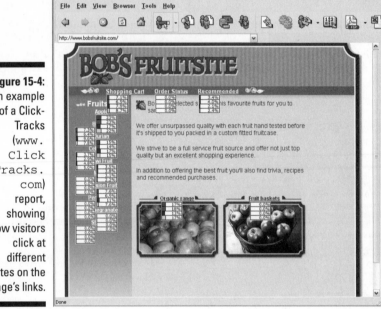

Figure 15-4: An example of a Click-Tracks (www. Click Tracks. com) report, showing how visitors click at different rates on the page's links.

Here are a few of the top traffic-report programs:

- **WebTrends:** www.WebTrends.com
- **Urchin** (owned by Google): www.Urchin.com
- **HBX Analytics:** www.WebSideStory.com
- **ClickTracks:** www.ClickTracks.com
- **Omniture:** www.Omniture.com

Urchin starts at $199 a month, or you can buy the basic software to install on your server for $895. ClickTracks' base price is $49.95 a month or $495 for the software. Of course, prices go up from there, depending on the features you want and the amount of traffic your site gets.

Chapter 16

Working with Bid-Management Tools

. . . .

In This Chapter

▶ Understanding bid management

▶ Using proprietary bid managers

▶ Working with third-party bid managers

▶ Using a bid-management firm

. . . .

*H*ere's the challenge: As your PPC campaigns grow, as you broaden your scope and start working with multiple PPC systems, and as you add more keywords to your campaigns, things get complicated. Imagine dealing with a $20,000-a-month campaign across, say, four PPC services — or six or seven — with 5,000 keywords. In effect, you're managing 20,000 keywords (or 30,000 or 35,000). How are you going to manage all that?

At the time of writing, managing two PPC campaigns — one for Yahoo! Sponsored Search and one for Google AdWords — is a very common occurrence. When MSN joins the PPC game, three PPC campaigns will be the norm, with many companies also running campaigns through systems such as ePilot, Searchfeed, Quigo, and many others. Managing all this information gets complicated.

Why Bid Management?

What's so complicated? Can't you set the campaigns up and let them run? Well, if you're asking that question, you've been skipping through this book. Certainly you haven't read Chapter 7, in which I talk about bidding.

In Chapter 7, I show you some situations in which you can get into real trouble if you just let your campaigns run themselves. I review one situation, bids for the term *vioxx attorneys,* in Table 16-1.

Table 16-1	The Difference between the Bid Price and the Click Price	
Bid Position	**Max Bid**	**Actual Paid**
#1	$40.00	$5.51
#2	$5.50	$3.51
#3	$3.50	$3.01

Imagine that's you in Position #1. You've decided that you want to dominate the #1 position, so you've bid eight times higher than #2. Then you left the campaign to run.

Now, let's say the person managing position #2 has read this book, specifically Chapter 7. He decides to test your resolve, so he bids $39.99. What effect does this have on his click price? Nothing; he still pays $3.51 per click. How about your click price? It just increased 625 percent, from $5.51 to $40 per click. Wait a few days and then come back and check your campaign. Ouch!

This is an extreme example, but an example nonetheless of the dangers of not managing your campaigns well.

Designing the Ideal PPC Manager

A number of tools, generically known as *bid-management* tools, are designed to help you manage your PPC campaigns — designed, primarily, to help you manage your bids. But before I show you these tools, imagine what the ideal tool would be. It would be more than just a bid-management tool, it would be a PPC-campaign tool. It would allow you to do these things:

- Enter your ads and keywords into a single program.
- Import ads and keywords from a spreadsheet or database.
- Sign up for PPC campaigns from within that single program.

✔ Automatically tag URLs for tracking purposes (see Chapter 15).

✔ Submit ads and keywords from the program to the PPC services.

✔ Automatically check click prices and positions every few minutes.

✔ Automatically pause your campaigns at particular times and days, such as in the evenings and on weekends.

✔ Manually review and adjust bids for all campaigns on all the PPC services.

✔ Set up "rules" for automatic bid adjustments.

✔ Hide your maximum bid from competitors — the software knows what you're really willing to pay for a click, but bids based on temporary competitive conditions.

✔ View campaign reports showing click-throughs, ROI, and so on (that is, incorporate the features I show you in Chapter 15).

✔ Make your coffee, tea, and hot chocolate, just the way you like it.

You want to be able to manage all campaigns from one place, view all the bids in one place, make all the changes in one place. Oh, and this tool should be well-designed — easy to learn and easy to use. This is the ideal. It's hard to find, but there are some tools that come close.

Your ideal tool would check prices and positions, maybe every half hour, and adjust bids according to rules you've defined, rules that tell the program what you would do in various situations if you noticed the position change yourself and changed the bid manually. For instance, you could tell the program to look for situations in which you can drop one position and save 50 percent; if it finds such a situation, it will automatically drop the bid to take the new position.

Some bid managers actually do have this sort of *rules-based bidding,* as Atlas OnePoint calls it. Atlas has around 20 different rules to play with, including the following (notice that some of these rules reflect what you discover in Chapter 7 . . . we'll look at Atlas OnePoint in more detail in a moment):

✔ **ROAS Bid Strategy:** Changes a bid based on the return on advertising spend (ROAS), allowing you to increase the bid if the return allows for a higher price or reduce it if the bid is too high.

✔ **Max Bid Gap Jammer:** Adjusts your bid to 1 cent below your next highest competitor, *jamming* him (forcing him to pay as much as he's bid).

✔ **Don't Jam Me:** Moves your bid below a competitor who is jamming you to jam him and avoid paying too much.

- ✔ **First Gap:** Bids inside the first bid gap within a specified set of positions.

- ✔ **Daily-Rank Adjustment:** Adjusts the rank based on the time of day.

- ✔ **Multiple Day – Bid Adjustment:** Adjusts the bid for two or more consecutive days.

- ✔ **Multiple Day – Rank Adjustment:** Adjusts the rank for two or more consecutive days.

- ✔ **Bidding War Eliminator:** Eliminates ratcheting up of bids due to competitive bidding by dropping out of the competition; it moves you to a specified position if the additional cost is less than or equal to an amount you enter.

- ✔ **Relative Listing:** Moves your ad above or below a specified competitor.

- ✔ **Caboose Rule:** Moves your keyword bid to the minimum allowed by the search engine and then jams the bid above.

A number of bid-management tools are available with a wide range of features and capabilities. Note, however, that to some degree, the bid managers are dependent on the system they are working with; as you've seen, Google's ranking mechanism is very different from Yahoo!'s, so there are rules that will work with Yahoo! but not with Google.

By the way, you will have noticed, in this chapter and the previous, that these reporting and bid-management tools focus on ROAS — return on advertising spend — rather than the more familiar (and more important) return on investment. ROI requires more information — ROI calculations require the gross-profit figures rather than just sales revenues — so it's easier for these systems to make ROAS calculations. Of course, at the end of the day, it's ROI that you need to calculate.

Using Proprietary Bid Managers

At the time of writing, MSN is a bit of an unknown; it's in beta testing, so it's hard to tell what tools it will provide to manage large campaigns. Google and Yahoo! will assist larger advertisers in managing their campaigns, both through the use of special tools and by providing staff to assist.

Yahoo! bundles its Search Optimizer together with Yahoo! Marketing Console (the reporting tool I mention in Chapter 15). The package begins at $249 a month for campaigns with 500 or fewer ad/keyword listings (and Yahoo! sometimes runs free trials so you can check it out without cost). It isn't as sophisticated as, say, Atlas OnePoint's tools, which I discuss in the next section, but it is much simpler to use. The tool lets you "day-part" — turn campaigns on and off automatically according to the time of day or day of the week.

As for bidding rules, Search Optimizer's bid management is simpler than some bid-management tools. In fact Search Optimizer doesn't use bidding rules so much as bidding and performance targets. You can set performance targets based on ROAS or CPA (cost per acquisition) and then define the desired ROAS or CPA and the maximum ROAS or CPA you're willing to accept (see Figure 16-1). In addition, you set other constraints: the bid range and the position range you want to work within. Search Optimizer then, based on the tracking you set up (see Chapter 15) adjusts bids with the aim of meeting those targets. You can choose to automatically accept Search Optimizer's recommended bids or to accept them manually.

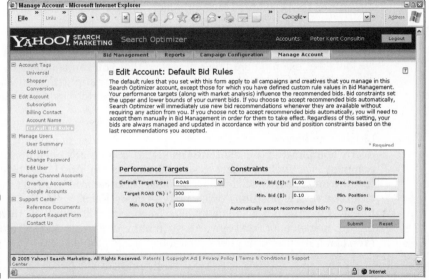

Figure 16-1:
Yahoo!
Search
Optimizer.

Of course, working with a tool such as Search Optimizer, provided by the PPC systems themselves, has the added advantage of rapid response. Search Optimizer works in near real-time, whereas third-party tools are generally limited to the number of times they can check and adjust bid prices.

Using Atlas OnePoint BidManager

Atlas OnePoint's (www.AtlasOnePoint.com) suite of PPC management tools are perhaps the best known in the business and work with probably the widest range of systems. It provides the following Web-based tools — so you can access them from anywhere — that work in conjunction with each other:

✔ **MasterList:** Use this tool to enter keywords and ads and submit them to the search engines.

✔ **BidManager:** Manage bids on multiple PPC systems.

✔ **ProfitBuilder:** Track campaign results for any online campaign.

You can manage your ads, keywords, and bids on a wide range of different PPC systems (probably more than any other tool): Google, Yahoo! (14 different national sites), Miva, Blowsearch, Enhance, GoClick, Kanoodle, LookSmart, Mirago, myGeek, Search123, Searchfeed, and Turbo10.

In addition, however, the system also feeds data to a variety of shopping directories (see Chapter 14): Shopping.com, Froogle, NexTag, mySimon, Shopper.com, and Yahoo! Shopping.

Atlas OnePoint has around 20 bidding rules — you saw some of them when we looked at example bidding rules. Note that you can combine these rules, running them in sequence to adjust bids in a very sophisticated way. This is not a simple piece of software; it's a very "feature rich" system that can take some time to learn.

Is Atlas OnePoint the answer to your prayers? Maybe, maybe not. It was overly complicated the last time I used it, though that's been a while, and the company is actively working to simplify the system. And it can be expensive, too; the most basic package — to manage 50 keywords in up to ten PPC systems and review positions twice a day — costs $79.95 a month. Not too bad, but 50 keywords is a small campaign. To check 1,000 keywords three times a day, for instance, or 500 keywords six times a day, costs $649.90 a month. (You can have the tools check positions up to 48 times a day.)

Finding Other Bid-Management Tools

A variety of other third-party bid-management tools are available, such as the following:

✔ **BidHero** (www.Clicktracks.com/products/bidhero): From the publisher of the excellent ClickTracks tracking software (see Chapter 15). In fact, this system is a ClickTracks add-on, so you can manage your campaigns, from bidding to tracking, through a similar interface. It's only $69 a month, but handles only Yahoo! and Google campaigns.

✔ **KeywordMax's BidDirector** (www.KeywordMax.com/bid_director.html): Manages Yahoo!, Google, Miva, Espotting, and Kanoodle, starting at $199 a month.

✔ **Bid** (www.websidestory.com): This product is from WebSiteStory, the company that publishes the popular HitBox and HBX Analytics Web-traffic analysis tool. Bid manages bids on Google, Yahoo!, LookSmart, Miva, and Kanoodle, and is integrated into the HBX Analytics product.

✔ **BidRank** (www.BidRank.com): This is software that runs on your computer. There are two different versions, though: one for Yahoo! and one that handles Google and a dozen other systems. Combined, the two cost around $30 a month to manage 100 keywords.

✔ **Dynamic Bid Maximizer** (www.KeywordBidMaximizer.com): Also software running on your computer, and also in two versions, one for Yahoo! and one for about 11 other systems, including Google. Starts at around $40 a month for both.

✔ **PPCBidTracker** (www.PPCBidTracker.com): There are two versions of this system, one for the U.S. market (seven PPC services), and an International version (through Yahoo!, Miva, and Google). The system works with ShopTracker, a program for submitting data to shopping directories. Prices start at $50 a month for the U.S. version.

✔ **PPC Pro** (www.PPCManagement.com): Starting at $30 a month for Yahoo!, Google, Miva, Enhance, and Kanoodle.

Build Your Own Bid-Management Tool

I spoke recently with a company that spends $2 million each month on PPC campaigns. How does it manage that? Using a third-party bid-management tool? Well, no. It worked closely with Yahoo! and Google and built custom tools to manage its campaigns.

These firms have APIs (Application Programming Interfaces) designed to allow other companies to write software that sends data to and receives data from the PPC systems; after all, that's how companies selling third-party bid-management systems have created these systems. So, some large advertisers have chosen to use the tools provided by the large PPC firms in conjunction with their own customized applications.

For the *many* readers out there with $2 million-per-month PPC campaigns, I suggest you look into this option.

Using a Bid-Management Firm

Here's another strategy: Pay someone else to manage your PPC campaign. Many companies are eager to run your PPC campaigns for you; in fact, some of the software companies mentioned earlier will sell you their software or use the software to manage your campaigns for you.

Using a bid-management firm is tempting and can be a good idea in some cases. But I should also note that a number of companies I've spoken to about this haven't been very happy with the results. It's easy to set up a PPC campaign and manage it; what's hard is managing it well, and some bid-management firms *don't* manage it well, meaning increased costs and lost opportunities.

But even if the campaign is being managed well, it can still be an expensive proposition. You may end up paying as much to manage the campaign as you do in click costs. And if you have a large campaign, the management cost may be so much that you can hire full-time staff to manage the campaign.

In particular, small campaigns are very expensive. If you want to spend $100, even $1,000 a week, you'll probably spend more managing the campaign than actual click costs.

It's a bit of a Catch-22 for the firms in this business (a business that, it appears, has high levels of dissatisfaction). If you're running a small PPC campaign and don't have the time to manage it, you'll find hiring a PPC firm very expensive — you'll pay a very high management fee compared to the click cost. On the other hand, if you're managing a very large PPC campaign, tens or hundreds of thousands of dollars a month, you'll pay so much in management fees that you'll be tempted to hire your own full-time PPC staff. Which is exactly what many companies do.

Chapter 17

Avoiding Click Fraud

· ·

· ·

In Chapter 3, you find out about *conversion ratios,* the proportion of the people coming to your site who carry out the desired action — who buy from you, become a sales lead, and so on.

If 100 people click your ad but only one buys, you have a conversion ratio of 1:100. Why would 99 people click but not buy? Clearly there are many possible reasons:

✔ On arriving at your site, they realize that what you're advertising is not what they really want.

✔ Your price is too high.

✔ They prefer another brand of product.

✔ They're not yet ready to buy.

✔ . . . and on and on.

There's another category of non-converter (unfortunately, in some cases, the *largest* category): the clicker who never intended to buy from you in the first place, who only clicked so that you would be charged the click fee, the clicker who clicked in order to defraud you!

Click fraud has been described as a *billion-dollar problem* by the president of Snap.com. Exaggeration? The PPC business is a $5-billion-per-year business, and some estimates of click fraud are as high as 20 percent. I'll do the math for you; 20 percent of $5 billion is $1 billion. One click fraud–monitoring company (Click Assurance) says that it's found campaigns with click-fraud levels as high as 80 percent, with an average of 18 percent. That's right, as many as 20 percent of all clicks could be fraudulent. (Actually some estimates go as high as 50 percent, but I find this high end to be implausible . . . though it could be true in some categories.)

Understanding Click Fraud

How does click fraud work? There are two main types:

- ✔ Fraud intended to make money through context ads
- ✔ Fraud intended to hurt you financially or damage your PPC competitive position

PPC is an unusual form of advertising in that it actually encourages click fraud in a number of ways. There's no way you can fraudulently view a newspaper ad, fraudulently watch a television ad, or fraudulently listen to a radio ad. But with PPC, two important characteristics come into play. First, the people viewing your ad determine how often you will be charged the click fee. Second, thanks to the wonders of content match, or contextual advertising, any Tom, Dick, or Harriet can get into the advertising business and share click fees.

Fraudulent use of contextual advertising

As you discover in Chapter 13, *contextual advertising* is the process of placing PPC ads on non-search sites, that is, on "content" sites. A number of PPC systems have contextual-advertising programs, but the most widely used is Google's AdSense program.

Consider this all-too-common scenario. The scammer finds a group of high-click-price keywords and then builds a Web site (or maybe several Web sites) that contain plenty of related keywords. Our scammer signs up for the AdSense program and begins running ads on his site.

Then, you guessed it, he begins clicking the ads. Each time he clicks an ad, Google earns the click fee and credits a portion of the fee to the scammer's account. Simple, eh?

Hurting you financially

The second main form of fraud is clicking on competitors' ads in order to hurt them. Company A wants to get the bulk of the clicks for a particular keyword, but finds that it's way too competitive. The price of the clicks for the top positions is more than A wants or can afford to pay.

So Company A begins clicking on the ads placed by Companies B, C, and D. This has several effects:

- ✔ Company A's competitors waste money, something that may be gratifying to Company A in and of itself (call it the "spite factor").

- ✔ The competitors' conversion rates go down, so their ROIs go down, too. They may decide the ads are no longer competitive and drop out, allowing Company A to get high positions at lower costs.

- ✔ In some cases, competitors will drop their ads to lower positions in order to lower click-costs, so that their daily budgets last throughout the day.

- ✔ Competitors may run through their daily budgets earlier in the day, at which point their ads are removed, allowing Company A to get high positions at lower costs the remainder of the day.

It's hard to imagine that this fraud can really go on, but believe it; it's happening. As I mention earlier, PPC actually *encourages* fraud. It's just too easy! In many cases, people see their competitors' ads and click them because . . . well, just because. In other cases, they're more devious and do it as part of an underhanded scheme.

Oh, and it's not necessarily competitors clicking on your ads; it could be anyone who wants to hurt you. Do you have any disgruntled employees? Any vendors you haven't paid in a while? Any customers you've upset?

Different Fraud Tactics

Click fraud has a number of tactics:

- ✔ **Dumb clicking:** The crudest type of click fraud is sitting in front of a computer and clicking ads. This is how click fraud began, but this has a number of problems. First, if you click too quickly, the PPC system will probably discount all but the first click. These days, the PPC companies also look for large numbers of clicks coming from a single source — and that means from a particular IP (Internet Protocol) number. If a large number of clicks come from a particular IP number, they'll be ignored.

    An *IP number* identifies a computer; all the computers connected to the Internet at any particular moment have unique IP numbers.

- ✔ **Smarter clicking:** Some people, realizing that PPC systems track IP numbers, are a little smarter. They click from different computers in different locations — at work, at home, in a library, using a laptop with WiFi in a Starbucks, WiFi in a bar, WiFi in a bookstore . . .

✔ **IP switching:** All that running around is a real hassle, so some people use programs to switch IP numbers so the clicks seem to come from different computers. (It's done through proxy servers, if you need some geek terminology.)

✔ **Programmed clicking:** It's possible to build programs — called *hitbots* — to automate clicking. A scammer could write a program that searches for a variety of different keywords and clicks on a variety of different ads over and over again. Of course, hitbots are generally combined with the switching of IP numbers.

✔ **Outsourced clicking:** All this clicking, in particular if you're running around from computer to computer, can be terribly tiring. If you're a big click-fraud mogul, you don't want to work up a sweat, after all. Many scammers hire people to do the clicking for them. In May 2004, *India Business* ran an article called "India's Secret Army of Online Ad 'Clickers'." That article stated that a "growing number of housewives, college graduates, and even working professionals across metropolitan cities are rushing to click paid Internet ads to make $100 to $200 per month."

✔ **Multiple-system clicking:** It's said that some scammers spread their fraudulent clicks across multiple systems; if a competitor is using Google, Yahoo!, Miva, and LookSmart, the scammer can click on ads presented through all four systems, making it harder to identify the fraud.

Incidentally, some companies are even contacting sites that carry AdSense ads and offering fraudulent clicking services. "We'll click on your ads a thousand times a month," they'll say, "if you split the ad income with us."

Watching for Impression Fraud

Another form of fraud, which certainly isn't as common as the forms of fraud I've already mentioned, is called *impression fraud,* and it only targets Google PPC.

As you find out in Chapter 9, one of the criterion used by Google for determining where a PPC ad will rank is CTR — *click-through rate.* The more often your ad is clicked, the higher it ranks, which means that in some cases, ads with lower bids actually rank above ads with higher bids.

So, here's how impression fraud works. An advertiser who wants to rank high for an ad removes his ad from the campaign for a while. He then displays the competing ads thousands of times on his browser, using some kind of bot to search using the keywords that pull up the ad. The bot doesn't click the ads, it simply runs the search, reducing the CTR of the ads. Because the ad is being displayed far more often, and yet is not being clicked upon any more often, its click-through rate drops.

Now the fraudster can begin running his ad again. His competitors, with their low CTRs, are likely to be pushed down in the ranks, allowing him to get high positions at low bid prices. In some cases, the competitors' ads may even be dropped; if the CTR drops below a particular rate, Google will nix the ad.

Of course, the competitors are not *directly* hurt; the scammer is not clicking on the ads and running up click charges. But they are hurt indirectly. The whole point of pushing them down is to take sales away from them, so they lose sales revenue. And competitors may try to regain rank by bidding more, so they pay more for the same results they had before.

How serious of a problem is this? Google claims it's not very important. (Remember, it only hits Google because of the way Google determines rank.) It's a more complicated form of fraud, and Google claims to be running scripts that look for sudden dramatic increases in ad impressions and reduction in click-through rates. But a number of advertisers swear they've lost thousands of dollars because of it.

What Are the PPC Companies Doing about Click Fraud?

The PPC companies understand that click fraud is a huge problem. The companies are sometimes accused of not caring about click fraud because, after all, they still make money from the clicks, even if you're losing money. But click fraud actually reduces ad revenues and threatens the entire business model. Just as e-mail spam has dramatically reduced the effectiveness of e-mail marketing — and thus hurt e-mail marketing firms — click fraud has the potential to dramatically reduce the effectiveness of PPC ads, and seriously hurt, or even kill, the PPC companies.

How can click fraud reduce ad revenues? As I've explained, fraud reduces conversion rates and thus ROI. And every time a firm's PPC ROI drops below profitability, the PPC firms lose a customer. With click fraud at such high rates, this must have happened many times already. Those firms take their ad dollars out of the system and spend them elsewhere. Furthermore, all the bad press about click fraud scares off other companies; they never even try. If click fraud amounts to 20 percent of all clicks, as some observers claim, one could argue that 20 percent of all the PPC companies' revenues are due to click fraud. But what about their losses? How much money is being lost because companies are dropping out of the game?

And the real fear is that eventually the PPC business becomes totally unviable. What would Google be without PPC revenues? In real trouble! *Ninety-eight percent* of Google's money comes from PPC, so without it, Google would be a company without a business model.

Still, it's hard to ignore all the complaints of PPC advertisers who claim that the PPC companies have been slow to react and perhaps haven't reacted very effectively. In any case, the major PPC companies are worried, and they should be. They are, in fact, spending a lot of money developing systems to identify and eliminate click fraud.

Another strategy used by the PPC companies is the lawsuit. Google began filing lawsuits in November 2004 against a company called Auctions Expert International, which it claimed had joined its AdSense program and was clicking on ads displayed in its own pages in order to make money, defrauding Google and its customers in the process. "This lawsuit against Auctions Expert," said Google, "demonstrates the success of our anti-fraud system and that we will take legal action when appropriate."

On the other hand, various search engines are now being sued themselves, Google included, by irate click buyers who feel that the PPC firms have been very cavalier about taking responsibility and issuing refunds for click fraud.

Protecting Yourself

So how do you deal with click fraud? Here are a few things you can do:

- ✔ **Track conversion ratios carefully.** As discussed in Chapter 15, you must track conversion ratios. Remember, even if fraud is taking place, if you're still making money from a keyword, then it's still worth using the keyword. In the same way that a toy store in a shopping mall continues doing business even though it knows it's losing money through shop lifting, click fraud is simply, for many companies, a cost of doing business.

- ✔ **Avoid contextual advertising.** Avoid contextual advertising, in particular Google's contextual advertising, and you are entirely avoiding one of the two main forms of click fraud. This is particularly important if you are buying very expensive keywords. Of course, if contextual ads are still profitable, then *don't* avoid it! (See the first item on this list.)

- ✔ **Avoid very expensive keywords.** They are targets not only in contextual ads but also in the regular search-engine ads. Of course, again, if the keywords are still making money . . .

- ✔ **Place ads lower on the page.** You're less of a target for fraud if your ads are below the fold. You'll pay less for clicks, too, and your ROI may actually be better. But you may not get enough clicks to be worthwhile.

✔ **Specify the maximum spend per day.** You'll avoid runaway fraud in which you're charged thousands of dollars before you notice.

✔ **Check your traffic-analysis software.** If you see a sudden large jump in PPC traffic to your site, in particular combined with a drop in conversions, find out why. If you see large numbers of clicks coming from the same IP number or network, you probably have a problem.

✔ **Block particular sites.** If you use Google's AdSense contextual advertising, and you see suspicious clicks coming from a particular site, you can block the ads from being placed on that site (see Chapter 13).

✔ **Use a fraud-detection tool.** As I explain later in this chapter, a number of fraud-detection tools can tell you if your PPC campaign is being hit.

✔ **Learn how to complain!** If you find evidence of click fraud, contact the PPC firm immediately and *push*. The PPC companies have a reputation for not handling fraud complaints very well, so you may have to be really insistent. If you can show evidence of unusual click activity, it should pay attention.

✔ **Call your lawyer.** If you can identify who is doing the clicking — if you know who owns the computers identified by the IP number of the computers doing the clicking — immediately get a lawyer to send him or her a "cease and desist" letter along with the evidence.

Identifying Click Fraud

What, then, does click fraud look like? How can you identify it? One thing you can do is to look at the click statistics reported by the PPC companies and the visits from the PPC companies reported by your Web analytics software. Note, however, that there will always be a discrepancy; the PPC company will generally report more clicks than your software picks up, for a variety of reasons. ClickTracks, a publisher of a good analytics tool, suggests these reasons for why the PPC companies measure higher numbers than analytics software:

✔ *Between the time the visitor clicks on a link in the search engine results and the time the page is successfully loaded in his or her browser, any number of things can happen, like:*

✔ The visitor changes his/her mind and clicks his/her browser's Back button.

✔ He/she clicks the 'stop' button.

✔ He/she clicks the 'home' button.

✔ He/she closes the browser altogether.

✔ Your data center router is burdened and not transferring data quickly.

✔ Your pages are taking too long to load.

✔ The visitor starts having network problems, and data doesn't go through.

✔ His/her 2-year-old son toddles in and pushes the 'power' button on the CPU.

So don't expect the two numbers to match exactly; the analytics companies suggest that even a 10 or 20 percent difference is fairly normal.

A number of things you might see in your traffic logs and in your PPC provider's stats might indicate possible click fraud:

✔ **Your CTR (click-through rate) suddenly increases to an implausibly high rate.** For instance, you're getting one click every 100 times the ad is displayed; then, suddenly, it leaps to one click for every four times the ad is displayed.

✔ **Your Web site traffic from the PPC ads suddenly increases without a corresponding increase in sales.**

✔ **You see a lot of traffic coming through proxy servers.** This may suggest that someone's trying to hide his IP number (you can find lists of public proxy servers here: www.publicproxyservers.com).

✔ **Many of the referring URLs don't seem to last long before the pages disappear.**

✔ **Many of the referring domains are owned by a single company or are anonymously owned.** Check out www.DomainsByProxy.com, a company that helps people register anonymous domains.

✔ **A referring page, or a small number of referring pages, seem to be sending a lot of traffic.**

✔ **A lot of the traffic is coming from overseas.**

It can be hard to understand traffic logs. If you're not much of a geek, and if you have a small PPC budget, it's not practical to closely monitor your logs. However, if your company spends tens or hundreds of thousands of dollars a year — I know one company that spends a couple of million dollars a *month* — then *someone* in your organization should understand traffic logs intimately and should closely monitor what's going on. Hey, 20 percent of $100,000 a month is, um, lots of money — enough to pay someone to watch closely.

Some Web traffic–analytics companies now provide tools designed specifically for tracking click fraud. For example, Urchin, a log-analysis company owned by Google, has a special Click Fraud Tracking Module that tracks repeat clicks, providing the IP number of the computer and the ad source.

Using a Click Fraud Detection Service

If you have a large PPC campaign, you should seriously consider using a click fraud–detection program or service. These companies can provide more detailed information and provide reports that should help simplify the process of getting a refund from the PPC service. Such services may cost you $50 to $100 a month, sometimes more, so if your campaign is small, it's just not worth it. If you spend a lot on PPC, adding a click-fraud system is really a very small additional cost. For instance, using WhosClickingWho to monitor half a million clicks a month would cost a little under $500 a month — around one-tenth of a penny per click.

Click-fraud systems can protect you in various ways:

- ✔ **Track clickers across multiple PPC systems.** If someone clicks PPC ads on Google, Yahoo!, Kanoodle, and Miva, the detection service can sometimes identify the different visits as being the same person.

- ✔ **Identify infrequent clickers with multiple IP numbers.**

- ✔ **Generate reports that you can submit to the PPC firms to get a refund.**

- ✔ **Identify visitors by IP address.**

- ✔ **Display a warning.** Who'sClickingWho, for instance, can pop up a warning message to someone who's clicked one of your ads several times (see Figure 17-1).

Figure 17-1:
A Who's-
Clicking-
Who
warning
message,
displayed
when
someone
clicks a PPC
ad several
times.

Please read ☒

Your internet location has been detected visiting this site more than 5 times via links from one or more pay-per-click search engines.

We appreciate the opportunity to serve you and thank you for your visits. To protect our customers from higher prices by keeping advertising dollars down, we routinely examine recurrent visitations from PPC Search Engines.

Please help us pass the savings on to you by bookmarking our site for future reference.

Thank you for visiting and please enjoy browsing our site!

Powered by
Who's Clicking Who?™
PPC Auditing Service
ClickMinder™ Patent Pending. All Rights Reserved.

Here are a few click-fraud systems you can check:

- ✔ **Who'sClickingWho:** www.WhosClickingWho.com
- ✔ **ClickLab:** www.ClickLab.com
- ✔ **AdWatcher:** www.AdWatcher.com
- ✔ **KeywordMax:** www.KeywordMax.com
- ✔ **CoreMetrics:** www.CoreMetrics.com

Some companies will manage the process for you. They'll track your traffic to identify fraud and then handle the process of getting a refund for you from the PPC firms:

- ✔ **Alchemist Media:** www.AlchemistMedia.com
- ✔ **Click Assurance:** www.ClickAssurance.com

Click Assurance will audit your PPC traffic for free; it makes money when it identifies click fraud — it earns a portion of the refund it gets you from the PPC companies.

Complaining to the PPC Service

If you're sure you have a click-fraud case, complain. If that doesn't work, complain again. Right now, this is a difficult situation, and victims of click fraud are often angry, feeling that the PPC firms are in the position of being plaintiff, prosecution, judge, and jury, all wrapped up in one package. What hope do you have of winning?

Well, it is possible to win. You need to document everything as carefully as possible (which is why those click-fraud reports from the detection programs and services can be so useful). Then call and keep calling. If you reach someone who clearly is not being helpful or who doesn't seem to understand what you're saying, ask for the fraud department or click-fraud department or ask for a supervisor.

If you have the evidence, do not take no for an answer. The PPC companies know they've got a public-relations problem, so if you can reach the right people in the organization, there's a chance you *can* get a refund.

Part IV
The Part of Tens

The 5th Wave   By Rich Tennant

"You know, it dawned on me last night why we aren't getting any hits on our Web site."

In this part . . .

This book explains how to get into the PPC game and do it well. There's enough information to keep you busy for quite a while and to help you build a strong foundation for your click-based advertising campaigns.

But let's face it, there's always more to learn. I'll start by explaining how you can sell PPC ads for yourself — how to partner with a PPC network, place PPC ads on your own Web site, and share in the ad revenues.

I also show you a few interesting tools to help you manage your PPC campaigns, from programs that check bid prices on various different systems to a neat little tool that shows you what sort of ads will appear on your Web pages if you place ads on your site for Google, from Google's secret *Google Suggest* tool, to a tool that quickly cleans keyword lists.

I also point you in the direction of some useful sources of information so you can keep on top of things in the PPC world.

Chapter 18

Ten Ways to Make Money Selling Clicks

In This Chapter

▶ Generating traffic and picking keywords

▶ Using Google AdSense

▶ Working with other PPC systems

▶ Creating your own PPC system

Most of this book explains how to use PPC to sell your products or promote your Web site. But there's another side to the PPC coin; you can make money by selling clicks. The concept is simple: You place PPC ads on your Web site and get paid when people click the ads.

You can make money from clicks in a number of ways, from partnering with PPC firms to setting up your own PPC software. This chapter shows you ten ways to make money by getting into the advertising-sales business, selling clicks to advertisers. You will become what is known in the PPC business as a *publisher* — the guy or gal publishing the site that the ads sit on.

Generating a Lot of Traffic

The first thing you need to do is, not surprisingly, have a site with enough traffic to make it work. You want plenty of visitors to your site, and you want those visitors to view lots of pages. This is really a "page impression" game. The more pages shown to visitors — the more page impressions — then the more ads are displayed and the more clicks you could get.

Let's say your site gets 500 page views a month. That could mean, perhaps, 50 clicks a month, which would mean very little money. You need to have a site that generates thousands of page impressions a month, hundreds of thousands or more, ideally.

How do you create a lot of traffic? One of the best ways, if you really under-stand the "art," is Search Engine Optimization. If you win at this game, you can generate a lot of traffic to your site, some of which will convert to clicks on your PPC ads. (I doubt if I've mentioned this so far, but I wrote a book called *Search Engine Optimization For Dummies* [Wiley] that you really should take a look at.)

One common strategy is to create large amounts of content — lots and lots of text spread over many pages — on pages that are easily indexed by the search engines. (I know of people with literally hundreds of thousands of pages designed to carry PPC advertising.)

Some sites that carry advertising have used another, long-term strategy. In fact, many sites that carry advertising were not built for that purpose; rather, the site grew in popularity over the years, just through word of mouth and perhaps a little PR, and the owner realized he had enough traffic to make money from the account by placing PPC advertising on the site. The strategy, in effect, is to build a truly useful site that people will visit and revisit, and that other site owners will link to.

Picking High-Value Keywords

If you want to build a site to sell clicks, consider carefully the subject matter of your site and the pages on which you will place PPC ads before you begin. You might as well pick a subject matter with high-value keywords — content that will cause PPC ads to be placed with high click values. It's often just as hard to get traffic that will click on 10-cent-per-click ads as it is to get traffic that will click on $10-per-click-ads, so, to maximize your profit, go for the $10-per-click ads!

Some keywords have very high bid values, in the tens of dollars. For instance, when I looked a moment ago, the top three click prices for the term *denver attorney* through Yahoo! are $7.75, $7.74, and $5.74. On the other hand, the top three terms for the term *soccer* are 70 cents, 69 cents, and 68 cents. For those of you who are math-challenged, that means you'll earn around *ten times* the income from clicks on the *denver attorney* ads compared with the *soccer* ads.

There is, admittedly, one downside to targeting expensive clicks. Very expen-sive clicks are often very competitive; it may be harder to get the traffic to your site if you are competing for high-value clicks. But that isn't always the case.

How do you pick high-value keywords? One way is to guess about subjects that may be very popular — not popular in the sense that many people search on them, but in the sense that many companies are willing to spend a lot of money to get the business. *paris hilton,* for example, is a very popular search term, but it's a low-cost click because people searching on this term aren't normally looking for something to buy. Any business that involves lots of money and heavy competition is likely to have high click prices; anything to do with attorneys, for instance, and in particular anything to do with legal advice related to hot litigation — *vioxx,* for example.

Check your guesses by using the Yahoo! bid tool: `http://uv.bidtool. overture.com/d/search/tools/bidtool`. There's also a nifty little tool called Keyword Burner (`www.KeywordBurner.com`) that grabs keyword price and click data from Google for $47 a month. And you can check large numbers of bid prices through Yahoo! by using a tool such as Wordtracker (Chapter 4).

Other services provide you with lists of expensive keywords. TopPaying Keywords.com, for instance, will sell you a list for $199 (and you can buy quarterly updates for $50). Its recent database contained 56 keywords with bid prices over $20, one over $40, and over 7,000 between $1 and $19.99. These are the #3 bid prices, not the top bids, because the company selling the list feels that #3 is more representative of the real price being paid for a click. (As you find out in Chapter 7, people often bid high but pay significantly lower in the first couple of positions.) So when the database shows a click price of, say, $45, the actual top price can sometimes be significantly more.

Buying Clicks to Sell Clicks

Another way to generate traffic to your site is to use PPC. Some publishers use the second- and third-tier PPC systems, or target cheaper keywords, in order to get enough traffic to a site that carries more expensive PPC ads. In other words, you buy the traffic at low costs and "re-sell" it at higher click prices.

You have to use this strategy very carefully, though. Make sure you have enough "spread" between click prices to make it work.

Combining and Experimenting with Ad Systems

The PPC systems you sign up with will probably have a clause in their Terms and Conditions mandating an exclusive relationship; if you use, for instance, Google AdSense, you can't have another company's ads on the same page.

Still, it's sometimes worth running different systems on your site at the same time. On the other hand, some Web sites *do* run multiple ad types on the same page. They just hope they don't get caught. It's very common to find Google AdSense ads running alongside a variety of different companies' ads, despite Google's terms and conditions; it's so common, in fact, one has to wonder whether Google really cares.

Signing Up with Google AdSense

The largest and best-known system that small publishers can use to sell PPC ads is Google's AdSense program (http://AdSense.Google.com). AdSense provides you with AdWords ads to run on your site. It's really quite easy; Google provides a little piece of code that you drop into your pages, and when the pages load, the script contacts the Google servers for ads to place into those positions.

Google sends a check every month (assuming your income is over $100 each month). How much will Google pay you for each click? Good question. Problem is, I don't know the answer, and Google ain't saying! Here's exactly what Google says about the subject of your earnings:

> Although we don't disclose the exact revenue share, our goal is to enable publishers to make as much or more than they could with other advertising networks.

Well, anyway, many thousands of sites carry AdSense ads. . . . Hey, it's Google; it can do what it wants. Google's reports will tell you the total number of page and ad unit impressions, clicks on the ads, the click-through rate, the effective CPM (cost per thousand ad impressions), and your total earnings, so you can figure a few things out. But Google won't tell you what percentage you earn on each click.

Experimenting with Different Features

There's more to making money from clicks than just placing ads on your site. Experiment with the various tools provided to you. For instance, if you're working with Google AdSense, try installing Search boxes on your site.

Visitors to your site will be able to use the Google Search box to search within your site, or across the entire Web. When Google displays the results, it includes AdWords, and if the searcher clicks those ads, you get paid.

Another neat little tool is the Google Link Units. These were introduced early in 2005, but so far, not many publishers use them. They are little blocks of links, as you can see in the window on the left in Figure 18-1. Clicking one of the links opens a page (on the right in the figure) containing a list of AdSense ads. You won't get paid when someone clicks the links, but you will get paid when they click an ad in the resulting page.

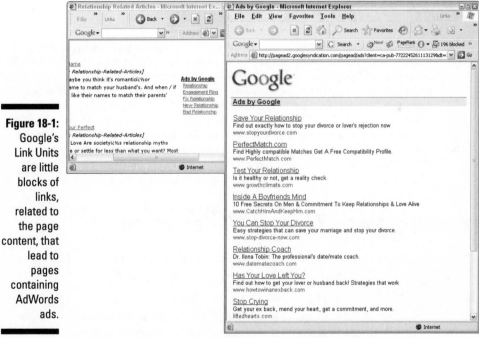

Figure 18-1:
Google's Link Units are little blocks of links, related to the page content, that lead to pages containing AdWords ads.

Working with the Yahoo! Publisher Network

Yahoo! has been distributing its ads for some time, but only through larger sites. Yahoo! recently began opening up the system to "publishers of all sizes" through the new *Publisher Network* (http://publisher.yahoo.com). As with Google, you can integrate various tools into your site, such as the new Y!Q, a search tool that searches the Yahoo! index for information related to the information on the page the visitor is reading (the reader sees a little Search Related Info link).

At the time of writing, the network is not yet fully operational. In order to use it, you must apply to join the beta program. By the time you read this, however, it will probably be up and running.

Finding Other PPC Systems

MSN, at the time of writing, does not have a publisher's program, but it quite likely will sometime soon, so keep your eyes open. There are many other systems, however, that do allow small Web publishers to integrate ads into their pages; in fact, these smaller systems *have to* do this. Google has billions of searches through its own site and its large partners. Small companies have to scramble to find distribution. What companies have content distribution? You can try just about any of the second-tier search-results PPC companies and the content-placement companies we've looked at elsewhere in the book (Chapters 11 and 13, respectively).

Creating Your Own PPC System

You might consider installing PPC software on your own site, contacting merchants that would want to reach your visitors, and selling advertising to them directly.

A number of these systems are available, such as iWeb Hyperseek (www.hyperseek.com), K-Search (www.turn-k.net/k-search), Searchawy (www.mewsoft.com), Softbiz Pay Per Click Script (www.softbizscripts.com), and inClick (www.inClick.net). You can find more by visiting script libraries, such as www.HotScripts.com and www.perfectscripts.com, and searching for *ppc* and *pay per click*. Or find a small specialty PPC site running PPC software that you like and ask it what it's using.

Check these out carefully, though. Some won't do content placement but are designed as search engines with integrated PPC — the ads are placed on the search-results pages.

Thinking about Affiliates

Here's another way to sell clicks. Rather than displaying PPC ads on your site, display links and ads pointing to affiliate programs; you won't get paid when someone clicks on your site, but you will get paid when someone clicks and then buys something or provides lead information.

If you'd like to find out the type of products and services that you can make money with by pointing people to, visit some of the major affiliate networks: **Commission Junction** (www.cj.com), **LinkShare** (www.LinkShare.com), and **ClickBank** (www.ClickBank.com).

Chapter 19

Ten Ways to Stay Up-to-Date and Track Down the Details

In This Chapter

▶ Learning more about the individual PPC services

▶ Finding professional PPC training

▶ Finding PPC services and tools

▶ Keeping up-to-date with goings-on in the PPC systems

▶ Finding people to help you

There's always more to learn, about any subject. I'm sure someone could create a university course on PPC that would cover more than just the few hundred pages you find here. So where do you go next if you want to continue your education? If you want to learn about new PPC tools and services, and learn how others are making PPC work for them? The sections that follow highlight a few possibilities.

Let Me Help Some More

Visit my site (www.PPCBulletin.com/). You can find the links in this chapter, and from the entire book, to speed your work. I'll also post links to a few other interesting tools that I run across.

The PPC Systems Themselves

Virtually all the PPC systems provide some kind of online help, though it varies in quality greatly. Nonetheless, it's worth spending a little while getting to know the system, especially if you're about to invest a lot of money in one of the major systems. Look carefully for links to Help or Support.

Yahoo! hides away much of the support information for some reason; if you've already logged in to your account, look for the little gray Support Center link at the bottom of the page. (Note to Yahoo! Web designers: Small text displayed at the bottom of a page in an indistinct color like gray says to the user, "nothing important here!") Otherwise, you can find the Resource Center on the login page, with links to information about various Yahoo! services.

Google offers a Help link, at the top right of your management console, that takes you to quite an extensive information area. Google also provides a forum for AdWords users at `http://groups.google.com/group/adwords-help`.

The Google Learning Center

Google's AdWords Learning Center takes your education one step further (`www.google.com/adwords/learningcenter`). The Learning Center is distinct from the Help area mentioned previously. You'll find dozens of different lessons in both text format and Flash multimedia — over seven *hours* of training in the minutiae of working with Google AdWords. There are lessons about click fraud, "overdelivery," managing a budget, and geo-targeting. You can find information on site targeting and reports, ROI tracking, and creating landing pages.

If you want to totally immerse yourself in the Google AdWords system, this is the training course for you. After you've completed it, cough up your 50 bucks and register for the *Google Advertising Professional Exam* (`http://ibt.prometric.com/google`), which will look cool on your resume or business card.

By the way, you can also find lots of interesting statistics related to PPC, for various businesses — Automotive, Entertainment, Financial Services, and so on — here: `www.google.com/ads/metrics.html`.

Yahoo!'s Training Manual

Yahoo! has a training manual, the *Yahoo! Search Marketing Advertiser Handbook,* over 100 pages of information about working with Sponsored Search. However, it's hidden away somewhere, and I haven't figured out how to find my way through the site to the manual. You may receive an e-mail pointing you to the book, but if you miss the e-mail among all the spam for "physical enhancements" and requests that you help someone steal $50M from Nigeria, here's the direct URL: `http://searchmarketing.yahoo.com/rc/srch/eworkbook.pdf`.

SearchEngineWatch

SearchEngineWatch (www.SearchEngineWatch.com) is one of the top sites for keeping up-to-date with changes in the search-engine world. It tends to focus more on organic search results, but there's still plenty of information about PPC, too, including lots of articles about the business and forum areas dedicated to PPC.

The SearchEngineWatch forums are really valuable features; they often have 150 or so people online, sometimes many more, and overall have tens of thousands of messages. It's a great place to find answers. SearchEngineWatch has more than 40 different forums, such as forums on Google AdWords, on Yahoo! Sponsored Search, on other PPC systems, on search engine marketing in general, on search engine advertising, and so on. This site really is a *must see* site for information gathering.

There's a lot of free information in this site, including the forums, but you also have a subscription option — $99 a year — that provides a lot of additional articles and information with a lot more detail.

WebMasterWorld

WebMasterWorld (www.WebMasterWorld.com) is another great place to talk with others in the business. It has very popular forums on a wide variety of Web-related subjects, including Yahoo! Publisher Network, Yahoo! Search Marketing (Overture Pay Per Click), Pay Per Click Search Engines, Google AdWords, Google AdSense, and so on.

It is a pay site, though; it costs $89 for six months or $149 for a year, but if the PPC business is your sole business or an important part of your responsibilities, you'll quite likely find it worth the three bucks a week for access to the combined knowledge of hundreds of professionals.

PayPerClickSearchEngines.com

PayPerClickSearchEngines.com is a good site to check out if you're interested in trying the third-tier PPC systems. It has a directory of 659 PPC systems, many of which are single-site services (that is, you can place PPC ads on a particular site). You may be able to use this system to track down specialist PPC systems that match your business, such as WeddingsFirst (yep, just for wedding sites) and 101HomeResources.com (check out the Specialty subcategory in the directory).

In addition, the site has plenty of other resources, such as PPC system reviews, information about PPC-management tools, and a large list of special offers from PPC services.

Pandia

Pandia (www.pandia.com/optimization/ppc.html) is a site about *all things search-related,* from how to search to using the search engines to promote your site. It has lots of information on Search Engine Optimization, and some useful information on PPC, too, including links to various PPC systems and tools.

Open Directory Project's PPC Category

Visit the Open Directory Project's (www.dmoz.org) Pay-Per-Click Advertising category (http://dmoz.org/Computers/Internet/Web_Design_and_Development/Promotion/Pay-Per-Click_Advertising). You can find links to literally hundreds of PPC services, specialized PPC services (PPC for furniture, for agriculture, and so on), management tools, and more.

It's well worth a visit to the directory and a little time digging around in here. You can also access this directory through Google (http://dir.google.com); Google provides the same results, but instead of sorting them alphabetically, it sorts by Google PageRank, a measure of how popular a site is based on how many other sites (and the popularity of the sites) link to it.

Yahoo! Directory

Yahoo! Directory (http://dir.Yahoo.com) doesn't currently have a PPC category, but it does have a broader Internet Advertising category that's worth checking out (dir.yahoo.com/Business_and_Economy/Business_to_Business/Marketing_and_Advertising/Internet/Advertising). Much of this category is PPC-related, but there's another category, the Internet Promotion category, that covers other PPC links (dir.yahoo.com/Business_and_Economy/Business_to_Business/Marketing_and_Advertising/Internet/Promotion).

Other PPC Sites

Various other PPC sites can perhaps provide a little additional information (there's a lot of overlap). Pay Per Click Universe (www.payperclick universe.com) has a free monthly newsletter (subscribe, or read the archives at the Web site) and links to many useful tools. There's also Pay Per Click Analyst (http://payperclickanalyst.com); here, you'll find reviews of PPC systems to help you choose which ones to work with, the latest news from the PPC industry, information about new technical developments, reviews of useful tools for PPC advertisers, and plenty more. There's also Pay Per Click Guru (http://payperclickguru.com). It has a rating system that allows visitors to the site to rate various first- and second-tier PPC systems and also keeps track of current special offers, such as discounts on PPC service. There's also a handy comparison chart, comparing minimum bids and initial deposits across 17 different systems.

Search Engine Optimization For Dummies

Okay, there's not so much information about PPC in the wonderful book, *Search Engine Optimization For Dummies*, but I figure if you're reading *Pay Per Click Search Engine Marketing For Dummies* to learn about PPC, there's a very good chance you're interested in another acronym, SEO — *Search Engine Optimization*. Many companies that spend huge sums on PPC could invest just a fraction of their ad spend and kick off a great SEO campaign that would generate *free* clicks for years.

Did I mention that I wrote *Search Engine Optimization For Dummies?* No? Well, I did, and a fine book it is. Pick it up at your local bookstore or your favorite online bookstore, or download a shareware version at www.GetSEOBook.com.

Index

• B •